THE ROAD TO KELLS

Prehistoric archaeology of the M3 Navan to Kells and N52 Kells Bypass road project

THE ROAD TO KELLS

Prehistoric archaeology of the M3 Navan to Kells and N52 Kells Bypass road project

Fintan Walsh

With contributions by Shane Delaney, Ben Gearey, Thomas C B Hill, Emma J Hopla, Jim McKeon, Lorna O'Donnell and Jerry O'Sullivan

Academic Editor
Eoin Grogan

TII Heritage 12

First published in 2021 by
Transport Infrastructure Ireland
Parkgate Business Centre, Parkgate Street, Dublin 8, DO8 DK10

Library of Congress Cataloguing-in-Publication Data are available for this book.

A CIP catalogue record for this book is available from the British Library.

ISBN - 978-1-911633-26-6 (Paperback)
ISBN - 978-1-911633-27-3 (ePub)
ISBN - 978-1-911633-29-7 (POD)
ISSN - 2009-8480
TII Heritage 12

Copy-editing: Emer Condit
Cover design, typesetting and layout: Wordwell Books
Index: Geraldine Begley

Printed by: W & G Baird on paper sourced from sustainable forests
Front cover: Artist's impression of proceedings at a Late Neolithic ceremonial complex at Kilmainham (*Dan Tietzsch-Tyler*)

Contents

Foreword

Kells is known all over the world for its association with an illuminated gospel-book written on calfskin vellum by Columban monks c. AD 800. In this latest publication in the TII Heritage series, we discover another 'Book of Kells'. The original text of this book was not written in carefully inked characters on vellum but was written on the landscape, in foundation trenches and boundary ditches, pits, post-holes, hearths and myriad other marks of human life. Deciphering these features is a very expert form of palaeography requiring the trained eyes of experienced field archaeologists. Translating them into an accessible book that we can all read and enjoy is yet another challenge. Fintan Walsh, Irish Archaeological Consultancy Ltd and the production team at Wordwell Group have done an admirable job in meeting this challenge in *The Road to Kells*.

The story begins with Mesolithic hunter-gatherers, who foraged in a forested primeval landscape and left traces of a campsite on a gravel ridge in Cakestown Glebe, overlooking the River Blackwater. It continues, chapter by chapter, over a span of c. 5,000 years, recording the homes, burial-grounds, work and worship of Neolithic, Bronze Age and Iron Age communities. It brings us at last to the threshold of history, in the Iron Age/early medieval transition period, when we meet agricultural workers on tillage land in Kilmainham, stoking the cereal-drying kilns that would secure their surplus grain harvest for the winter. Kells was not yet the seat of a famous monastery but had already become a central place in the region, with a tribal capital at Commons of Lloyd, on the hill that overlooks the town today.

A national road project delivers many benefits: shorter, safer journeys; enhanced economic opportunities; and a better quality of life in the towns and villages bypassed along the way. When we embark on these projects we sometimes discover other, unexpected benefits. In this case we have discovered the long prehistory of Kells and its hinterland. TII is committed to publishing archaeological discoveries on our national transport infrastructure projects in a variety of printed and digital media. We are delighted to bring you a new perspective on Kells in this latest title in the TII Heritage series and to congratulate everyone involved in bringing the work to completion.

Peter Walsh
Chief Executive
Transport Infrastructure Ireland

Acknowledgements

Several archaeological consultancies were involved in the investigations that preceded construction of the Navan to Kells and N52 Kells Bypass section of the M3 Clonee to North of Kells national road scheme. Margaret Gowen & Co. Ltd carried out the environmental impact assessment, which included some targeted geophysical survey by GSB Prospection Ltd, and Bartlett Clark Consultancy carried out blanket geophysical survey on the whole Navan to Kells section. Irish Archaeological Consultancy (IAC) Ltd carried out the preliminary test excavations and the archaeological excavations described in this book.

The excavations were commissioned by Meath County Council with funding from the National Roads Authority (now Transport Infrastructure Ireland). Ministerial Directions for the work were issued by the National Monuments Service, on behalf of the Minister for Environment, Heritage and Local Government, in consultation with the National Museum of Ireland. The engineering consultants for this phase of the M3 project were N3 Meath Consult, a joint venture of consulting engineering firms Arup, Halcrow Barry and RPS. The archaeological contracts were administered by Project Engineers Peter Thorne and Thomas Meagher of N3 Meath Consult and, on this section, by Resident Engineer Gillian Cogan. At Meath County Council National Roads Design Office the Senior Engineers were Nicholas Whyatt and John McGrath, the Project Archaeologists were Mary Deevy, Maria FitzGerald and Clare Crowley, and the Project Liaison Officer was Catherine Anderson. IAC Ltd and Meath County Council are grateful to the many landowners along the M3 route who facilitated our work on the road scheme.

The resulting book is based on the work of many colleagues. Shane Delaney was Senior Archaeologist for the project and oversaw all of the work, from testing through to post-excavation analyses and reporting. Fieldwork was managed by Shane Delaney, Tim Coughlan, Rob Lynch and Conor Gormley with support from the IAC Ltd office by Colette Rynhart, Carmel Mythen and Maeve Tobin. The excavations directors were Dave Bayley, Tim Coughlan, Carmel Duffy, Catriona Gleeson, Amanda Kelly, James Kyle, Patricia Lynch, Ed Lyne, Ciara MacManus, Gill McLoughlin, Fintan Walsh and Yvonne Whitty. David Swift was logistics supervisor for the on-site works. We are grateful to all of the archaeological supervisors, site assistants and surveyors who worked on the excavations, though we cannot list them all here. The machinery for topsoil-stripping and spoil management was provided by Joe O'Brien Plant Hire. Post-excavation analyses and reporting were managed at IAC Ltd by Gill McLoughlin, Maeve Tobin, Aoife McCarthy and Fintan Walsh, with assistance in report production from John Winfer and Michelle Brick. The figures in the preliminary and final excavation reports were by Graeme Kearney and Paul Higgins.

Specialist contributions were by Enid Allison and John Carrott (insect remains), David Brown (dendrochronology), Jennifer Coughlan (human bone), Niamh Doyle (post-medieval pottery), Ben Gearey with Emma Hopla and Thomas Hill (palynology), Eoin Grogan and Helen Roche (prehistoric pottery), Cathy Johnson (glass beads), Susannah Kelly (finds conservation), Susan Lyons (plants), Stephen Mandal (petrology), Margaret McCarthy (faunal remains), Jacqueline McDermott (metal objects), Alva McGowan (finds drawings), Eimear Nelis (chipped stone objects), Joe Norton (clay pipes), Ellen O Carroll (wood), Richard O'Brien (coarse stone objects), Lorna O'Donnell (charcoals), Ian Riddler and Nicola Trzaska-Nartowski (bone combs), Rachel Sloane (giant Irish deer bones at Newrath), John Stafford Langan (coins) and Angela Wallace (metallurgy). Radiocarbon dates are from the ^{14}CHRONO Centre at Queen's University Belfast and the Scottish Universities Environmental Research Centre. The figures for this volume are by Hugh Kavanagh (maps, site plans) and Dan Tietzsch-Tyler (artist's reconstructions). Eoin Grogan (Maynooth University) gave invaluable support as academic adviser for the project.

The final draft of the book was reviewed by TII Senior Archaeologist Mary Deevy and TII Archaeologist Emer Dennehy and prepared for publication by TII Archaeologist Jerry O'Sullivan. The book was copy-edited by Emer Condit, designed at Wordwell and was printed by W & G Baird.

The archaeological results presented in this book are based on reports by the individual excavation directors, including analyses by specialist contributors, but the authors are responsible for the final interpretations and, of course, for any errors. All of the original excavation reports on which the book is based may be consulted on the Internet in the TII Digital Heritage Collections at the Digital Repository of Ireland (https://repository.dri.ie/catalog/v6936m966).

CHAPTER 1

People of the Blackwater

Jim McKeon and Fintan Walsh

People of the Blackwater

The M3 Clonee to North of Kells motorway scheme traverses one of the richest archaeological landscapes in the country. Here, in the catchment areas of the River Blackwater and River Boyne in County Meath, there are prehistoric ritual and funerary monuments that are national treasures, such as the passage tomb cemetery of Loughcrew on Sliabh na Calliagh (Illus. 1.1), the Hill of Tara, the Hill of Slane, the Hill of Ward, and the great passage tombs of Newgrange, Knowth and Dowth in the bend of the Boyne known as Brú na Bóinne. As one of the key places in the history and prehistory of this region, the fertile agricultural land around Kells is similarly rich in archaeology. The ancient royal ceremonial complex at Teltown

Illus. 1.1 County Meath has an exceptionally rich heritage of prehistoric funerary monuments. Aerial view of part of the passage tomb cemetery at Loughcrew on Sliabh na Calliagh, Co. Meath, c. 15 km west of Kells (*Paul Naessens*).

(Tailtiú) is 5 km ESE of Kells. Much closer to the town, on its western outskirts, the Hill of Lloyd may have been the site of an ancient royal fort and assembly place. Kells itself is most famous for its fabulously illuminated eighth-century gospel-book. The town retains some of its early medieval built heritage, including a round tower, an early church or shrine chapel and high crosses, on a monastic site associated with St Columcille (Columba) of Derry and Iona (Illus. 1.2).

Taken all together, these sacred places do not speak for only one period but for most of prehistory and early history. They have been part of the cultural landscape almost since women and men first set down roots and began farming the land. Over several millennia, people worshipped at these places, built new monuments and modified or adapted existing ones to carry out their own particular rites and ceremonies. Then came Christianity, literacy and the end of prehistory. From that time onwards everything changed—not only in how and where people worshipped and disposed of their dead but also in almost every aspect of Irish society.

Illus. 1.2 An early monastery at Kells was endowed by the Uí Néill king of Tara Diarmait mac Cerbhaill in the sixth century. It was granted to Columban monks fleeing Viking attacks on Iona, in the Hebrides, in the early ninth century. A round tower and several high crosses form part of their legacy in Kells today (*Wikimedia, Stephen Keaveney*).

The principal rivers in this rich archaeological landscape, the Blackwater and the Boyne, were the major routeways of prehistory and early history, connecting people and places across the region. Our national roads fulfil that role today, and the M3 is now the principal way of travelling from Dublin in the east, across County Meath, on through County Cavan as the N3, and ultimately linking with the road network of the North of Ireland. Many archaeological sites were discovered, excavated and recorded along the route of the M3 motorway before it was built. These sites bear witness to the ancient communities of people who lived, worked and buried their dead in this special landscape.

The M3 Navan to Kells and N52 Kells Bypass run through the fertile, low-lying landscape of the River Blackwater catchment (Illus. 1.3 and 1.4). In total, 43 archaeological sites were excavated and recorded on this part of the scheme (Illus. 1.5 and 1.6) (Table 1.1), including some of the most important prehistoric sites discovered along the entire route. The aim of this book is to provide an easily

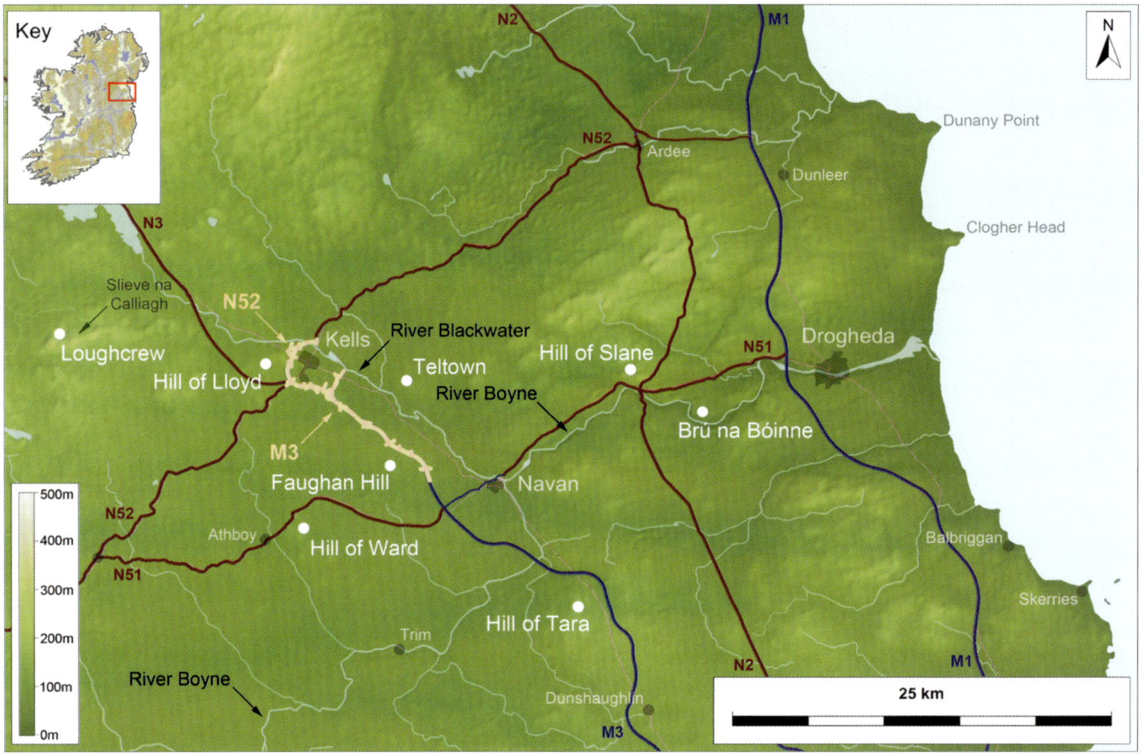

Illus. 1.3 Location map of the M3 Navan to Kells and N52 Kells Bypass road project, showing some of the more important archaeological locations in the hinterland of Kells (*IAC Ltd*).

Illus. 1.4 Aerial view of Kells, with the M3 motorway to the south, the N52 Kells Bypass and Hill of Lloyd to the west, and the River Blackwater winding around the northern outskirts of the town (*Ordnance Survey of Ireland*).

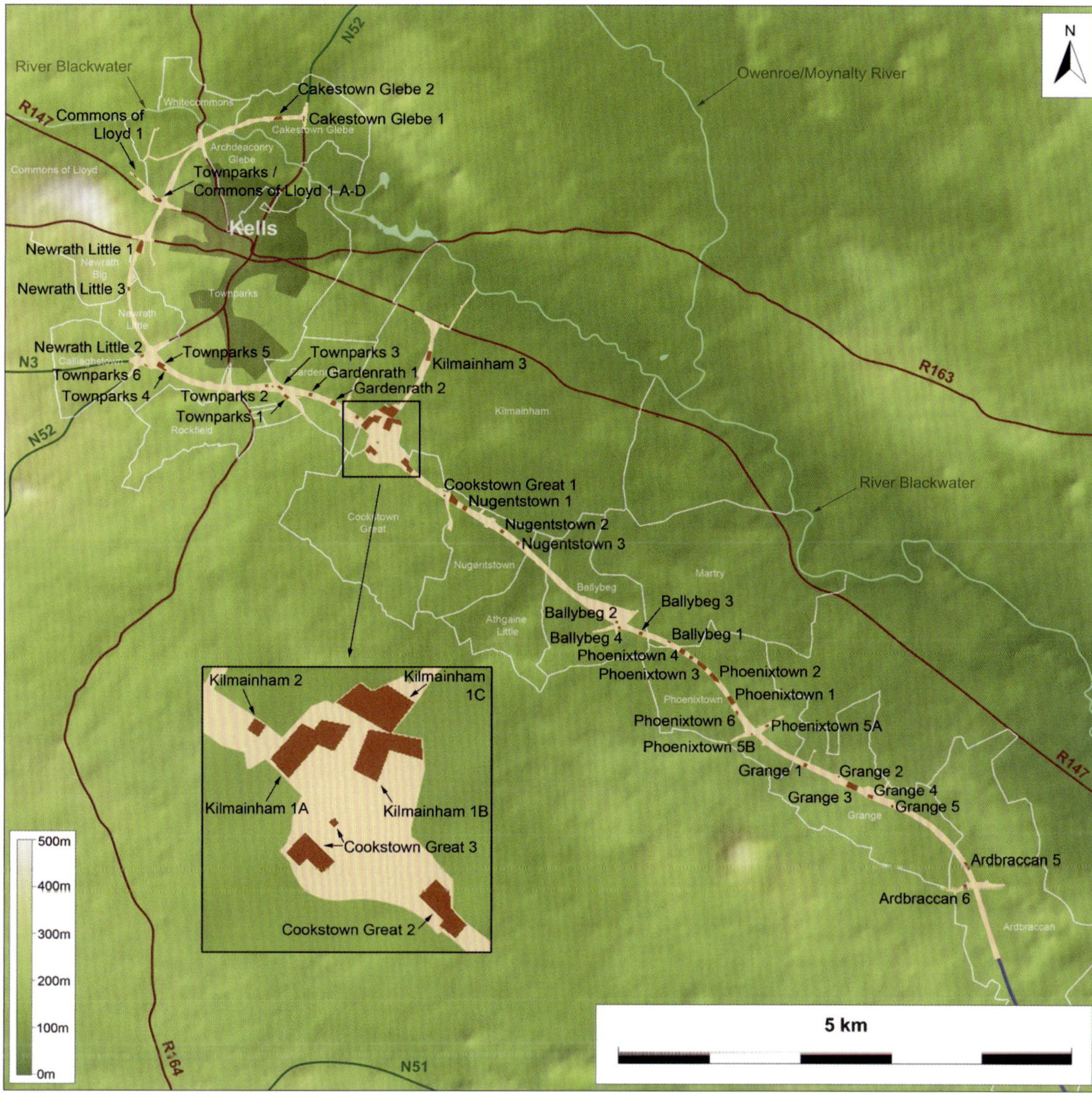

Illus. 1.5 M3 Navan to Kells and N52 Kells Bypass: 43 archaeological sites were excavated along the road project, representing all periods from early prehistory to early modern times (*IAC Ltd*).

digestible summary of the evidence from the prehistoric excavations on this section of the M3 in their cultural landscape context, rather than a site-by-site gazetteer of the excavated sites. Sites dating from the early medieval, later medieval and post-medieval periods were also recorded along this section of the motorway but they are not discussed in this book.

Chronologically, the book covers a period of about 5,000 years. The story begins c. 4500 BC at a Late Mesolithic cooking place just outside Kells, and ends during the time of transition between later prehistory and the early medieval period, heralded by the arrival of Christianity c. AD 400. Chronological periods in archaeology are continually refined and updated in response

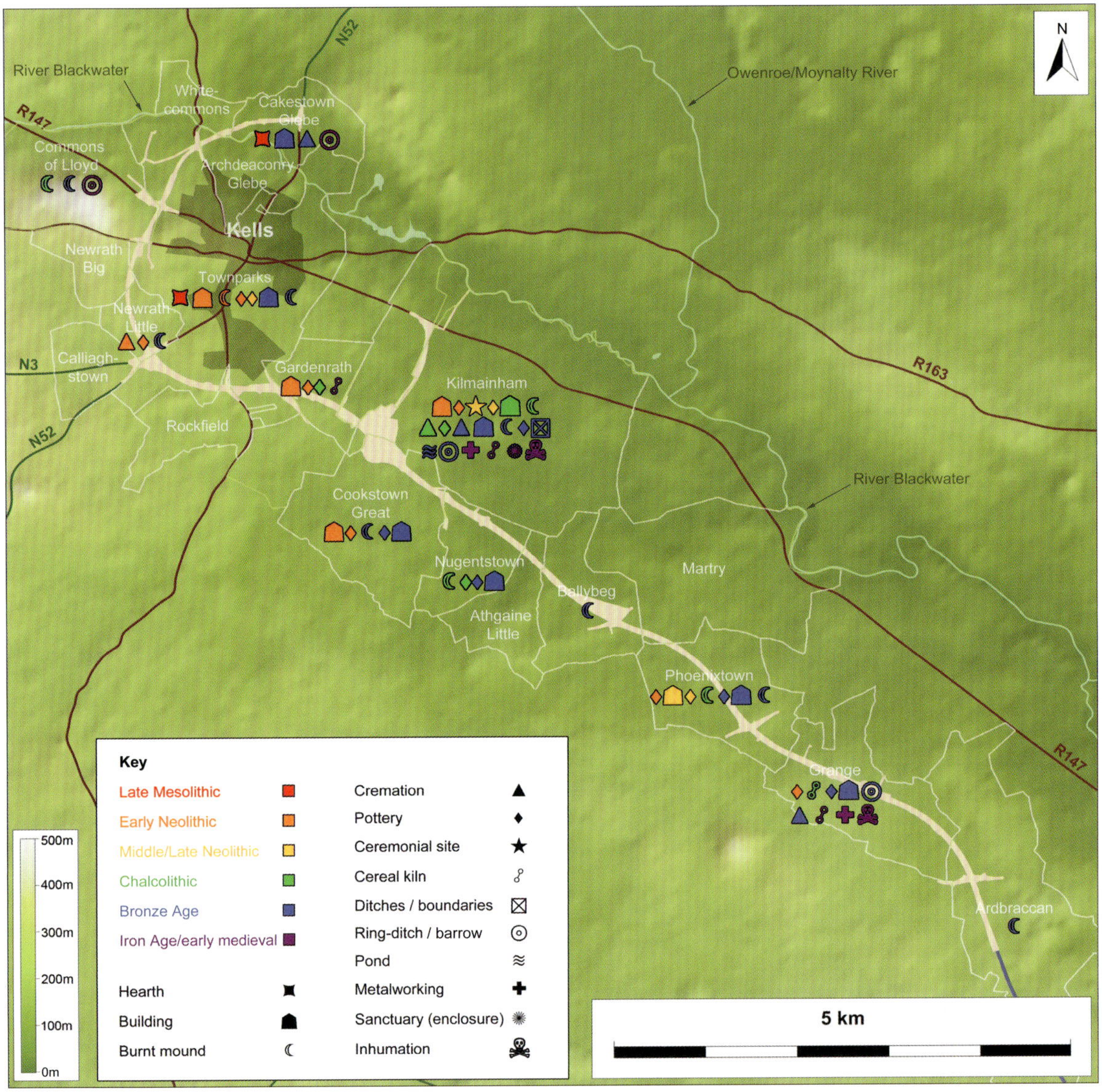

Illus. 1.6 M3 Navan to Kells and N52 Kells Bypass: summary map of the main prehistoric discoveries in each townland along the project route (*Hugh Kavanagh*).

to ongoing research, so the periods used in this book are not set in stone but serve simply as a framework and guide. Throughout the book, radiocarbon dates are given in calibrated form (i.e. in calendrical years) at a two-sigma level (95%) of statistical confidence. Full details of the dates, including lab reference codes, sample material and uncalibrated measurements, are given in Appendix 1.

Table 1.1—Excavated archaeological sites on the Navan to Kells and N52 Kells Bypass section of the M3, with the main periods represented on each site.

SITE NAME	Undated	Mesolithic 8000–4000 BC	Neolithic 4000–2450 BC	Chalcolithic 2450–2200 BC	Bronze Age 2200–800 BC	Iron Age 800 BC–AD 400	Transitional AD 400–500	Early medieval AD 500–1169	Late medieval AD 1169–1600	Post-medieval / early modern AD 1600–1900
Ardbraccan 5	■									■
Ardbraccan 6					■					
Ballybeg 1					■					
Ballybeg 2										■
Ballybeg 3					■					■
Ballybeg 4										■
Cakestown Glebe 1	■									■
Cakestown Glebe 2		■			■	■				■
Commons of Lloyd 1					■	■		■		
Cookstown Great 1			■			■				
Cookstown Great 2					■					■
Cookstown Great 3			■		■			■	■	■
Gardenrath 1				■	■					
Gardenrath 2			■	■	■		■			■
Grange 1					■		■			
Grange 2			■			■	■			
Grange 3				■	■		■	■		■
Grange 4			■		■			■		
Grange 5				■			■			
Kilmainham 1A			■		■		■			
Kilmainham 1B			■	■	■	■	■			■
Kilmainham 1C			■	■	■	■	■	■	■	
Kilmainham 2					■	■				

SITE NAME	Undated	Mesolithic 8000–4000 BC	Neolithic 4000–2450 BC	Chalcolithic 2450–2200 BC	Bronze Age 2200–800 BC	Iron Age 800 BC–AD 400	Transitional AD 400–500	Early medieval AD 500–1169	Late medieval AD 1169–1600	Post-medieval / early modern AD 1600–1900
Kilmainham 3			■		■	■				■
Newrath Little 1			■							
Newrath Little 2					■					
Newrath Little 3					■					
Nugentstown 1	■				■					
Nugentstown 2			■							
Nugentstown 3				■	■					
Phoenixtown 1			■	■	■					
Phoenixtown 2									■	
Phoenixtown 3			■		■				■	
Phoenixtown 4										■
Phoenixtown 5			■							
Phoenixtown 6			■		■					
Townparks 1					■					
Townparks 2		■	■							■
Townparks 3					■			■		■
Townparks 4	■									
Townparks 5			■							
Townparks 6			■							
Townparks / Commons of Lloyd 1				■	■					■
Totals	2	3	17	11	26	9	8	5	4	12

Archaeology and the M3

This book describes the prehistoric archaeology of the M3 Navan to Kells and N52 Kells Bypass road project. This section of the M3 is part of the much larger M3 Clonee to North of Kells national road scheme, which was one of the biggest public infrastructure projects in the history of the state. It involved the construction of 61 km of new motorway/dual carriageway along the primary route, as well as the single-carriageway Kells Bypass, with all associated link roads and bridges, and two toll plazas.

The full suite of archaeological investigations on the M3, including work on route selection and the environmental impact statement, included research in early maps and documentary sources, aerial reconnaissance, architectural heritage surveys, archaeological geophysical instrument surveys and archaeological excavations. Prior to the intensive manual excavation of individual sites, there was an extensive programme of test excavations by hand and by machine (under continuous archaeological supervision) throughout the entire footprint of the road project. In total, 167 archaeological sites were discovered and excavated on the M3, representing all of human history and prehistory in the region, from the Mesolithic period to early modern times. The 43 sites described in this book, on the Navan to Kells and N52 Kells Bypass section of the M3, were all excavated by IAC Ltd between 2005 and 2007.

Some of the investigations along the M3 Clonee to North of Kells project have already been published in books, conference proceedings and collected excavations summaries, including, most notably, *Places along the Way* (Deevy & Murphy 2009) and *Harvesting the Stars* (O'Connell 2013). For more detailed technical information on individual archaeological sites described in this book, readers may consult the Excavation Final Reports that are listed in Appendix 4 and that are now available on the internet, free to view and download, in the TII Digital Heritage Collections at the Digital Repository of Ireland (www.repository.dri.ie).

Archaeology of the River Blackwater catchment

Mesolithic period (c. 8000–4000 BC)

There are tentative glimpses in the Irish archaeological record of Upper Palaeolithic (literally 'Ancient Stone Age') people (Dowd & Carden 2016) but the first well attested population is not seen in Ireland until around 8000 BC, in our Mesolithic ('Middle Stone Age') period. These first people were semi-nomadic hunter-gatherers. Their campsites are found in low-lying places near to coasts, rivers and lakes. Such locations allowed them access to fish, one of the staples of their diet, which they supplemented by hunting (particularly wild pig) and by seasonal foraging for shellfish, berries and hazelnuts.

On the M3 Navan to Kells and N52 Kells Bypass project, evidence of these earliest people was found at two sites. At Cakestown Glebe 2, on a raised gravel ridge overlooking the River Blackwater, just north of Kells, a campsite or cooking place was represented by a Late Mesolithic hearth and post-holes, and by a stone tool typical of that time (a butt-trimmed mudstone flake). At Townparks 2 there was possible evidence for another campsite, with post-holes, chipped flint and a hearth dated to the Late Mesolithic/ Early Neolithic period. The most spectacular Mesolithic find from the M3 was not found on our section, however, but 30 km south-east at Clowanstown 1, on the Dunshaughlin–Navan section. Here, a fishing/mooring platform and four conical fish-traps, woven from slender rods, were found in peat deposits that had infilled a small lake (Chapter 3) (Mossop & Mossop 2009).[1]

Neolithic period (c. 4000–2450 BC)

The Neolithic revolution may have begun as early as 10,000 BC in the so-called fertile crescent that extends from the Nile in modern Egypt to the Tigris and Euphrates river valleys in modern Iraq and Syria. This saw the transformation of human cultures across the Middle East and then Europe from semi-nomadic hunting and gathering to more sedentary lives centred on livestock farming and cereal cultivation. As local populations expanded, people moved further inland and established permanent settlements, clearing forests for agriculture as they went. The Neolithic revolution reached Ireland c. 4000 BC. As elsewhere, this began a time of major social change and a greater concern for territory. Large ritual and funerary monuments were constructed (megalithic tombs), farmsteads with strong timber houses now appeared in the landscape, and the first Irish pottery also dates from this period. Early Neolithic houses were typically rectangular in plan and built with large timbers. By the Middle and Late Neolithic, houses were of various forms and generally less robust in their construction. Current evidence indicates that these innovations in the Early Neolithic period were introduced by an immigrant population of first farmers who either displaced or intermixed with the thinly scattered population of hunter-gatherers.

County Meath is graced with some of the best-known Neolithic ritual and funerary monuments in Ireland. These include the passage tombs of Brú na Bóinne—focused on Newgrange, Knowth and Dowth—and of Loughcrew and the Hill of Tara. Other megalithic tombs in the county include an isolated court tomb at Cornaville North and a wedge tomb at Edengera.

The Hill of Tara is c. 20 km south-east of Kells. The Tara complex includes funerary monuments and other earthworks of several periods, from the Neolithic to early medieval times. Excavations at the Mound of the Hostages (Duma na nGiall) confirmed that it was a passage tomb that had been reused for burials during the Bronze Age (Ó Ríordáin 1955; O'Sullivan 2005).

The archaeological landscape of Loughcrew covers at least eight townlands, roughly 15 km west of Kells. It features a number of Neolithic passage tombs, in addition to numerous cairns and standing stones, passage tomb art and rock art (Shee Twohig *et al.* 2010). A survey by archaeologists from the University of Cambridge, using lidar (airborne laser survey), has found many new monuments in the landscape around Loughcrew, including ancient field boundaries, small enclosures, and aligned post/pit features associated with a standing stone (Shell & Roughley 2004; Shell 2005). These add significantly to the record of this landscape published by the Archaeological Survey of Ireland in the inventory for the county (Moore 1987), which was based on traditional sources such as maps, aerial photographs and field inspection.

Roughly 27 km east of Kells, at Brú na Bóinne, the three great passage tombs at Newgrange, Knowth and Dowth are surrounded by over 30 smaller tombs, as well as pit circles, Neolithic houses, enclosures, passage tomb art, standing stones and cairns. These sites occur along the banks of

1 The fish-traps from Clowanstown were conserved and now feature in the permanent exhibitions of the National Museum of Ireland.

the River Boyne, a location that undoubtedly influenced this concentration of ritual and funerary activity. The passage tomb complex at Loughcrew is only c. 10 km from the River Blackwater, which flows north of Kells and joins the Boyne at Navan. Both rivers are navigable. They would have formed arterial routeways in prehistory, linking Loughcrew and Brú na Bóinne, and facilitating trade and communication between inland settlements and the Irish Sea coast. If this was the case, then the Neolithic sites discovered along our modern motorway project around Kells were ideally placed along this riverine highway.

The Neolithic sites found on the M3 Navan to Kells and N52 Kells Bypass project included the remains of a ceremonial post-built timber circle, with other building remains and Grooved Ware pottery, at Kilmainham 3, c. 1 km south-west of the River Blackwater. Grooved Ware is a Late Neolithic pottery type often found in association with ritual/funerary activity. There was also abundant evidence of domestic activity along this section of the M3, including at least eight Early Neolithic houses with associated features and finds, located within 3 km of each other, just south of Kells. Most of this early settlement evidence was discovered during the open excavation of an unusually large area on the site of a motorway intersection at Kilmainham/Cookstown Great (Illus. 1.7). At Kilmainham 1C alone there were the

Illus. 1.7 Aerial view from south-west of Kilmainham and Cookstown Great. The site of a motorway interchange provided the opportunity for a large-scale investigation of a multi-period prehistoric site (*Studio Lab*).

remains of at least a dozen prehistoric timber structures of one sort or another, including two Early Neolithic post-built houses (Structures 1 and 3) (Illus. 1.8 and 1.9). This is an extraordinary concentration of building remains on a single site—albeit a very large one in a rich agricultural landscape.

The majority of the structural evidence was for rectangular buildings. This is a common plan form for Early Neolithic houses. Many other examples are now known from across the region, including one from elsewhere on the M3, at Johnstown 1 (Elder & Ginn 2009). Another major site that testifies to a settled Neolithic population was excavated in advance of an industrial development at Townparks, on the north-west side of Kells and close to the banks of the River Blackwater. This was a multi-period site that included Neolithic occupation evidence (pottery and chipped stone tools), a curvilinear ditch and a palisade enclosure (undated) (Rohan 2006; 2007).

The settlement evidence recorded on the M3 provides valuable information on the domestic life and subsistence strategies of Neolithic communities and adds significantly to their known distribution in the region. Much of the recent information of this sort has come from pre-development excavations on linear project sites, including gas pipelines and national road schemes. Such linear projects typically allow only a narrow ribbon of the landscape to be investigated. Neolithic settlement on these projects is often represented by small clusters of features including one or

Illus. 1.8 Manual excavation, sampling and recording of pits and post-holes of an Early Neolithic house at Kilmainham 1C (*IAC Ltd*).

two houses, or none, but Grogan (2002, 524) argued that agglomerated settlement was a feature of life in the Early, Middle and Late Neolithic periods in Ireland. On the M3, the large, open-area excavation at Kilmainham/Cookstown Great confirms that Neolithic settlements were sometimes very extensive, with multiple houses dispersed over a large area. Settlements like this were permanent and potentially of long duration. Similarly, at Knowth there were five phases of Neolithic settlement (Grogan 2002, 522), and at Newgrange it has been suggested that there was a long pattern of continuing occupation or reoccupation, albeit by small groups (Cooney & Grogan 1994, 44; Grogan 2002; 2004). With reference to our own evidence from excavations on the M3, we can surmise that there was a large and well-established Neolithic population in the region, and we can say with full confidence that some of these people formed settlements on the lands around Kells, near the banks of the River Blackwater.

Chalcolithic period (c. 2450–2200 BC)

The first use of metal in Ireland occurred during a transitional time between the Late Neolithic period and the Early Bronze Age. This is variously known as the Chalcolithic, Copper Age or Beaker period. Copper was used for tools and ornaments, mostly simple axes and daggers. Gold was used for personal ornaments, like the beaten gold lunulae worn around the neck. The introduction of metalworking came with a distinct cultural package that included new pottery types (Beakers) and funerary monuments (wedge tombs), among other things. Wedge tombs are mainly distributed in the west and south-west of Ireland, but Beakers have been recovered from numerous excavated sites across the country, so it can be safely said that settlement at this time was widespread across the island.

We saw above that the introduction of farming in the Neolithic period was associated with an influx of people. Was this also true of the changes that occurred in the Chalcolithic period? There is new interest, and recent research, in the possibility of a major westward migration of people across Europe in this period, with a consequent displacement of local populations (Olalde et al. 2018). The evidence for this is lacking in an Irish context. In any case, migration alone would not explain all the technical and cultural changes at this time, which may owe as much to a diffusion of ideas and fashions, or, conversely, the complete absence in Ireland of the crouched inhumation burials that are associated with Beaker pottery elsewhere. Carlin (2018, 199) addressed this conundrum in a recent review of the Beaker phenomenon in Ireland and concluded, pungently, that 'The Beaker complex was a regionally divergent, socially constructed phenomenon, not a biological condition. The presence of people with a different (Steppe-related) genetic heritage in Britain or Ireland certainly does not explain the spread of Beaker pots to these islands or the adoption of new ideas, objects and practices in the third millennium BC.'

County Meath has its fair share of Chalcolithic sites. At Brú na Bóinne there was Chalcolithic settlement and ritual activity at Monknewtown, Newgrange and Knowth (Sweetman 1976; O'Kelly et al. 1983; Eogan 1984). Elsewhere along the M3 motorway route Chalcolithic evidence was recorded on several sites, particularly in the form of Beaker pottery. In our section, from Navan to Kells and the N52 Kells Bypass,

Illus. 1.9 (a) Kilmainham 1C: plan of the excavated features on the western part of the site. The remains of at least a dozen prehistoric buildings were recorded on this large and complex excavation site, including Early Neolithic post-built houses Structures 1 and 3 (*IAC Ltd*).

Illus. 1.9 (b) Kilmainham 1C: plan of the excavated features on the eastern part of the site (*IAC Ltd*).

Social and ceremonial places in later prehistory

The excavated archaeological sites on the M3 Navan to Kells and N52 Kells Bypass project show us the everyday life of later prehistoric communities. We have to look beyond the road scheme, however, for the great ceremonial places where these communities gathered for seasonal and religious events. There are at least two and possibly three such sites near Kells: Teltown, the Hill of Lloyd and Faughan Hill.

Teltown is the best known of the three sites. This landscape of ancient earthworks and early church sites is located 5 km south-east of Kells, in a bend of the River Blackwater on its northern bank. The prehistoric origins of Teltown have not been demonstrated by archaeological investigation but it shares some characteristics with similar sites of known prehistoric origin. At its centre is the large royal earthwork enclosure called Ráith Airthir. It was the site of an annual assembly (*Óenach Tailtiú*) at the festival of Lughnasa, presided over by the early kings of Tara (Binchy 1958; Bhreathnach 2011).

The Hill of Lloyd is less than 2 km from Kells and overlooks the town from the west. Faughan Hill is c. 8 km south-east of Kells. Both places have panoramic views and a direct line of sight with each other. In addition, the Hill of Tara, the Hill of Ward (another potentially important ceremonial site) and Teltown are all visible from Faughan Hill. Recent investigation by the Discovery Programme using lidar analysis and geophysical surveys at both sites, and limited excavations at Faughan Hill, confirmed that the two hilltops are ringed by concentric ditched enclosures of large diameter, with multiple smaller features that were probably ring-ditches or possibly round-houses (Illus. 1.10 and 1.11) (Dowling & Cahill Wilson 2014; Dowling 2015).

There are at least 74 hillforts in Ireland, and some other hilltop enclosures may also date from this period (Lock & Ralston 2017; Grogan 2005b, 112).[2] Only a few have been investigated. From this limited dataset it seems that the construction and use of hillforts commenced in the Late Bronze Age and continued throughout the Iron Age and into the early medieval period (Grogan 2005a, 217). The hilltop enclosures on the Hill of Lloyd and Faughan Hill can be classified as hillforts, though the remains are complex and include features of other periods too.

Hillforts were not principally occupation sites or even military fortifications. They were used for social and ceremonial gatherings that might have included inaugurations and religious festivals, funerals, fairs, martial displays and athletic contests. The construction of hillforts represents the cohesion of the communities that used them, and the power and prestige of their chiefs. They could be potent places in mythology: Faughan Hill is identified as the burial place of the legendary Niall of the Nine Hostages, the eponymous ancestor of the Uí Néill kings of early medieval Tara (Bhreathnach 2005; Byrne 1973, 77).

2 Lock & Ralston (2017) map over 500 Irish sites in the online *Atlas of Hillforts of Britain and Ireland*, but include numerous marine promontory forts, hillslope enclosures and miscellaneous other enclosures that would not be classified as hillforts by the Archaeological Survey of Ireland.

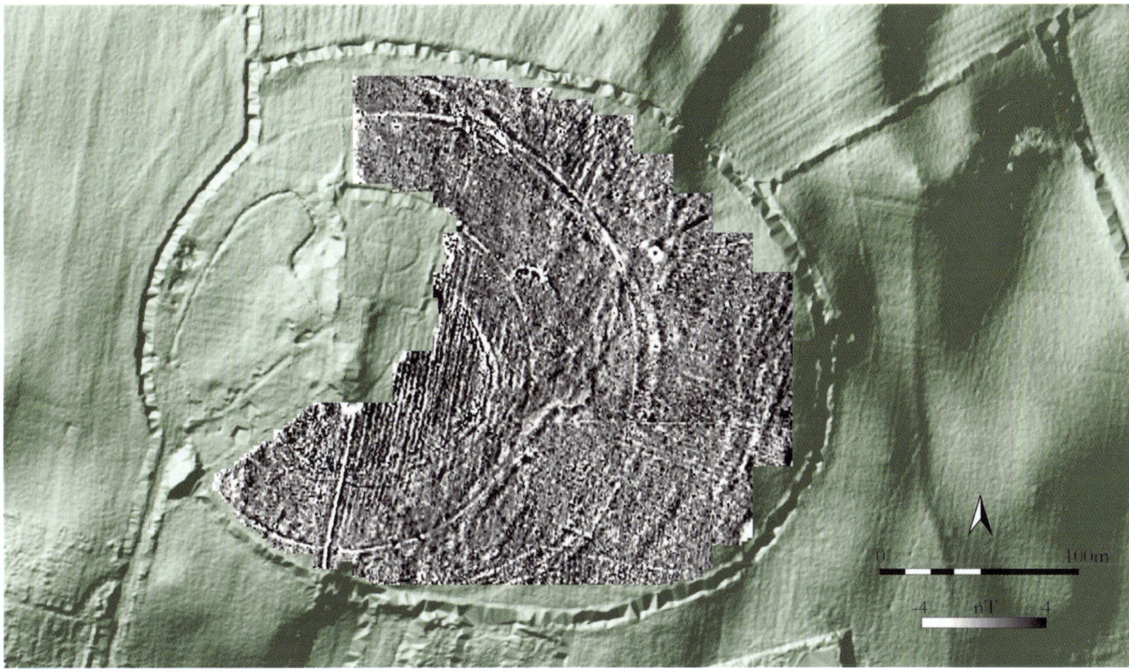

Illus. 1.10 The Hill of Lloyd overlooks Kells from the western outskirts of the town. An archaeological geophysical survey for the Discovery Programme confirmed the concentric earthworks of a large hilltop enclosure or hillfort (*Dowling 2015, fig. 13*).

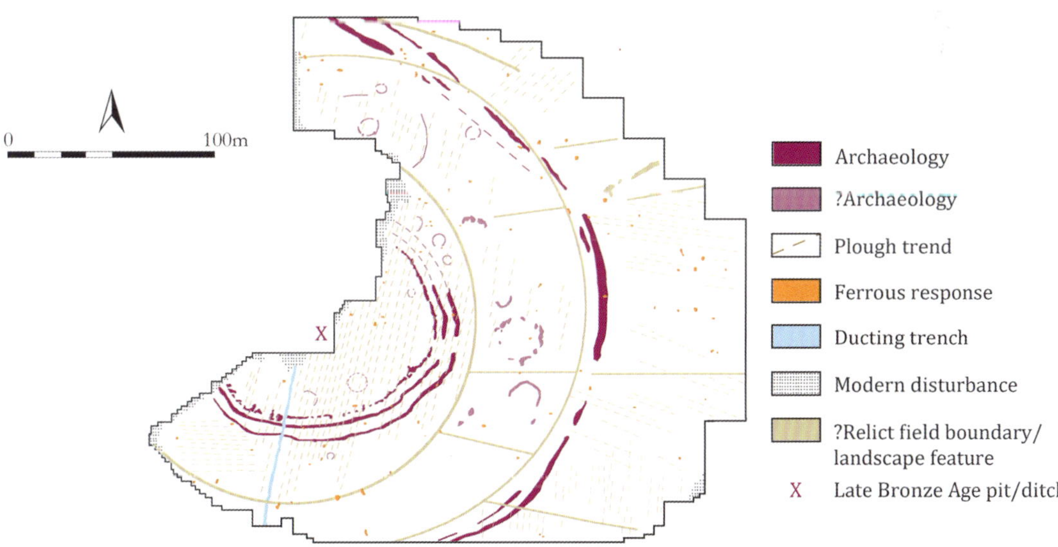

Illus. 1.11 Interpretive plan of the archaeological geophysical survey of the Hill of Lloyd, showing the concentric earthworks of a large hilltop enclosure, or hillfort. The unsurveyed area (left) is a community park containing the 'Spire of Lloyd', an 18th-century folly (*Dowling 2015, fig. 14*).

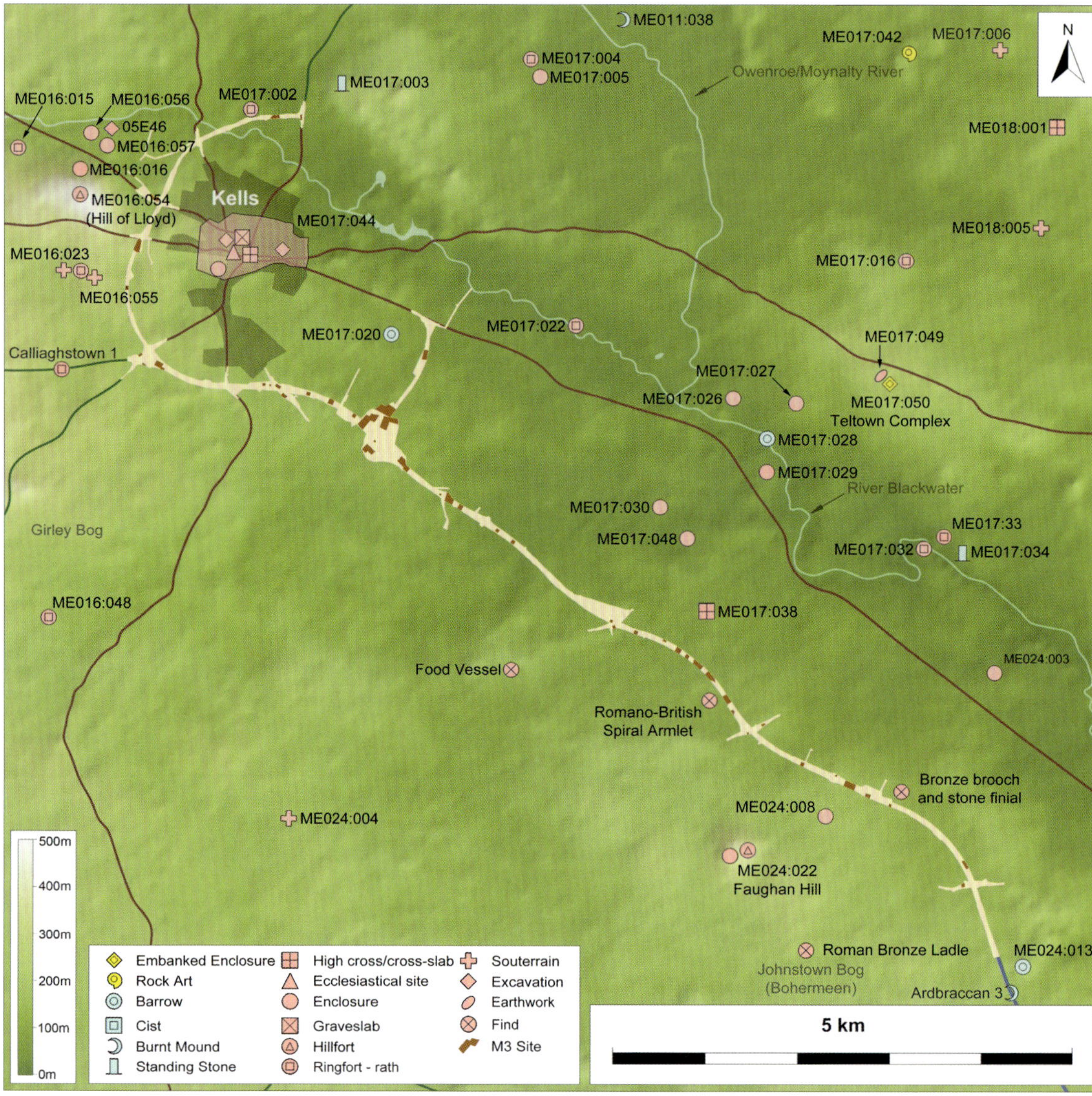

Illus. 1.12 M3 Navan to Kells and N52 Kells Bypass, with a distribution map of archaeological monuments (SMR Nos) and selected find-spots in the environs (*IAC Ltd*).

most of the evidence is from one site, at Kilmainham 1C (Illus. 1.9). Here there were Beaker pottery sherds, possible building remnants, pits, and a metalled platform or mound that seemed to be an outdoor working area. In all, Beaker pottery was recovered from four sites on this section: Gardenrath 2, Kilmainham 1C, Kilmainham 1B and Nugentstown 3. At Phoenixtown 6, a complete barbed-and-tanged flint arrowhead of Chalcolithic type was found. Three other sites yielded no diagnostic artefacts but did return Chalcolithic radiocarbon dates: Gardenrath 1, Grange 5 and Townparks/Commons of Lloyd 1.

Illus. 1.13 Roman bronze ladle (NMI No. P1000/WK3) from Bohermeen Bog, Co. Meath. Objects like this attest to the long-distance contacts of late prehistoric communities in the River Blackwater catchment (*National Museum of Ireland*).

Bronze Age (c. 2200–800 BC)

This period heralded the appearance of true bronze technology in Ireland. Bronze, an alloy of copper and tin, was now used to produce a greater variety of tools, weapons and ornaments, while gold was also used increasingly for personal ornaments. By the Late Bronze Age, Ireland, like much of Europe and Britain, had become a more hierarchical society with a dominant aristocratic warrior caste. This was a time of warfare, ostentatious displays of wealth, gift exchange, alliances and increased trade. Powerful chiefdom societies emerged and appear to have centred their power on large hilltop enclosures or 'hillforts'. There are at least 74 and possibly 90 known examples of these hillforts in Ireland. According to Grogan (2005b, 123), they were not only places of strategic military importance, power and influence but also symbols of communal pride and cohesion, reflecting a sense of collective identity for the people of the territory they commanded.

The typical settlement sites from this period feature round-houses, isolated or in small groups and sometimes found in ditched or palisaded enclosures. The most commonly discovered archaeological sites of the period are the burnt mounds, known as *fulachtaí fia*, which resulted from hot-stone water-boiling in pits or troughs, usually in bogs or similar environments with naturally high water-tables. (For a recent comprehensive study of burnt mounds in Ireland, see Hawkes 2018.)

There were major changes in ceramic traditions and burial practices. The heyday of the megalithic tomb was over. Pyre cremation gradually became the dominant funerary practice. Individual burials in pits or cists became the preferred method of disposing of the remains of the dead, either in isolation or in cemeteries, often in an urn and sometimes accompanied by smaller 'food vessels'. Barrows and ring-ditches became common burial monuments in the Middle to Late Bronze Age. These are commonly found to contain central cremation pits or cremated bone deposits and funeral pyre debris, either in or beneath a central mound or in the fill of the enclosing ditch.

Funerary and settlement sites dating from the Bronze Age occur throughout County Meath. In the 1980s the *Archaeological Inventory* for the county (Moore 1987) listed over 60 barrows and ring-ditches, and 22 cist burials. The number has greatly increased in the intervening years, principally owing to pre-development investigations. The online Sites and Monuments Record of the Archaeological Survey of Ireland (www.archaeology.ie) currently lists over 200 barrows and ring-ditches and over 30 cist burials. There is a cluster of barrows on the Hill of Tara and at least 17 secondary burials were inserted into the earth covering of the Mound of the Hostages (O'Sullivan 2005, 240). Barrows also form part of the Loughcrew complex, and Bronze Age burials were recorded at Fourknocks, c. 15 km south of Newgrange (Ó Ríordáin & Waddell 1993, 123–4). Other Bronze Age funerary sites in County Meath include cemeteries at Keenoge (Mount 1995) and Bettystown (Eogan 1998; 1999), and a ring-ditch with burial urns at Staleen (Campbell 2004). Further east, a number of Bronze Age house and settlement enclosures were discovered along the route of the M1 Northern Motorway–Drogheda Bypass project (e.g. Nelis 2012; Russell 2003a; 2003b). Burnt mounds are common and numerous examples have been recorded on pre-development projects in County Meath.

Bronze Age funerary and settlement evidence was recorded along the entire length of the M3 motorway scheme, including at least five buildings, five barrows or ring-ditches, three urn burials, and a 'flat cemetery' of pits with cremated bone, at Ardsallagh 2 (Clarke & Carlin 2008). Bronze Age pottery sherds were recovered from at least nine sites, representing food vessels, collared and cordoned urns and domestic wares. Over 40 sites had evidence of the hot-stone technology associated with burnt mounds (O'Connor 2007, 2).

A similar variety of archaeological evidence was recorded on the M3 Navan to Kells and N52 Kells Bypass section. Two Bronze Age barrows were excavated. One of these, at Grange 3, was a large example established in the Middle Bronze Age, with a ditch that was recut at a later date. Grange 3 also featured settlement evidence from the Middle and Late Bronze Age. Two round-houses, metalled surfaces or 'hard standings' and several pits and post-holes were excavated. The finds comprised domestic pottery and a large quantity of stone tools. Several other buildings were recorded along this part of the motorway, including two D-shaped buildings at Cookstown Great 3 and some small huts at Kilmainham 1C. Bronze Age pottery was recovered from several sites. This included cordoned urns, vase urns and a fine bipartite vase from Phoenixtown 3. Although they are more

Illus. 1.14 A post-built ceremonial enclosure at Lismullin 1, c. 20 km south-east of Kells, was the most important Iron Age site discovered on the M3 motorway scheme. In this image virtual timber posts have been inserted in post-holes identified on the excavated site (*Archaeological Consultancy Services Ltd*).

commonly associated with burials, some of these pots had previously been used in a domestic context. Finally, 15 burnt mounds, dating from the Late Neolithic period to the Bronze Age, were discovered along this section of the motorway.

Iron Age (c. 800 BC–AD 400)

Iron replaced bronze as the main metal used for manufacturing tools and weapons in Ireland around 800 BC. Unlike copper and tin (the components of bronze), iron ore was widely available from major sources like the Antrim basalts and Wicklow pyrites, as well as from rock outcrops and bogs (bog ores) across the country (Raftery 1994, 147). Pottery is a reliable indicator in the archaeological record of human activity in most periods but, for unknown reasons, there is a dearth of native Irish pottery from this period.

In County Meath the Hill of Tara continued in use into the Iron Age as a place of major ceremonial importance: the complex includes a large, hilltop enclosure from this period known as Ráith na Ríg (Roche 2002). To the east, in Brú na Bóinne, the mound of the great passage tomb at Knowth was the focus for an important Middle Iron Age cemetery (Eogan 2012, 13–44). Closer to Kells, the hillforts on the Hill of Lloyd and Faughan Hill were probably major Iron Age ceremonial centres, and Teltown was the site of a great annual assembly of the Uí Néill and their followers. It has been suggested that Kells itself originated as a royal fort or *dún* where early Uí Néill kings resided before their inauguration on Tara, though this may have been on the Hill of Lloyd and not on the site of the present town (Ní Bhrolcháin 2011, 50; Simms 1990, 1). Evidently the warrior aristocrats who commanded these hillforts had access to valuable goods from far beyond their own territories. This is suggested by finds of high-status objects of Late Iron Age date and possible Roman provenance in the district, like the Roman bronze ladle from Boheermeen Bog and the spiral armlet from Phoenixtown (Illus. 1.12 and 1.13) (Kelly 2002; Dowling 2015, 17–18).

Despite the continuing importance of these focal places in the landscape, archaeological evidence for settlement and funerary sites of the Iron Age was elusive in Ireland until recent years, when pre-development excavations on public infrastructure projects added a good deal of new information (e.g. Becker 2009; 2012; McQuade et al. 2009, 149–78). All along the M3, there was evidence from the period for crop-processing, metalworking and some funerary monuments. The exceptional discovery on the motorway route was a large, circular, post-built ceremonial enclosure at Lismullin, c. 20 km south-east of Kells and 2 km from Tara (O'Connell 2013) (Illus. 1.14). On the Navan to Kells and N52 Kells Bypass section there were cremation pits, a barrow, cereal-drying kilns, metalworking pits and assorted other pits and post-holes. Many of the excavated features returned radiocarbon dates spanning the transitional period between the Late Iron Age and the early medieval period (AD 400–500). Taken all together, the evidence attests an Iron Age population in the area but does not include any explicit evidence (e.g. enclosures, houses, hearths) for domestic habitation sites.

Early medieval period (c. AD 500–1169)

The early medieval period saw some of the greatest social, technical, environmental and economic changes in all of Irish prehistory and early history. There was a marked increase in population and, in contrast to the preceding Iron Age, there is abundant evidence of settlement. The landscape is still dotted with remains of the homesteads and stockyards (earthen raths/ringforts and stone cashels) that were built in great numbers from the sixth century onwards. The defining aspect of this period was the conversion from paganism to Christianity, which began some time during the fifth century. The new religion was accepted slowly at first, before spreading across the country and growing in influence. Ever since those early years the Church has left an abiding imprint on the cultural landscape of the island. Most importantly, perhaps, with Christianity came the written word, the end of prehistory, and thus a coda to our story in this book.

For most of this period Ireland was divided into numerous petty kingdoms or *tuatha*, allied to regional overkings. Kells and its hinterland were in the important regional kingdom of Brega of the Southern

Uí Néill, who also held Mide, to the west. The great passage tomb mound at Knowth became a royal seat of the kings of north Brega; it was enclosed by a ditch and houses were built on top of it (Eogan 2012). Tara, in the kingdom of Mide, retained its importance as the symbolic seat and inauguration place of the Uí Néill high kings. Teltown is recorded in this period as the site of a great assembly or fair that had origins in late prehistory. It was located on the Slí Assail, which was identified in the Annals of the Four Masters as one of the great highways of Ireland that allegedly converged on Tara (Geissel 2006, 9–10). There are numerous surviving ringforts in County Meath and also some good examples of the lake-dwellings of the period known as crannogs. A royal crannog at Lagore was investigated by the famous Harvard Expedition in the 1930s (Hencken 1950).

West of Teltown, the Slí Assail passed through Kells. There was now a monastic settlement here, situated on a prominent ridge south of the River Blackwater and overlooked by the Hill of Lloyd from the west. An ancient fording place probably influenced the choice of site. One derivation of the name Kells is 'Ceanannas' or 'Ceanannas Mór', meaning 'great residence'. It is recorded as a royal seat of the king of Tara, Diarmait mac Cerbhaill, in the sixth century. He probably endowed the first monastery. In the early ninth century it was granted to monks from Iona, the Hebridean monastery founded by St Colmcille, who were retreating from Iona following a devastating Viking raid recorded by the Annals of Ulster in AD 806. Their new home in Kells became a wealthy monastery. The world-famous Book of Kells may have been made there or brought from Iona and finished at Kells. In any case, it was kept at Kells until the 17th century. A small stone church or shrine chapel known as St Columba's House, a round tower and a group of elaborately carved high crosses are the main physical relics of the monastery that can be seen in Kells today.

The archaeological evidence for this period from the M3 Navan to Kells and N52 Kells Bypass project is very limited. It mostly relates to manufacturing or crop-processing (i.e. metalworking sites and cereal-drying kilns). This is in striking contrast to the archaeology of the more southerly part of the M3, where several large and complex early medieval settlement and funerary sites were recorded, at Baronstown, Castlefarm, Collierstown, Dowdstown and Roestown (Deevy & Murphy 2009). As we said above, however, that is another story.

CHAPTER 2

Landscape and environment

Lorna O'Donnell, Ben Gearey, Thomas C B Hill, Emma J Hopla and Jim McKeon

Landscape and environment

Topography, geology and land use

Jim McKeon

The landscape of County Meath is a rich mosaic of rivers and smaller streams, low hills, rolling farmland, peat bogs, woodland and, in the east, an Irish Sea coastline.[1] Central Meath, the part traversed by the M3 motorway, is low-lying and flat or gently undulating (50–100 m OD). It is drained by two major rivers—the Boyne and the Blackwater—and their many tributaries. There are low hills to the west and north-west of the county, on the fringes of a drumlin belt that extends into neighbouring Cavan and Westmeath. Farming, especially pastoral or livestock farming, is the main land use, but the soil is fertile and tillage is also practised. There are large-scale commercial farms in the south and east of the county, and stud farms typically in historic demesne settings. Smaller, mixed-use farms are more common in the hilly upland landscape of the north and west. In the heart of Meath, Navan is the county town, with a population of almost 37,000. Elsewhere along the M3 corridor, Dunshaughlin and Kells are smaller centres of commerce and community life, with populations of about 4,000 and 6,000 respectively.

The River Boyne and River Blackwater are designated Special Areas of Conservation (SAC No. 002299) (NPWS 2020) for their alluvial woodlands and populations of salmon, otter and lamprey (an ancient jawless fish). The Blackwater contains a healthy population of brown trout and most stretches provide good angling in season, from March to September (Inland Fisheries Ireland 2020). The Blackwater is the largest tributary of the Boyne and is fed by Lough Ramor in County Cavan. It flows in a south-easterly direction, passing north of Kells on the way to its confluence with the Boyne at Navan. It drains most of north County Meath and is itself fed by tributaries, including the Moynalty River and the Yellow River.

Broad-leaf woodlands and smaller copses are a common feature of the Meath countryside. Mature trees surround many archaeological monuments, especially ringforts and historic graveyards. Larger woodlands are still found on some of the old demesne landscapes that developed around mansion houses of the 18th and 19th centuries. Among today's tree species, oak is scarce but alder, beech and sycamore are abundant. Ash, hazel and hawthorn flourish

1 This section is largely based on two sources for landscape and land use in County Meath: ***The Making of Meath*** (2007) by Robert Meehan and 'Landscape Character Assessment' (Appendix 7) in the ***Meath County Development Plan 2013–2019*** (Meath County Council 2013).

Illus. 2.1 View south-west over Grange and Phoenixtown, with the Grange 3 excavation site in the foreground. The flat, fertile land in central County Meath is suitable for tillage as well as livestock farming (*Studio Lab*).

Illus. 2.2 View north-east over Archdeaconry House towards Cakestown Glebe on the north bank of the River Blackwater, with the Cakestown Glebe 2 excavation site at top right. The landscape around Kells has frequent low hillocks and ridges formed by glacial sands and gravels (*Studio Lab*).

in the hedgerows that divide farmland and border local roads. Of these, oak, ash, hazel, hawthorn and alder are native trees. Beech and sycamore are among the broad-leaf trees introduced on landed estates in the post-medieval and early modern periods.

The underlying land-forms are a combination of solid geology and glacial deposits. Throughout most of County Meath, limestone of the Carboniferous period, 354–298 million years old, is the dominant rock type. The calcareous soils derived from limestone nourish the rich grass pastures of the county. Namurian shales (Carboniferous period) form some of the hills, including Tara and Skreen. Ordovician and Silurian shales and sandstones, 495–410 million years old, are the underlying geology of the Kells area.

Overlying the solid bedrock geology of County Meath, the subsoils are mostly stiff silts formed on glacial till, typically with a combined depth of 5 m or more. The topsoils are mostly grey-brown podzolics, which are versatile, well-drained soils suited to arable and pastoral farming (Illus. 2.1). In the upland areas to the west and north-west the soils are less fertile and the topography more varied, so the landscape here is better suited to livestock farming, or to forestry and rough grazing on the wetter areas of peat and peaty gleys. Locally, the area around Kells is mostly characterised by the low sand-and-gravel ridges (eskers), hillocks and hollows (kames and kettles) that are the legacy of melting glaciers (Illus. 2.2). Between the ridges and hillocks drainage is often poor, forming pockets of wetland where peat has formed. Otherwise, the overlying soils around Kells are brown earths, which are well-drained, mature soils ideally suited to arable farming.

Pollen evidence from Kilmainham and Newrath Big

Ben Gearey, Emma J Hopla and Thomas C B Hill

As part of the M3 archaeological programme, natural deposits with the potential to yield evidence for past vegetation change and human activity were sampled at several locations (Illus.2.3). The sites investigated represent a range of different sedimentary contexts, including floodplain deposits at Castletown Tara and Pottlebane; marl and peat from an infilled open water body (via hydroseral succession) at Newrath Little; and shallow organic deposits associated with surface water ponding in a natural hollow (topogenous accumulation) at Kilmainham. The age range of these deposits is broad, with the majority of the Newrath Little sequence dating from the Late-glacial period but also spanning the early Holocene (i.e. after c. 9750 BC). Some of these sequences can be regarded as providing 'snapshots' of vegetation change at particular places and times. The sample sites in Kilmainham and Newrath Little (Illus. 2.4) are most relevant to the Navan to Kells and N52 Kells Bypass section of the M3 and the results from those locations are summarised here.

Pond site at Kilmainham 1C

Pollen analysis at Kilmainham 1C was carried out on deposits of well-humified silty peat, 0.6 m thick, sampled from a low-lying hollow (the former pond). The peat deposit sealed a scatter of waterlogged wood, including worked pieces. Radiocarbon dates from the top and base of this deposit are statistically inseparable (top: 1930–1695 BC, Beta-235626; base: 1890–1640 BC, Beta-235627), which suggests either that the deposit accumulated rapidly or that one or both of

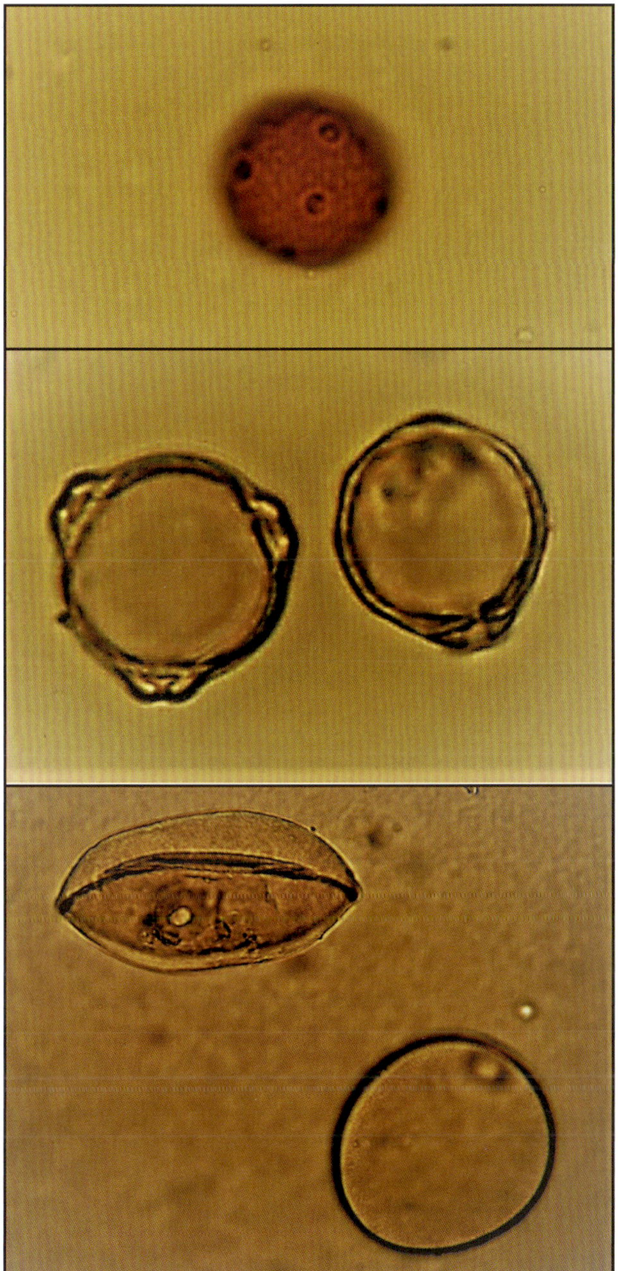

Illus. 2.3 Ancient pollen grains recovered from waterlogged deposits at several sample sites along the route of the M3 Clonee to North of Kells national road scheme indicate a constantly changing mosaic of pasture, tillage and woodlands in the prehistoric landscape. From top: plantain (*Plantago*), a common pasture weed; birch (*Betula*), an early post-glacial coloniser; and oats (*Avena*), a cultivated cereal crop (*Ben Gearey*).

the dates is in error. Error is less likely and the consistency between the two determinations suggests that the deposit dates largely from the Early Bronze Age. Chronological (Bayesian) modelling indicates that the sequence covers the period 2060–1675 BC (95% probability; base boundary), and probably 2025–1775 BC (68% probability), to 1510–1125 BC (92% probability; top boundary), and probably 1390–1214 BC (68% probability). (For details of the chronological analysis see Gearey et al. 2011; for original calibrated date ranges see Appendix 1.) The sediments accumulated relatively quickly in a shallow pond or pool. The basal deposit, underlying the peat, was a yellow-brown silt, which was not radiocarbon-dated but which seems to represent a much earlier period of accumulation.

The pollen data represent a snapshot of the local vegetation. Although the record is comparatively short in terms of chronology (perhaps four centuries), its value is enhanced by the fact that the source area is likely to have been relatively small. Thus the pollen record reflects vegetation that grew within an area that can probably be measured in terms of tens of metres around the pond.

Woodland consisting of alder–hazel–oak (*Alnus–Corylus–Quercus*) is indicated, with perhaps some willow (*Salix*) and elm (*Ulmus*), but there is also good evidence for open grassland. Although herbs other than wild grasses (Poaceae) and ribwort plantain (*Plantago lanceolata*) are

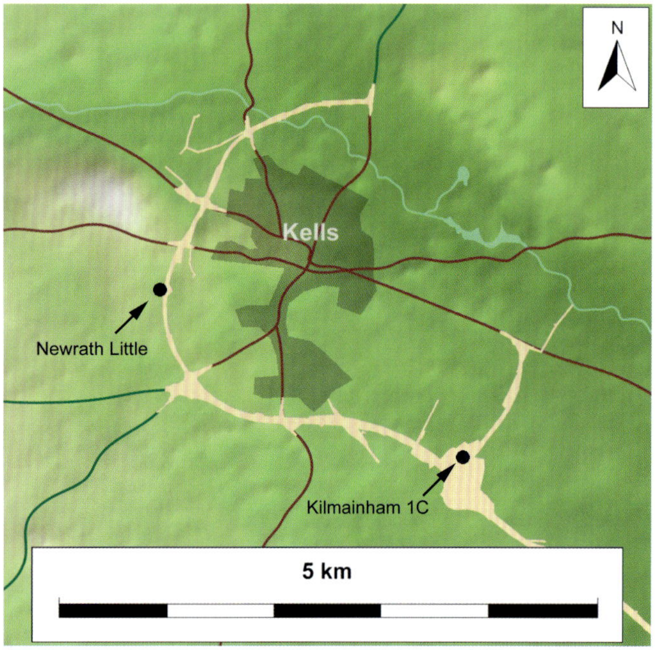

Illus. 2.4 M3 Navan to Kells and N52 Kells Bypass, showing locations of peat-sampling sites for pollen analysis at Newrath Little and Kilmainham. Samples at Newrath Little were from a small wetland area with peat overlying clay marl, silts and gravels. Samples at Kilmainham 1C were from silty peat deposits in an infilled pond that contained worked timbers (hazel, alder) and driven posts (oak) (*IAC Ltd*).

poorly represented, a comparatively wide range of taxa are present. These include docks (*Rumex*), clover (*Trifolium*-type), dandelions (Lactuceae), tormentil (*Potentilla*-type) and meadow rue (*Thalictrum*-type), all of which are indicative of grassland environments. Tall herbs such as meadowsweet (*Filipendula*) and ferns (Pteropsida monolete, indeterminate) and common polypody (*Polypodium vulgare*) indicate damp, probably shady environments, within or at the fringes of the pond. Members of the rose family (Rosaceae) are continuously present. This is a very large family, including a wide variety of fruiting trees, shrubs and perennials. Among these, *Rubus*-type, which is a pollen type including blackberries and raspberries, is recorded in trace values towards the middle of the zone. Occasional grains of cereal-type may reflect local tillage, although this pollen type can include wild grasses.

From this evidence we can say that the Bronze Age landscape around the pond at Kilmainham was a mosaic of woodland, pasture/grassland, waste or disturbed ground (i.e. ruderal environments) and tall herb communities. The range and character of the herbs recorded very strongly suggest a human presence, with vegetation created and maintained by pastoral farming but with arable cultivation also possible. It is highly likely that alder and willow were growing on the poorly drained soils around the pond, with oak, hazel and elm established on the better-drained slopes nearby, but the precise structure and distribution of the vegetation cannot be discerned from the pollen. Another feature of the record is the fact that the percentages of trees/shrubs and herbs show very little fluctuation across the diagram, indicating little significant change in the relative area of woodland and grassland during the period represented by the sample.

The tree/shrub cover might have been relatively open, with tracts of grassland among the trees. Alternatively, the pond could have been at an interface between discrete areas of closed woodland and grassland. Another possibility is that the pond was located within a stand of woodland in an otherwise open landscape that had previously been cleared of woodland cover. The persistence of woodland throughout the record could mean that the local woodland may have been managed in some way or that livestock farming was relatively unintensive, perhaps a form of 'forest farming'.

Palaeoentomological (beetle) analysis sheds further light on both the pond deposits and the surrounding Bronze Age landscape (Allison et al. 2011). The beetles indicate still, shallow but not necessarily permanent standing water in the hollow. There is also evidence for damp, shady woodland, in the form of insects associated with both oak and hazel. Other elements of the beetle fauna indicate grasslands and grazing animals. Some material that may have derived from a bird's nest could indicate trees and shrubs overhanging the sampling site. This tends to support the hypothesis that the pond was located in an area of woodland within an otherwise relatively open grassland landscape, although it is not possible to determine the exact spatial extent of these environments.

The archaeological record complements the pollen evidence and also indicates that the sampling site was a focus for human activity. Kilmainham 1C was an unusually large excavation site with evidence for settlement, ritual and industrial activity from the Early Neolithic to the medieval period. There was a burnt mound with a wood-lined trough immediately adjacent to the pond,

Illus. 2.5 Newrath Little: this wetland area near the N52 Kells Bypass provided a core sample for fossil pollen analysis. An excavation site at Newrath Little 3 can be seen in the background (*Ben Gearey*).

and the remains of another mound some 50 m to the west. Within the pond itself there were worked timbers, including several posts driven into the base and a number of split planks. The posts and planks were all of oak. They are interpreted as the collapsed remains of a platform providing access to the water. (Two of the oak posts produced unexpectedly early dates, suggesting reused timbers: see Chapter 7.) Other pieces of wood, including a chisel-pointed stake (hazel) and a log (alder) with axe marks at both ends, were found within the pond sediments. The removal of at least some of the screening woodland around the site, presumably to provide better access to the water, is suggested by the worked wood in the base of the pond. The pond was probably used as a waterhole for grazing animals and was possibly a source of water for the nearer of the two burnt mounds. The sediment infilling the pond probably reflects natural processes rather than a single event and may have been accelerated by the effects of trampling by humans and animals around the site.

Illus. 2.6 Newrath Little: the cored sediments from the wetland sampling site were dominated by pre-Holocene marl, a calcareous deposit that formed in open bodies of standing water (*Ben Gearey*).

A wetland area at Newrath Little

This small area of wetland (Illus. 2.5) was located some 600 m north of the archaeological site at Newrath Little 3, on the margins of the N52 Kells Bypass. Coring identified a sediment sequence up to 4.0 m deep, consisting of c. 1.0 m of peat over c. 2.5 m of calcareous marl (Illus. 2.6), underlain in turn by a thin, well-humified peat unit, then grey silts and clays over basal gravels. The marl was strongly laminated, with variations in organic content. Pollen assessments were carried out at 0.16 m intervals along the sample core. Three radiocarbon dates were obtained: (a) from the base of the lower peat deposit (depth 3.71 m), (b) at the transition from lacustrine marl to fen peat (depth 0.99 m), and (c) at the transition from fen peat to organic mud (depth 0.30 m).

Examination of the two basal peat samples (depths 3.68 m and 3.84 m) recorded low concentrations of poorly preserved pollen. A calibrated date of 13,620–13,170 BC (Beta-235620) indicates that the basal peat began to accumulate during the climatic amelioration of the Woodgrange Interstadial (cf. Lowe et al. 2004). The transition from basal peat to organic marl indicates the replacement of a semi-terrestrial environment with open water on the sampling site. The pollen record implies a largely open environment with grasses and sedges and other herbs, including rock rose (*Helianthemum*-type), sorrels/docks (*Rumex*) and meadowsweet, and an aquatic

Giant Irish deer from Newrath Little

After the main phase of the investigations was completed on the M3 motorway scheme, ongoing construction works were monitored by archaeologists. During the works, skeletal remains of at least two giant Irish deer (*Megaloceros giganteus*) were found in a small wetland area in Newrath Little. The deer remains were found in a deposit of marl, 2.5 m thick, beneath 1.0 m of overlying peat. Marl is a calcareous white clay-silt that forms in open bodies of standing water. In Ireland, marl deposits are commonly found beneath fen peat in infilled lakes and ponds.

The giant Irish deer was a tall, powerful animal, much bigger than any modern species of deer in Ireland, with magnificent spreading antlers (Illus. 2.7). It stood to about 2.1 m in height. Its antlers were up to 3.65 m in span and weighed up to 40 kg.

The remains found at Newrath Little were a complete skull with antlers (Specimen 1), a fragment of skull with a single antler attached (Specimen 2) and a fragment of antler. Like modern deer, giant Irish deer shed their antlers each year in early spring and grew new ones for the autumn mating season. As the animals from Newrath Little were carrying fully grown antlers, they must have died between autumn and spring. Malnutrition during these colder months would have increased the vulnerability of the animals to starvation, disease and fatal accidents. Other deaths in a herd could result from the injuries sustained in fighting between the males during the autumn rutting, exacerbated by the huge loss of energy expended in the rut. Both circumstances would have made the animals vulnerable to wolves.

A fragment of one antler from Newrath Little was dated to 11,480–11,210 BC (Poz24082) before the onset of the last extreme cold spell of the glacial period and long before the first humans ventured into the region.

Illus. 2.7 Giant Irish deer (*Megaloceros giganteus*) roamed the landscape of Ireland long before the arrival of the first people. The skull and antlers of this specimen were found beneath the fen peat infilling a former lake in Newrath Little (*John Sunderland*).

flora including alternate-leaf water milfoil (*Myriophyllum alterniflorum*). Woody taxa including birch (*Betula*) and heather (*Calluna vulgaris*) are attested and juniper (*Juniperus communis*) also expanded, suggesting that soils had stabilised sufficiently to allow scrub to become established. Such vegetation is typical of the early Post-glacial period in Ireland. The presence of hazel/sweet-gale (*Corylus avellana*-type) pollen at this time is not typical and probably reflects some reworking of the sediments in this basal zone with redeposition of pollen from secondary sources. Giant Irish deer bones from the base of the profile also date from this period (see text box, 'Giant Irish deer', below).

A subsequent decline in juniper, followed by birch, reflects climatic deterioration during the late Interstadial and the onset of colder conditions during the Nahanagan Stadial, resulting in an open, treeless, tundra dryland around the sampling site. The pollen data show a phase of birch and willow expansion and the development of closed woodland, with hazel subsequently expanding to replace these shrubs and become the dominant woody taxa. Pine (*Pinus* sp.) is often seen to expand at this time (e.g. Molloy & O'Connell 2004), but its rise seems to have been delayed until later at Newrath. Elm also increased later, but percentages of oak remained low. A radiocarbon date of 8010–7650 BC (82.5%) (8180–7610 BC at 2σ; Beta-235619) at a depth of 0.99 m may be slightly too young (i.e. too late in the sequence) for the subsequent establishment of hazel woodland indicated by the pollen record. The date of 4620–4450 BC (87.8%) (4680–4450 at 2σ; Beta-235618) at a depth of 0.3 m also appears too young. Alder should have appeared by this time but is recorded at trace levels only. Rootlet penetration can cause a 'younging' effect in dated peat samples. Alternatively, there may be a hiatus in the upper part of the record. A subsequent fall in hazel and elm coincides with a peak in grasses, sedges and other herbs, including low peaks in ribwort plantain and dandelions, and trace values of other herbs. These changes imply the opening up of the woodland canopy—an effect of human settlement and associated activities throughout the Neolithic period and the Bronze Age.

It is very clear that most of the deposits analysed represent the period from the Woodgrange Interstadial (c. 13,000 BC), through the Nahanagan Stadial (c. 10,950 BC), to the opening of the Holocene (c. 9750 BC). The precise timing of these climatic shifts is unclear from the available data, but the pollen record indicates vegetation typical of the open, scrubby environments that persisted during the Late-glacial period. During this time, sediment deposition shifted from inorganic sandy silt to well-humified peat, with poorly preserved or sparse pollen, to lake marls, then back to peat accumulation as the water body eventually infilled and was colonised by vegetation.

The expansion of birch, followed by hazel and other trees, including elm and pine, is also typical of the early Holocene. It is unclear how much reliance may be placed on the two radiocarbon dates at the lower and upper boundaries of the peat (Beta-235618 and Beta-235619, above), as they both appear too young for the corresponding pollen spectra.

Evidence for human activity in the record is restricted to the decline in trees/shrubs and the rise in herbs, including 'anthropogenic indicators' (e.g. ribwort plantain), in the final, uppermost zone of the sample core. The date or precise character of this is unclear, especially given the uncertainty surrounding the uppermost date and the possible presence of a hiatus in this part of the record.

Wood charcoal from excavated sites

Lorna O'Donnell

Charcoal from archaeological sites provides evidence of how woodlands were exploited in the past. Identification of the species represented in a charcoal assemblage can indicate the character and diversity of local woodlands. The contexts from which the charcoals are recovered—for instance, a post-hole, a hearth or a funerary pyre—can reveal whether particular wood types were favoured for construction, for domestic fuel or for ritual acts. The trees and shrubs most frequently appearing in the charcoal record of excavated sites on the M3 Navan to Kells and N52 Kells Bypass project are oak (*Quercus*), hazel (*Corylus*), alder (*Alnus*) and ash (*Fraxinus*). A variety of other trees and shrubs are also represented, including birch (*Betula*), elm (*Ulmus*), holly (*Ilex*), spindle (*Euonymus europaeus*) and willow (*Salix*), as well as blackthorn (*Prunus spinosa*) and wild/bird cherry (*Prunus avium/padus*) and other, unidentified members of the Maloideae.[2]

Oak is an exceptionally strong and durable species that was often favoured for construction in early Irish history and prehistory. It can reach a height of 40 m and live for 1,000 years or more (Hickie 2002, 60). There are two native species of oak in Ireland. They prefer different habitats but cannot be distinguished by wood anatomy (i.e. from close examination of the charcoals). The sessile oak (*Quercus petraea*) thrives on less fertile acidic soils, often in hilly areas. The pedunculate or common oak (*Quercus robur*) grows on heavy lowland soils and tolerates flooding (ibid.). Hazel often occurs as an understorey to oak (Illus. 2.8). It is a medium-sized deciduous tree or shrub and can reach a height of 12 m. It tolerates a wide range of soils but favours calcareous soils especially (Lipscombe & Stokes 2008, 102). When it is felled, the stools produce fast-growing clusters of long, pliable branches, making it ideal for coppicing and for use in woven panels of wattlework. Hazelnuts were an important wild food source in prehistory and are often found on domestic habitation sites in all periods. Alder (Illus. 2.9) is a fast-growing tree that reaches 20 m in height. It prefers dry soils but has a high tolerance of wet conditions and is commonly found on riverbanks and wetland margins (Stuijts 2005). The wood is easily worked and was favoured in antiquity for making wooden bowls and cups. Ash is a fast-growing tree that typically reaches 20 m in height and can reach 35 m. It tolerates a range of soils but favours calcareous soils, on limestone (ibid.). It is a light-loving tree and, in prehistory, can be an indicator of clearances for settlements, crops and grass pasture. The wood is tough but elastic. It is excellent for tool handles and, of course, is used in making hurleys.

Three case-studies are presented here in order to examine woodland cover in detail: charcoal from excavations in Kilmainham, Phoenixtown and from all the *fulachtaí fia* along the project route (Tables 2.1, 2.2 and 2.3).

2 Maloideae (formerly called Pomoideae) is the name of a large sub-family of the Rosaceae that includes flowering and fruiting trees and shrubs like crab-apple (***Malus sylvestris***), rowan (***Sorbus aucuparia***), whitebeam (***Sorbus aria***) and hawthorn (***Crataegus monogyna***).

Illus. 2.8 The first people to colonise the Irish midlands would have encountered dense forests of oak (centre) and elm with an understorey dominated by hazel. Oak and hazel were among the most frequent types of wood in charcoal samples from the excavated archaeological sites on the road project (*Lorna O'Donnell*).

Illus. 2.9 Alder is a fast-growing tree that tolerates poorly drained ground and is commonly found on riverbanks and wetland margins. It occurs frequently in charcoal samples from the excavated archaeological sites (*Lorna O'Donnell*).

Neolithic period

When the first farmers arrived in what are now the environs of Kells they would have found a landscape dominated by mature oak woodlands, with an understorey of holly and hazel. Birch, alder and willow would have flourished around any wetlands. Smaller flowering and fruiting trees of the Maloideae group would have grown on woodland margins. Clearing the woods to make space for cereal crops and grass pasture was an arduous undertaking for these first farmers, performed with stone axes as the main tools, probably aided by fire-setting.

Oak was widely used in Early Neolithic Ireland for the construction of houses (e.g. O Carroll 2011; Stuijts 2005; Smyth 2014, 34). Some of the earliest charcoal evidence from the M3 Navan to Kells and N52 Kells Bypass project is from rectangular, post-built houses at Kilmainham 1C (Structures 1 and 3). Oak was the main wood used in these houses, both as a construction material and as a fuel in domestic hearths. It dominates the charcoals recovered from most features, including primary contexts such as posts burnt *in situ* and hearths, and secondary contexts such as post-hole packing and pit fills. Various other wood taxa were also present at this site, including alder, ash, elm, hazel, holly, *Prunus* (a large genus of flowering and fruiting trees that includes wild cherry and blackthorn), Maloideae and willow.

Oak was also used for the construction of a rectangular, post-built Early Neolithic house (Structure 2) at Kilmainham 1A. It dominated the charcoals from some of the post-holes. The charcoal from other post-holes, however, included alder, ash, elm, hazel and *Prunus*. It may be that some of these were secondary or intrusive charcoals that were lying about on the occupation surface and became part of the infill of post-holes where oak timbers had decayed *in situ* or were removed.

At Phoenixtown 6 there was no identifiable house, but a hearth of Early Neolithic date included charcoals of alder, ash, hazel, oak, Maloideae and willow.

Oak features again as a preferred wood for construction in the Late Neolithic period, in the remains of a possible building (Structure VI) at Kilmainham 1C, which was represented by a right-angled arrangement of three post-holes. At Phoenixtown 5, possible building remains were represented by an L-shaped group of post-holes, with other, associated pits and a hearth, and Grooved Ware pottery sherds. The charcoals suggest that oak posts were used in at least two of the post-holes.

Overall, the charcoal data from excavated sites in Kilmainham and Phoenixtown demonstrate that oak and hazel were important components of the local landscape in the Neolithic period (Tables 2.1 and 2.2). But people had been busy clearing their local woodlands. There are some indicators for openings in the oak woodlands, for example the light-loving ash in Phoenixtown during the Early Neolithic period and in Kilmainham during the Chalcolithic period.

Chalcolithic period and Early Bronze Age

The clearance of Ireland's native woodlands began in the Neolithic period, but it is not until the Bronze Age that clearances are seen to begin on a significant scale in the country (O'Donnell 2017). On excavated sites at Kilmainham (see Chapter 6) pits with associated Beaker pottery sherds, of the Chalcolithic period, produced charcoals from a variety of species, including alder, ash, hazel and oak. Charcoal samples from burnt mound sites (*fulachtaí fia*) dating

Key to Tables 2.1, 2.2 and 2.3
E Neo = Early Neolithic; M/L Neo = Middle/Later Neolithic; Chalc = Chalcolithic; EBA = Early Bronze Age; MBA = Middle Bronze Age; LBA = Late Bronze Age; IA/E Med = Iron Age/early medieval

Table 2.1—Charcoal counts from excavated sites in Kilmainham (Sites 1A, 1B, 1C, 2 and 3).

Tree / shrub	E Neo	M/L Neo	Chalc.	EBA	MBA	LBA	IA/E Med	TOTAL
Alder	13	9	5	66	88	46	90	317
Alder / birch	—	1	—	—	—	—	—	1
Ash	25	20	82	55	57	11	79	329
Birch	—	—	—	—	—	—	45	45
Blackthorn	—	—	—	—	—	—	11	11
Cherry	—	—	—	—	1	—	4	5
Elm	4	28	—	3	—	—	3	38
Hazel	76	79	4	91	35	112	235	729
Hazel / Alder	—	—	—	—	—	1	—	1
Holly	5	1	—	1	—	—	7	14
Oak	1603	488	310	560	124	186	445	3716
Maloideae	58	3		6	8	7	24	106
Prunus	1	2	—	5	—	1	9	18
Spindle				1	—	—	—	1
Willow	4	1	—	2	—	—	11	18
TOTAL	1789	632	401	790	313	364	1060	5349

Table 2.2—Charcoal counts from excavation sites in Phoenixtown (Sites 1–6).

Tree / shrub	E Neo	L Neo	Chalc./EBA	MBA	TOTALS
Alder	2	6	32	59	99
Ash	17	20	44	157	238
Blackthorn	—	—	6	—	6
Buckthorn	—	—	—	—	0

Tree / shrub	E Neo	L Neo	Chalc./EBA	MBA	TOTALS
Cherry	–	1	–	2	3
Elm	–	–	9	6	15
Gorse	–	–	–	–	0
Hazel	1	34	57	134	226
Oak	10	197	22	162	391
Maloideae	1	5	4	48	58
Prunus	–	–	–	19	19
Willow	19	–	–	1	20
TOTALS	50	263	174	588	1075

Table 2.3—Charcoal counts from burnt mound sites.

Sampled sites	Ardbraccan 6, Ballybeg 1, Ballybeg 3, Commons of Lloyd 1, Cookstown Great 2, Cookstown Great 3, Kilmainham 1C, Newrath Little 2, Newrath Little 3, Nugentstown 2, Phoenixtown 1, Phoenixtown 6, Townparks 1, Townparks 6, Townparks/Commons of Lloyd 1					
Tree / shrub	L Neo	Chalc./EBA	MBA	LBA	IA	TOTALS
Alder	9	61	101	60	–	231
Ash	17	104	21	68	1	211
Birch	–	1	–	–	–	1
Blackthorn	–	–	6	–	–	6
Cherry	–	1	14	10	–	25
Elm	–	3	–	2	–	5
Hazel	36	284	122	106	–	548
Holly	–	2	1	–	–	3
Oak	66	119	67	120	–	372
Maloideae	3	5	12	10	–	30
Prunus	–	–	–	1	–	1
Willow	19	–	–	–	–	19
TOTALS	150	580	344	327	1	1452

from the Early Bronze Age had high values for alder, ash, hazel and oak (Table 2.3). At Phoenixtown, too, alder, ash, hazel and oak are the main trees identified during the Early Bronze Age. Hazel becomes more important in samples from Phoenixtown in this period and has higher values in samples from burnt mounds than at any other time. This could reflect oak woodland clearance, although values for oak remain consistently high for Kilmainham sites. (The samples here are from primary contexts like post-holes and hearths but also from secondary contexts such as surface spreads and infilled pits.) On the other hand, there is a significant increase at Kilmainham in the values for ash—which is an indicator of woodland clearance—in the Chalcolithic period to the Early Bronze Age.

Middle Bronze Age

Evidence for the Middle Bronze Age is mostly derived from buildings at Phoenixtown 3 and Kilmainham 1A. Charcoal was examined from pits and post-holes associated with a large round-house at Phoenixtown 3. The charcoal from post-holes suggests that ash and oak posts were used in the construction of the house. These are both good weight-bearing timbers, frequently found in the record of Bronze Age buildings in Ireland (O'Donnell 2017), but oak is more durable and is less prone to ground-level decay than ash. Charcoal from other Middle Bronze Age pit fills at Phoenixtown 3 included alder, ash, hazel, oak, Maloideae and wild/bird cherry. This charcoal probably derived from domestic hearths. At Kilmainham 1A, charcoals from the post-holes of another round-house included alder, ash, hazel, oak and Maloideae. Some of these would have been secondary inclusions in the post-hole fills so it is not possible to say with certainty what wood was selected for the building, but oak was probably the main construction timber.

In summary, alder, ash, hazel and oak were the dominant wood taxa during the Middle Bronze Age in excavated features at Phoenixtown and Kilmainham. Values for oak were lower than in the Neolithic period. Oak was favoured for construction in both periods but fewer post-holes (i.e. structural features) were available for sampling in the Bronze Age and this could partly account for lower oak values. Charcoal from burnt mounds also indicates some reduction of oak in the Middle Bronze Age, however, while alder, ash and especially hazel are still important. Overall, there appears to be some evidence in the charcoal data for a reduction in oak woodlands locally in this period.

Late Bronze Age

A four-post structure was recorded at Kilmainham 2. The charcoals from the post-holes included alder, ash, hazel, oak, Maloideae and *Prunus*. In another four-post structure, at Kilmainham 1C (Structure 7), at least one of the posts was oak. Charcoal remnants of hazel and oak posts burnt *in situ* were found in other contexts here. There was charcoal of alder, ash and oak in cremation pits at Kilmainham 1A. Alder, ash, hazel and oak were the main wood types represented in charcoal samples from burnt mounds in this period. Pollen analysis of peat from an infilled pond at Kilmainham 1 indicates that alder, hazel and oak were growing close to Burnt Mound 1 at this site (Gearey et al., above). The various beetle remains from the peat indicate hazel or oak woodlands nearby, and still, shallow water close to the site, providing suitable conditions for alder (Allison et al. 2011). Overall, in charcoal samples from excavated sites in Kilmainham and Phoenixtown, alder, ash, hazel and oak were the dominant taxa for this period.

Iron Age to early medieval period

The Iron Age and transitional Iron Age/early medieval period (AD 400–500) are mostly represented in the charcoal record by cereal-drying kilns excavated at Kilmainham. Hazel was the main fuel wood found in samples from three Late Iron Age cereal-drying kilns at Kilmainham 1C. Oak was also common, with smaller quantities of alder, ash, birch, elm, holly and Maloideae. Overall, hazel and oak are the dominant wood taxa from excavated features of this period at Kilmainham.

Charcoal was examined from seven cereal-drying kilns of the transitional Iron Age/early medieval period excavated at Kilmainham 1C. Many of the samples were derived from *in situ* burnt deposits in the kilns and thus provide primary evidence for fuel selection. (A caveat here is that charcoal from kilns may also represent a collapsed wooden superstructure, accidentally set on fire.) The dominant taxon was oak, followed by hazel, alder and ash, but several other wood types were also identified. Alder, ash, elm, hazel, holly, oak, Maloideae and *Prunus* were present in a kiln at Kilmainham 1A. Evidently people here were not selecting particular species as fuel for the kilns but were simply gathering what was easily available from the most frequently occurring trees in the area. Cereal-drying kilns did not need to be operated at a very high temperature—unlike, say, a smelting furnace or a cremation pyre—so particular wood species were not required for the kilns to be effective.

Charcoal from a single early medieval kiln at Kilmainham 1C was mostly hazel, with some ash, oak and wild/bird cherry (*Prunus avium/padus*). Samples from this kiln returned the highest values for hazel at Kilmainham, suggesting that it was abundant in the area at the time.

Conclusions

Charcoal data from excavated archaeological sites on the M3 Navan to Kells and N52 Kells Bypass project demonstrate changes in woodland use and environment in the vicinity from the Neolithic to the early medieval period. Overall, alder, ash, hazel and oak are the main wood types identified. A variety of other, smaller trees and shrubs are also represented, including birch, blackthorn, wild/bird cherry, holly, spindle and willow. Different types of woodland were exploited locally at different times, including dry oak woodlands, probably with a hazel understorey; scrub woodlands with flowering/fruiting Maloideae; and wet woodlands with alder and willow. Light-loving ash and Maloideae flourished as primal woods were cleared, but clearings that were not maintained would have been reclaimed by woodland within 10–20 years, with pioneer scrub trees such as birch among the first to appear. Oak was specifically selected for buildings, particularly in early prehistory, when it was in abundant supply. Higher values for ash and hazel in the Bronze Age indicate an increase in woodland clearance in that period, presumably for tillage and pasture. Hazel and oak were the main fuel woods in Iron Age cereal-drying kilns at Kilmainham. By the early medieval period values for oak had fallen significantly, but hazel seems to have been easily available locally and had become the dominant fuel wood.

CHAPTER 3

Hunters and gatherers

Shane Delaney

Hunters and gatherers

Situated on a raised gravel ridge overlooking the River Blackwater to the south, a small campsite identified at Cakestown Glebe 2 represents the earliest evidence for human occupation yet discovered in the Kells area. It was occupied in the later stages of the Mesolithic period, over 6,000 years ago. The people who camped here were hunters and gatherers. They left only slight traces of their presence, in the form of two hearths with some adjacent stake- and post-holes (Illus. 3.1). One hearth was dated to 4489–4356 BC (UBA-12070) using oak charcoal. The stakes and posts may have supported a cooking spit or a frame for smoking meat or fish. A butt-trimmed flake (mudstone) was found by one of the hearths (Illus. 3.2). This is a classic Mesolithic artefact and could have been used by these early inhabitants of the Blackwater valley as a cutting tool or a projectile head (e.g. for a fishing spear).

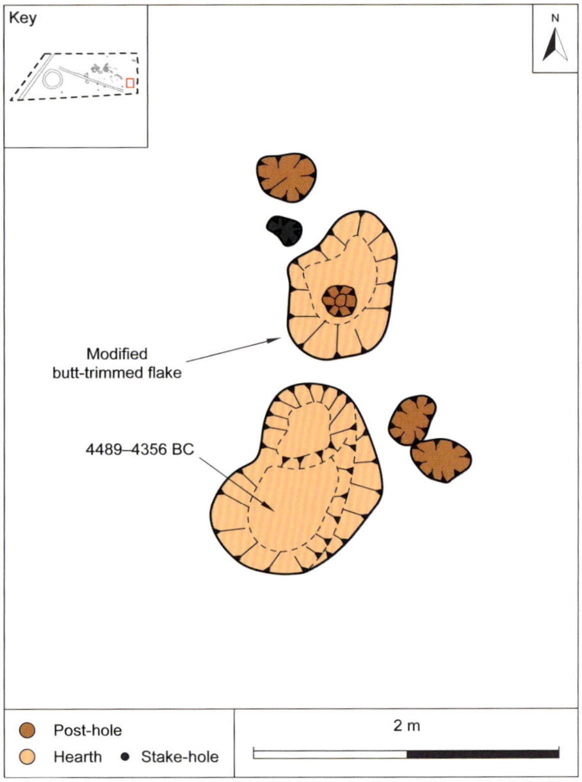

Illus. 3.1 Cakestown Glebe 2: plan of two Late Mesolithic hearths discovered on a gravel ridge overlooking the River Blackwater (*IAC Ltd*).

During the Mesolithic period in Ireland (c. 8000–4000 BC) there was a small, mobile population existing in a very different landscape from that of today—a landscape dominated by forests and wetlands. The social unit was probably a group of not more than 20 or 30 people. They lived in a landscape of primeval forests, rivers, lakes and extensive wetlands. These people, like the early settlers at Cakestown Glebe, would have travelled along the coast and used natural routeways around estuaries and along rivers and lakes to penetrate the primordial forests that covered the island.

The coast was easier to occupy and to move along. Estuaries were bountiful places for hunter-gatherers. Lakes and rivers were attractive settings too, as they provided wildfowl, fish and fresh water. There are examples in the Irish archaeological record

Illus. 3.2 Cakestown Glebe 2: this butt-trimmed flake is a classic Late Mesolithic artefact (Reg. E3158:246:1) and would have been used as a cutting tool or projectile head (*Mark Moraghan*).

of Mesolithic sites in all three settings. Ferriter's Cove in County Kerry (Woodman et al. 1999) is a coastal site where Mesolithic middens were found in sand-dunes. The site was occupied seasonally in the summer and autumn months. The campsite at Mount Sandel, Co. Derry, was on a ridge overlooking the lower reaches of the River Bann (Woodman 1981; 1985). In the midlands, Mesolithic sites have been found on the shores and islands of lakes, including Moynagh Lough, Co. Meath (Bradley 1991; 2001), Lough Derravarragh, Co. Westmeath (Mitchell 1972; 1990, 79), and Lough Boora, Co. Offaly (Ryan 1980; 1984).

The rivers and lakes could be navigated using canoes and rafts. We have evidence of Mesolithic dugout canoes from sites such as Brookend, Co. Tyrone, on Lough Neagh (Breen & Forsythe 2004, 31) and Carrigdirty, Co. Limerick, on the Shannon estuary (O'Sullivan 2001, 71). While no such canoes have yet been found in County Meath, mooring posts for vessels were discovered in a former lake at Clowanstown 1, on the Dunshaughlin to Navan section of the M3 (Mossop & Mossop 2009) (below).

Unlike the people of the Neolithic, this mobile population did not have knowledge of farming, but nature was bountiful to those who knew what food to look for and how to get it. Even the dense forests became in time a familiar habitat, as Ireland's hunter-gatherers became 'woodland dwellers' (Driscoll 2009, 110). Mesolithic people foraged for edible roots, fungi, nuts and berries. Hazelnuts were especially important. They caught trout, salmon and eels in rivers and lakes, and fished for inshore species from the sea. They supplemented their diet of fish with meat from wild pigs and hares. Seals could be killed on the coast. Shellfish provided a smaller mouthful but were a less dangerous proposition. Wildfowl were plentiful everywhere. For the leaner winter months they stockpiled whatever could be preserved: nuts, dried berries, and smoked meat and fish. The coastal campsite at Ferriter's Cove was occupied seasonally, in the summer and early autumn. Food debris from the site included the bones of wrasse, whiting and cod, and the shells of dog whelks, periwinkles and limpets. This marine diet was supplemented by wild pig, hare and birds. Fish dominated the food remains from Mount Sandel, on the River Bann, and included salmon, trout, eel, bass and flounder, supplemented by wild pig and birds. Food remains from hearths at Lough Boora also included burnt bones of wild pig, as well as pigeon, duck and grouse, brown trout and eel. It seems that nutritious food was in abundant supply for most of the year, and that the hunter-gatherers of the Irish Mesolithic were very skilful at obtaining it.

The site at Mount Sandel was unusual in that there was evidence for several huts—substantial, round buildings raised on earthfast stakes and posts. This is rare evidence of the living conditions and social organisation of an Irish Mesolithic campsite. Otherwise, the physical traces of Mesolithic people in the landscape are most often in the form of chipped stone artefacts—either individual finds of stone tools or scatters of tool-making debris. Early Mesolithic people in Ireland had a tool kit similar to their contemporaries elsewhere in Europe. It was based on the careful reduction of stone tools, from a prepared core, to create very small blades and flakes known as 'microliths'. For greater control, an 'indirect percussion' method was used, which involved striking a hardened bone or antler point against the stone rather than striking it directly with a hammer stone. These artefacts were used to form composite tools based on a wood, bone or antler haft. Late Mesolithic people in Ireland adapted their tool kit in a unique way not seen elsewhere in Europe. They developed a distinctive large flake and blade technology that relied on direct percussion. These later tools were likely to have been used for woodworking and food-processing, and may also have been used as the tips of fishing spears.

The mobile way of life of these early hunter-gatherers would have led them to be adaptable and to acquire knowledge of the raw materials required for their survival. The material used for stone tools was not consistent across the island; it depended on what was available locally. In the north-east flint was favoured; it occurs naturally in County Antrim. Elsewhere in Ireland flint is scarce and results only from transportation by glaciers. In the midlands chert was a common substitute for flint and was used almost exclusively by the people of Lough Boora. The people who came every summer to Ferriter's Cove, in the south-west, used a variety of stone types, including flint, greenstone and volcanic tuff (Woodman et al. 1999, 39). Clearly, adaptability was essential for survival and it is possible that raw materials were traded across the island, from one group to another.

The site at Cakestown Glebe 2 was on a ridge overlooking the River Blackwater, on its southern bank (Illus. 2.2). This is a typical location for a Mesolithic campsite. The river would have been a natural routeway, whether it was negotiated on foot along the banks or by canoe. More importantly, it provided a ready supply of fish and wildfowl. The river would have been broader and shallower in the Mesolithic period, making it easier to net or spear salmon and trout migrating upstream to spawn. Eels, too, would have been netted or trapped on their migration downstream to the open sea. Fine examples of Mesolithic fish-traps were discovered on the Dunshaughlin–Navan section of the M3 at Clowanstown 1 (Illus. 3.3 and 3.4) (Mossop & Mossop 2009). This site—during the Late Mesolithic—was located on the edge of a lake. Four conical fish-baskets, or

Illus. 3.3 Remains of Mesolithic fish-traps, woven from slender rods, were found in peat infilling a former lake at Clowanstown 1 on the Dunshaughlin to Navan section of the M3 (*Archaeological Consultancy Services Ltd*).

Illus. 3.4 Replica model of the Clowanstown 1 fishtrap (*Joe Hogan for the National Museum of Ireland*).

funnel-traps, were found here on the former lake bed, while a natural hollow, surrounded by upright stakes on the landward side, was a likely place for mooring canoes. The fish-traps and mooring posts produced dates in the region of c. 5300–4720 BC. Later Mesolithic tools, hazelnuts and burnt bone were recovered from a platform constructed at this location some 500 years later.

Other excavated sites on the M3 Navan to Kells and N52 Kells Bypass project produced Late Mesolithic radiocarbon dates: Cookstown Great 1 (4227–3978 BC, UBA-12113), Townparks 2 (4334–4179 BC, UBA-12114) and Kilmainham 3 (5620–5480 BC, SUERC-29340; and 5197–4913 BC, UBA-12091). The dates attest to Mesolithic activity across the landscape of the road project but offer little else. They come either from fills of pits and post-holes, where the integrity of the sample material is in doubt, or from obviously much later features, such as the Grooved Ware timber circle at Kilmainham 3. Cookstown Great 2 is different. This site alone offers us a rare glimpse of a place where a hunter-gatherer group made their campsite on high ground overlooking the river and sat around, no doubt, enjoying the warmth of their cooking fires as they repaired tools and fishing gear, told stories and made plans for the next day's work.

CHAPTER 4

First farmers

Fintan Walsh

First farmers

The Neolithic revolution was an international phenomenon that began c. 10,000 BC in the Middle East. Here in Ireland we define the Neolithic period as 4000–2450 BC. Our Early Neolithic was characterised by woodland clearance for cereal cultivation and livestock husbandry, and a proliferation of permanent settlements based around big, rectangular houses (Illus. 4.1). There is a remarkable similarity in the house types, pottery style (carinated pottery) and cereal crops (emmer wheat and barley) that appeared throughout Ireland in this first phase of sedentary settlement. There is a growing consensus that this cultural package was introduced by influxes of new migrants from what is now known as Britain and from the European mainland. Their presence in the archaeological record is conspicuous, though it lasts for only a short time, probably no more than c. 3800–3600 BC (Cooney et al. 2011, 562–675; McSparron 2008; Sheridan

Illus. 4.1 Artist's impression of an Early Neolithic landscape of primeval woodland with farmsteads and clearances (*Dan Tietzsch-Tyler*).

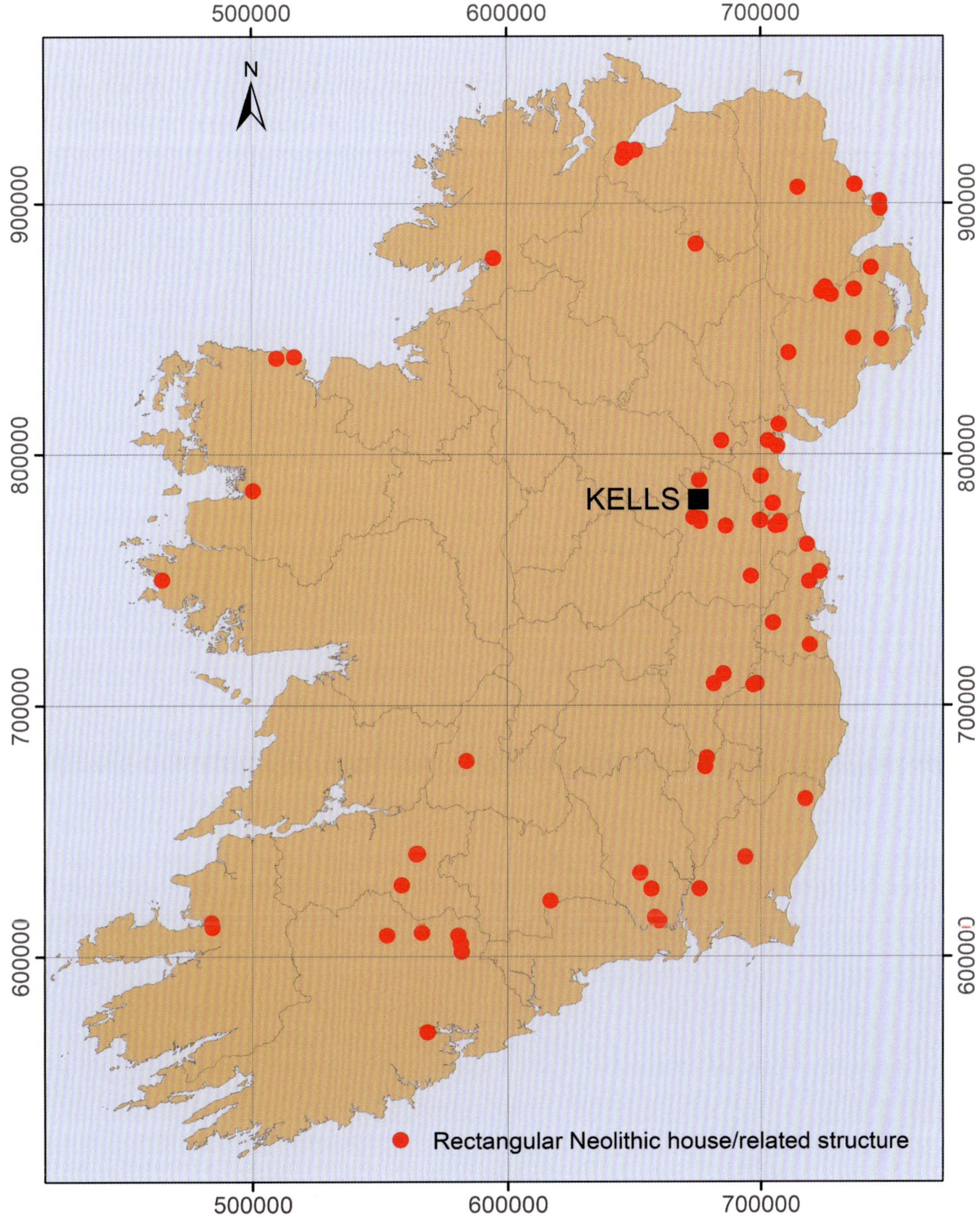

Illus. 4.2 Distribution map of known Early Neolithic house sites in Ireland. There are now over 100 excavated sites in the archaeological record (*Frank Prendergast*).

2010, 89–105; 2013, 283–300; Smyth 2014, 41–50).

Early Neolithic houses were a key feature of the changes happening at this time. They were typically large and rectangular, built with oak posts and planks, and with walls solidly footed in deep foundation trenches. These were not flimsy buildings for short-term shelter. They were built to last, and their permanence demonstrates a strong connection to the land. Though these houses were primarily homes for the Neolithic settlers, they were also likely to have been at the centre of social gatherings—a key element in maintaining community bonds. Much like rural Irish homesteads, they were an integral part of the fabric of society.

The robust construction of the houses has ensured their place in the Irish archaeological record, because large post-holes and deep foundation trenches are more likely to survive and be rediscovered. There are now over 100 recorded sites of excavated Early Neolithic houses in Ireland (Illus. 4.2). Our investigations on the M3 Navan to Kells and N52 Kells Bypass project have added eight more candidates to the corpus, as well as several lesser structures that might also have been roofed buildings (below).

Early Neolithic settlement in the River Blackwater valley

There were the remains of at least five Early Neolithic houses in the townlands of Kilmainham and Cookstown Great—at Kilmainham 1A, Kilmainham 1C and Cookstown Great 3. There was another at Gardenrath 2, less than 1 km to the north-west, and two others c. 2.3 km to the north-west at Townparks 5 (Illus. 4.3; Table 4.1). Evidence for other, smaller buildings included a post-built structure (Structure 5) at Kilmainham 1C and a possible hut at Kilmainham 1A (Structure 1). There are also numerous pits and post-holes in these townlands that potentially represent the remnants of other buildings of this period, though they did not reveal themselves in coherent ground-plans. Taken all together, these structural remains are evidence of extensive settlement in the area.

The houses were all associated with rich ceramic and lithic (chipped stone) assemblages, recovered from the buildings themselves and from adjacent features. Large pits around the houses at Kilmainham 1C and Townparks 5 contained substantial quantities of pottery. Hearths or cooking pits, smaller pits and stake-holes were also found immediately adjacent to the houses. Clearly, much of the business of daily life—e.g. food-processing and cooking, pottery manufacture, flint-working and other craftwork—was conducted in the outdoor areas surrounding the buildings.

Carbonised cereal grains such as emmer wheat and barley, along with hazelnut shell, were recovered from most of the buildings. These short-lived plant remains provided excellent samples for radiocarbon dating (as opposed to, say, charcoals from mature, long-lived trees) (Appendix 1). McSparron's (2008) study of radiocarbon dates from Early Neolithic rectangular houses in Ireland, focusing only on dates from short-lived species, concluded that the construction and use of this house type began between 3715 and 3650 BC and ended between 3690 and 3625 BC. The dates from similar buildings on our project fit well within this time-frame. Indeed, the dating evidence for the houses suggests the possibility of a dispersed rural community of contemporary Early Neolithic homesteads, extending over several square

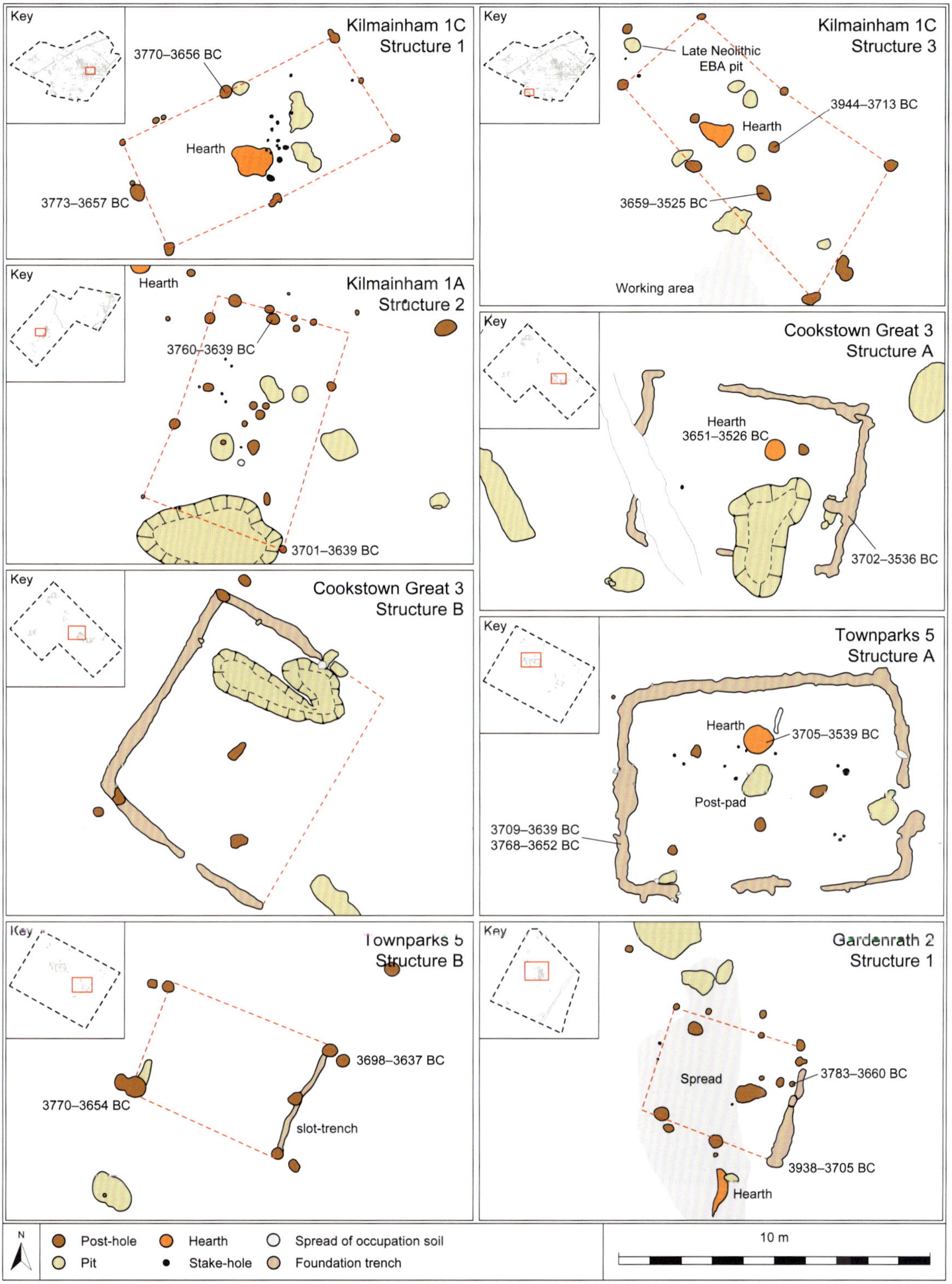

Illus. 4.3 Composite plan of Early Neolithic houses from sites in Kilmainham, Cookstown Great, Townparks and Gardenrath (*IAC Ltd*).

kilometres along the River Blackwater and its hinterland, with a core area in Kilmainham/ Cookstown Great.

The Early Neolithic farmers of the Blackwater valley were the pioneers who first cleared primeval woodland in this part of County Meath, ploughed and cultivated the land, and perhaps enclosed some of it with hedgerows or wooden fences. Land clearance on this scale would have been a collective endeavour and this, in turn, indicates a degree of social management or, at least, organised co-operation. This co-operative work was probably based on the shared values and group spirit of a tight-knit community rather than on the authority exercised by individuals in a hierarchical society.

Primeval woodland was not the only challenge faced by these pioneering Neolithic settlers. They had to protect their crops and livestock from bears, wolves and wild pigs. Also, like European settlers in North America in the early modern period or the Norse farmers who settled Greenland in medieval times, our first farmers may have had to defend themselves from attacks by native hunter-gatherers, who were already well adapted to the existing woodland environment, or, indeed, from attacks by other groups of Neolithic settlers. The burnt flint arrowhead recovered from an Early Neolithic house at Kilmainham 1A (Structure 2) is a grim reminder that the settlement may have suffered an attack at some stage.

Table 4.1—Early Neolithic buildings summary data.

Cookstown Great 3	Structure A (trench-built house)
Orientation	E/W
Dimensions	6.8 m x 5 m
Radiocarbon dates (2σ)	3702–3536 BC (UBA-11089), foundation trench
	3651–3526 BC (UBA- 11090), hearth
Charcoal	Mostly oak with some hazel from the foundation trench; oak, alder and hazel from a hearth
Plant remains	Hazelnut shell
Bone	—
Pottery	Carinated ware sherds from foundation trench (6) and hearth (7)
Worked stone	Flint flakes, modified piece and shatter from foundation trench and hearth
Cookstown Great 3	**Structure B (trench-built house)**
Orientation	NE/SW
Dimensions	7.2 m x 4 m

Cookstown Great 3	Structure B (trench-built house)
Radiocarbon dates (2σ)	–
Charcoal	Oak charcoal from internal pit and ‘occupation soil’ spread
Plant remains	–
Bone	–
Pottery	–
Worked stone	–
Gardenrath 2	**Structure 1 (trench-and-post-built small building)**
Orientation	NW/SE
Dimensions	4 m x 4 m
Radiocarbon dates (2σ)	3938–3705 BC (UBA-12042), foundation trench
	3783–3660 BC (UBA-12043), post-hole
Charcoal	Oak, hazel, alder and Maloideae from foundation trench; mostly oak from post-holes
Plant remains	–
Bone	Burnt bone fragments (unidentified) from a post-hole
Pottery	Carinated ware sherds (2) from post-holes
Worked stone	Flint flakes, blades (2) and shatter from pits, hearth and post-hole
Kilmainham 1A	**Structure 1 (possible hut or shelter)**
Orientation	NE/SW
Dimensions	4.6 m x 2.2 m
Radiocarbon dates (2σ)	–
Charcoal	Oak and hazel charcoal from a post-hole
Plant remains	Hazelnut shell
Bone	–
Pottery	Carinated ware sherds (5) from a post-hole
Worked stone	Flint flakes (3) from a post-hole

Kilmainham 1A	Structure 2 (post-built house)
Orientation	NE/SW
Dimensions	6.5 m x 4.5 m
Radiocarbon dates (2σ)	3701–3639 BC (UBA-12100), post-hole
	3760–3639 BC (UBA-12106), post-hole (internal)
Charcoal	Oak, hazel, elm from pits, post-holes and a 'habitation layer'
Plant remains	Hazelnut shell from a post-hole
Bone	–
Pottery	Carinated ware sherds (38) from internal post-holes, habitation layers and internal pits
Worked stone	Polished stone axe; flint and quartz scraper; flint flakes and shatter; arrow-head and arrowhead fragments (2); possible axe 'polishing stone'
Kilmainham 1C	**Structure 1 (post-built house)**
Orientation	NE/SW
Dimensions	8 m x 4 m
Radiocarbon dates (2σ)	3773–3657 BC (UBA-12896), post-hole
	3770–3656 BC (UBA-12895), post-hole
Charcoal	Mostly oak, with some alder and hazel, from post-holes, stake-holes and a hearth
Plant remains	Carbonised emmer wheat, club wheat, barley and a large quantity of indeterminate cereals
Bone	–
Pottery	Carinated ware sherds (4) from a post-hole
Worked stone	Flint knife from a post-hole; flint flakes (2) from a hearth
Kilmainham 1C	**Structure 3 (post-built house)**
Orientation	NW/SE
Dimensions	9.5 m x 5 m
Radiocarbon dates (2σ)	3659–3525 BC (UBA-13019), post-hole
	3944–3713 BC (UBA-12899), post-hole (internal)
Charcoal	Oak, alder, pomaceous fruitwood (Maloideae), hazel, elm, willow and holly from post-holes, internal pits and a hearth

Kilmainham 1C	Structure 3 (post-built house)
Plant remains	Hazelnut shells, carbonised wheat from internal pits and a hearth
Bone	–
Pottery	Carinated ware sherds from post-holes, internal pits and a hearth
Worked stone	Flint flake shatter and flint flake
Kilmainham 1C	**Structure 5 (post-built building?)**
Orientation	N/A
Dimensions	5.5 m diameter
Radiocarbon dates (2σ)	4060–3800 BC (SUERC-29347), oak charcoal
Charcoal	Oak from a post-hole
Plant remains	–
Bone	–
Pottery	–
Worked stone	–
Kilmainham 1C	**Structure IV (stake-built oval hut or pen?)**
Orientation	N/A
Dimensions	3.5 m diameter
Radiocarbon dates (2σ)	3776–3659 BC (UBA-12906), hazel charcoal
Charcoal	Hazel from a stake-hole
Plant remains	–
Bone	–
Pottery	–
Worked stone	–
Townparks 5	**Structure A (trench-built house)**
Orientation	E/W
Dimensions	9 m x 7 m
Radiocarbon dates (2σ)	3709–3639 BC (UBA-12049), foundation trench
	3768–3652 (UBA-12050), foundation trench
	3705–3539 BC (UBA-12051), from hearth

Townparks 5	Structure A (trench-built house)
Charcoal	Oak, ash, hazel, Maloideae, birch, alder, holly and elm from the foundation trench (mostly oak) and from an internal post-hole, hearth and stake-holes
Plant remains	Emmer wheat grains, unidentified cereal grains and hazelnut shells from an internal post-hole, hearth and stake-holes
Bone	Burnt bone from a hearth
Pottery	Carinated ware sherds from foundation trench (13) and internal features (47)
Worked stone	Chert laurel leaf arrowhead and flint shatter from foundation trench; pendant bead, burnt flint arrowhead tip and flake shatter from internal features
Townparks 5	**Structure B (trench-and-post-built building)**
Orientation	NW/SE
Dimensions	5.2 m x 4 m
Radiocarbon dates (2σ)	3698–3637 BC (UBA-12046), post-hole 3770-3654 BC (UBA-12408), post-hole
Charcoal	Mostly oak, from post-holes, also alder, holly, Maloideae
Plant remains	Small quantities of hazelnut shell and wheat grains from post-holes
Bone	Burnt bone fragments from post-holes
Pottery	Carinated ware sherds (2) from post-holes
Worked stone	—

Trench-built houses

A few of the Early Neolithic houses recorded on this section of the M3 were classic examples of a type found throughout Ireland, having large, rectangular ground-plans defined by substantial foundation trenches, internal hearths, and entrances in the south or east, where these could be identified. These houses were recorded at Townparks 5 (Structure A) and Cookstown Great 3 (Structures A and B).

The best-preserved example of a 'trench-built' house was Structure A at Townparks 5 (Illus. 4.4). This building had a hearth and several internal post-holes, which were probably for roof-support posts. Samples of charred cereal grain and hazelnut shell from, variously, a pit, the foundation trench (two dates) and the hearth, produced dates of 3768–3647 BC (UBA-12047), 3709–3639 BC (UBA-12049), 3768–3652 BC (UBA-12050) and 3705–3539 BC (UBA-12051). The smaller and simpler Structure B (below) at this site may have been an ancillary building rather than a dwelling house.

The two houses at Cookstown Great 3, Structure A and Structure B, were also large,

Illus. 4.4 Townparks 5: work in progress on the excavation of a trench-built Early Neolithic house (Structure A), viewed from north (*Hawkeye*).

rectangular and trench-built (Illus. 4.5). They were erected only 8 m apart, on level ground at the top of a gentle slope. Samples of hazelnut shell from the foundation trench and hearth in Structure A were dated to 3702–3536 BC (UBA-11089) and 3651–3526 BC (UBA-11090). Structure B was not dated, owing to a lack of suitable sample material.

Post-built houses

There were several other Early Neolithic houses that had large rectangular ground-plans but lacked the classic wall foundation trench. These houses were built instead with posts set in individual post-holes, which is rare in the archaeological record for this period in Ireland. The walls of these houses may have been made with horizontal planks attached to the upright posts, as opposed to the earthfast vertical planking that has been identified in houses with foundation trenches. They included houses at Kilmainham 1A (Structure 2), Kilmainham 1C (Structures 1 and 3), Townparks 5 (Structure B) and Gardenrath 2 (Structure 1).

Structure 1 at Kilmainham 1C is the best example of the post-built houses (Illus. 4.6). The stone-packed post-holes supported posts c. 0.1–0.15 m in diameter. There were *in situ* remains of a burnt oak post in one of the post-holes (Illus. 4.7). This is the wood most often found in the structural features of Early Neolithic houses. Inside the building there was a central hearth. Stake-holes clustered by the hearth probably represent cooking spits or drying racks. The charcoal from the stake-holes was hazel

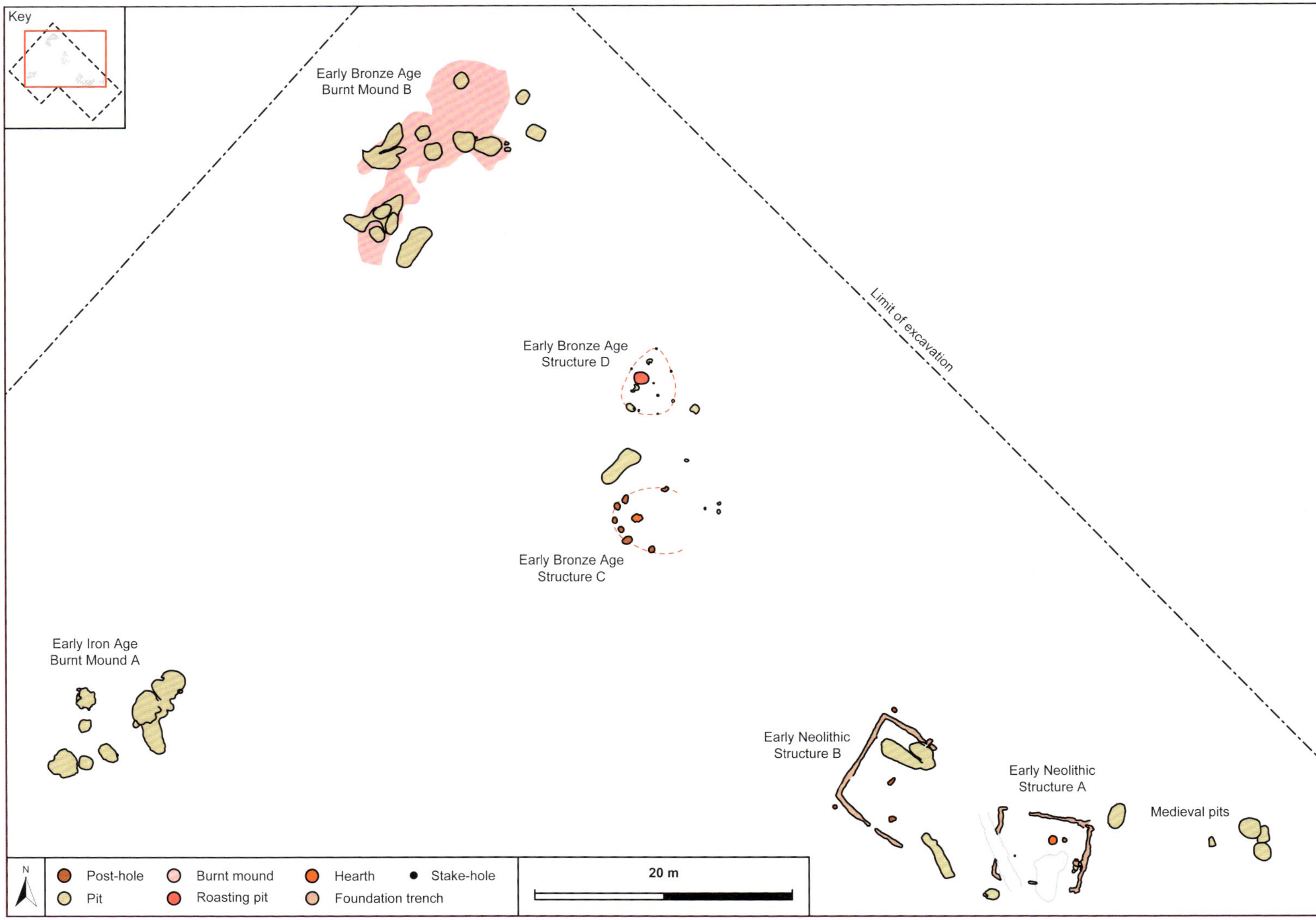

Illus. 4.5 Cookstown Great 3: plan of the excavated features, including Early Neolithic trench-built houses Structures A and B (*IAC Ltd*).

Illus. 4.6 Kilmainham 1C: work in progress on the excavation of a post-built Early Neolithic house (Structure 1), viewed from south-west (*IAC Ltd*).

and oak; the charcoal from the hearth was mostly oak. There were quantities of charred cereal grain in some of the post-holes associated with the house. This was mostly wheat, with some barley, including at least 346 emmer wheat grains and 500 indeterminate cereal grains. This is one of the largest assemblages of cereal grains from any context in Neolithic Ireland (Walsh et al. 2011). Samples of the wheat were dated to 3770–3656 BC (UBA-12895) and 3773–3657

Illus. 4.7 Kilmainham 1C: detail of a post-hole from a building (Structure 1), showing packing stones and remains of an oak post burnt *in situ* (*IAC Ltd*).

BC (UBA-12896). The sample grains came from secure, undisturbed deposits within two opposing post-holes. The results are in close agreement with a third date, from a hazelnut shell in a stake-hole, at 3765–3651 BC (UBA-12903).

The post-hole fills of Structure 1 at Kilmainham C also contained sherds of Early Neolithic carinated pottery. One large sherd, from the shoulder of a pot, was found at the interface between packing material and the post-pipe fill. This is interpreted as a votive offering, dedicating the house at its construction. There is a nearby parallel from Structure 2 at Kilmainham 1A, which was another post-built rectangular house (Illus. 4.8). Here, a fine polished stone axe was found lying horizontally at the base of a corner post-hole and was obviously placed there deliberately. The act of depositing special objects in Neolithic house foundations is not uncommon. According to Smyth (2014, 8), there are up to 20 excavated Irish examples where this has been recorded. They have a wide distribution and include, for instance, Ballyharry, Co. Antrim (Crothers 1996; Moore 2003), Cloghers, Co. Kerry (Kiely 2003), Monanny, Co. Monaghan (Walsh 2006; 2011c), Richardstown, Co. Louth (Byrnes 1999), Tankardstown South, Co. Limerick (Gowen 1988, 26–43), and, of course, Kilmainham.

Structure 3 was a second post-built house at Kilmainham 1C, located c. 80 m south-west of Structure 1. Again, this house had a hearth and internal and external pits and post-holes, which contained large quantities of ceramics, lithics and hazelnut shells. Samples of hazelnut shell from two post-holes were dated to 3944–3713 BC (UBA-12899) and 3659–3525 BC (UBA-13019). The gaps between these dates raises questions about the longevity of the house and the provenance of the samples. Could the later date represent an episode of repair or reconstruction?

Elsewhere, buildings such as Structure B at Townparks 5 and Structure 1 at Gardenrath 2 may have been smaller houses of rectangular plan, or simply stores or byres. The two buildings featured both post-holes and slot-trenches in the wall lines. Neither of them had a hearth. Samples of young oak charcoal and hazelnut shell from post-holes in the Townparks 5 (Structure B) building were dated to 3698–3637 BC (UBA-12046) and 3770–3654 BC (UBA-12048) respectively. Maloideae from a wall trench and hazel charcoals from a post-hole in the Gardenrath 2 building (Structure 1) were dated to 3938–3705 BC (UBA-12042) and 3783–3660 BC (UBA-12043) respectively.

Early Neolithic rectangular post-built houses like the ones described above are not common in Ireland, but they have been recorded elsewhere in the country, with examples from Pepperhill, Co. Cork (Gowen 1988, 44–51), and Ballyharry 1.1, Co. Antrim (Crothers 1996; Moore 2003). (The ground-plan of the latter house was not fully exposed.) They are more common in Britain, such as the 'longhouses' at Lismore Fields in Derbyshire (Darvill 1996; Davies 2009) and Parc Bryn Cegin, Llandegai, in Wales (Lynch & Musson 2001). Davies (2009) listed 25 examples of Early Neolithic houses ('longhouses') from Britain. Most of them were post-built and many of them were similar in size to the Kilmainham 1C houses, or within the same broad size range. For instance, Structure 1 at Kilmainham 1C (length 8 m by width 4 m) is somewhat smaller than the Llandegai 1 structure (12 m by 7 m) but larger than Lismore Fields 2 (LF2) (5

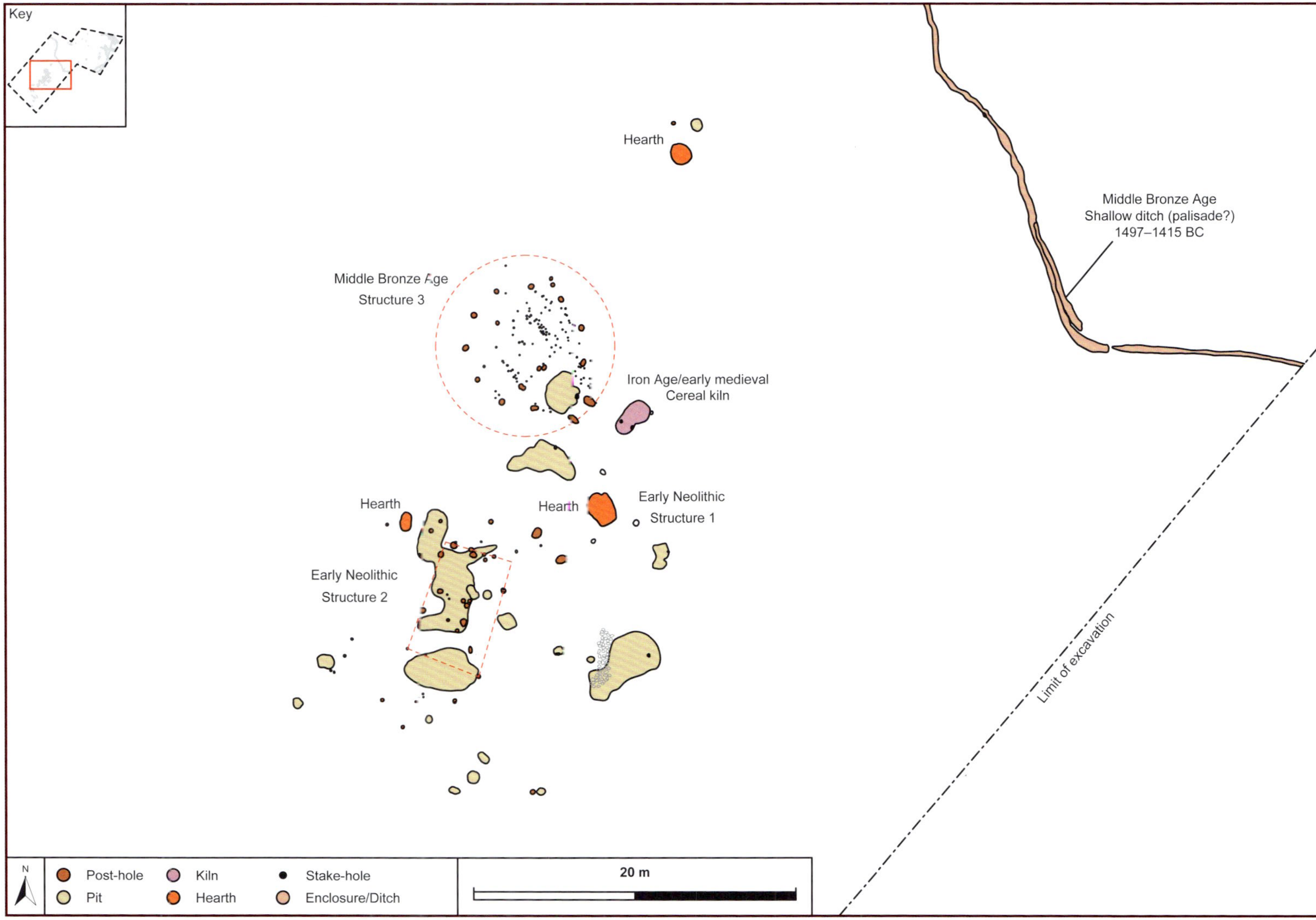

Illus. 4.8 Kilmainham 1A: plan of the main excavated features, including Early Neolithic post-built house Structure 2 and a smaller hut-like building, Structure 1 (*IAC Ltd*).

m by 5 m). As this style of construction is more common in Britain but rare in Ireland in this period, we can speculate that there were links between the Early Neolithic people of the River Blackwater valley and contemporary communities in England and/ or Wales. This suggestion is supported by general similarities in the ceramic and lithic evidence.

Other buildings

Some smaller and less well-defined buildings (Table 4.1) include Structure 5 at Kilmainham 1C, which was represented by a cluster of post-holes, stake-holes and pits but lacked Early Neolithic pottery, and Structure IV, a small stake-built structure with an oval plan, which may have been an ancillary building or animal pen associated with nearby Structure 1 at Kilmainham 1C (Illus. 1.9) (Walsh 2011a, figs 13 and 9).

At Kilmainham 1A, immediately beside the main house (Structure 2), there was another, contemporary but much smaller and flimsier, structure (Structure 1) (Illus. 4.8). This was a small, post-built hut or shelter, measuring only 4.6 m by 2.2 m, with a hearth at its centre, indicated by an area of burnt clay and sand. Five sherds from an Early Neolithic carinated bowl were recovered from one of the post-holes.

Dispersed Early Neolithic features

In addition to the houses and other buildings described above, there was other evidence of Early Neolithic activity all along the M3 Navan to Kells and N52 Kells Bypass project (Table 4.2). This was mostly in the form of dispersed features that did not form coherent patterns—typically pits and post-holes containing pottery and/ or producing radiocarbon dates from this period.

A cluster of post-holes and pits at Kilmainham 3 might have been the remains of a small hut (Whitty 2011, fig. 6). Here, a hazelnut shell was dated to 3702–3638 BC (UBA-12080). A similar group of pits and post-holes at Phoenixtown 1 was dated by Early Neolithic pottery inclusions (Lyne 2010, fig. 5). There were isolated pits or pit groups at Phoenixtown 6, Newrath Little 1, and Grange 2 and 4.

Table 4.2—Early Neolithic dispersed features (minor sites) summary data.

Grange 4	
Features	Group of three pits, post-hole and stake-hole
Radiocarbon dates (2σ)	—
Charcoal	Oak, hazel, Maloideae
Plant remains	—
Bone	Burnt bone fragments (unidentified)
Artefacts	Carinated ware sherds (six bowls), fossil bead, sandstone bead, chert wedge tool, flake and shatter, possible quartz shatter

Grange 2	
Features	Two pits
Radiocarbon dates (2σ)	3654–3527 BC (UBA-12074), hazelnut shell
Charcoal	Hazel, oak, ash, alder, *Prunus* sp., Maloideae, elm
Plant remains	Hazelnut shell
Bone	Burnt fragment
Artefacts	Carinated ware (two bowls), flint shatter
Phoenixtown 6	
Features	Pit or hearth
Radiocarbon dates (2σ)	3770–3654 BC (UBA-11107), hazelnut shell
Charcoal	Oak, hazel, ash, willow, alder, Maloideae
Plant remains	Hazelnut shells
Bone	–
Artefacts	Flint pressure flake
Phoenixtown 1	
Features	Group of five pits and nine post-holes and stake-holes
Radiocarbon dates (2σ)	–
Charcoal	Unidentified fragments
Plant remains	–
Bone	–
Artefacts	Carinated ware sherds (> two bowls), burnt flint flake
Kilmainham 1B	
Features	Group of three pits
Radiocarbon dates (2σ)	–
Charcoal	–
Plant remains	–
Bone	–
Artefacts	Carinated ware sherds (two bowls)

Kilmainham 3	
Features	Group of two pits and four post-holes (possible hut)
Radiocarbon dates (2σ)	3702–3638 BC (UBA-12080), hazelnut shell
Charcoal	Oak, hazel
Plant remains	Charred weed seeds, hazelnut shells
Bone	Burnt fragments (unidentified)
Artefacts	Flint flake, shatter, edge-retouched cutting tool, chert arrowhead tip
Townparks 6	
Features	Burnt spread with heat-affected stones and troughs or pits
Radiocarbon dates (2σ)	3749–3640 BC (UBA-11101), oak twig
Charcoal	Oak, alder, hazel, Maloideae
Plant remains	—
Bone	—
Artefacts	—
Newrath Little 1	
Features	Group of five pits
Radiocarbon dates (2σ)	3788–3661 BC (UBA-13960), hazelnut shell
Charcoal	—
Plant remains	—
Bone	—
Artefacts	Carinated ware sherds (3)
Cookstown Great 1	
Features	Shallow depression with possible occupation deposits, post-holes
Radiocarbon dates (2σ)	4227–3978 BC (UBA-12113), holly charcoal
Charcoal	Oak, alder, holly
Plant remains	Emmer wheat
Bone	—
Artefacts	Carinated ware sherds (four bowls)

Features of this sort may represent smaller or short-lived settlement sites, perhaps on the fringes of larger and more permanent settlements in the vicinity (but outside the lands investigated for the road project). At any rate, they certainly demonstrate that the landscape traversed by the road scheme was being fully occupied and exploited at the time. In fact, the frequency of such scattered and seemingly inconsequential features in the Grange/Phoenixtown area, towards the southern end of the road project site, hints at another Early Neolithic settlement area here, similar to the one described above in the core Kilmainham/Cookstown Great area.

Artefacts

Pottery

An assemblage of Early Neolithic carinated ware from the Kilmainham/Cookstown Great area, including the core and peripheral sites, represents at least 122 vessels. This is an important assemblage and is comparable to those at, for example, Lough Gur, Co. Limerick, and Monanny, Co. Monaghan (Ó Ríordáin 1954; Walsh 2006; 2011c).

At Kilmainham 1C most of the pottery sherds were found in large pits immediately adjacent to buildings (Structures 1 and 3) (Illus. 4.9). Sherds were also found in structural features of buildings (i.e. fills of foundation trenches and post-holes) at Kilmainham 1C (Structure 1), Kilmainham 1A, Townparks 5 and Cookstown Great 3.

Most of the vessels had short, gently curved necks, slight rounded or occasionally more angular shoulders, and deep rounded bowls. They were generally of good quality, well made and well finished, with thin-walled bodies and smooth surfaces. There were a few very fine pots, including Vessel 43 from Kilmainham 1C, which was of exceptional quality with a hard, brown-buff finish and a 'polished' outer surface (Illus. 4.10).

Worked stone objects

The chipped-stone 'tool kit' used by the people of Early Neolithic Ireland included scrapers, plano-convex knives, projectiles (both leaf- and lozenge-shaped) and a miscellany of edge-retouched tools. The manufacture of such tools typically produced a prolific

Illus. 4.9 Kilmainham 1C: excavation of a pit containing numerous sherds of Early Neolithic pottery, adjacent to a building (Structure 3) (*IAC Ltd*).

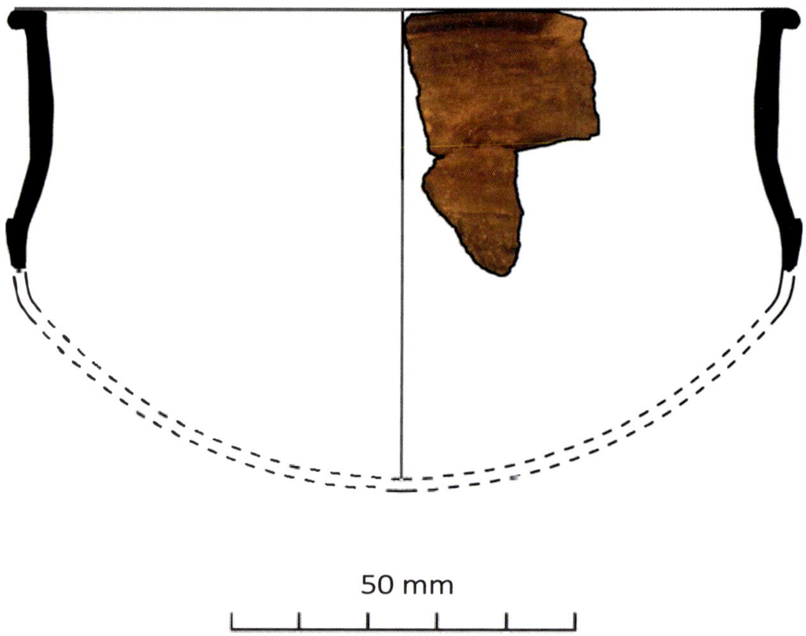

Illus. 4.10 Kilmainham 1C: reconstructed profile of a fine-walled Early Neolithic carinated pot, Vessel 43 (E3140:1343:42/55) (*Johnny Ryan and Alva MacGowan*).

amount of debitage or waste. All of this and more was found on the Early Neolithic settlement sites in the core Kilmainham/ Cookstown Great area. As with the pottery (above), the largest quantity of material was from sites in Kilmainham, and especially Kilmainham 1C). In contrast, sites in the Grange/Phoenixtown area produced only very small lithic assemblages. Most of the lithics were of flint but quartz and chert were also used.

A small number of finely produced knives were found at Kilmainham 1C (Illus. 4.11). They include a small, finely pressure-flaked plano-convex example, from a pit near Structure 1. Another knife was found in a post-hole of this building.

A very interesting collection of arrowheads or javelins was recovered from Kilmainham 1C, including examples at various stages of production, which indicates that this was a production centre. The evidence included a 'laurel leaf' (a possible javelin-type projectile head), two arrowhead blanks (the clearest indication of production), three unfinished arrowheads, and pressure-flaked leaf-shaped arrowheads (Illus. 4.12). This is an important assemblage, showing that the full range of Neolithic projectile types was known to the people of Kilmainham. These artefacts find parallels in Early Neolithic sites with an inferred history of defence or offence (Nelis 2011a), such as Donegore Hill and Lyles Hill, Co. Antrim (Mallory et al. 2011; Evans 1953), Thornhill, Co. Derry (Logue 2003), and Ballynagilly, Co. Tyrone (ApSimon 1976). Three arrowheads were also found at Kilmainham 1A, all in contexts associated with Structure 2. These items

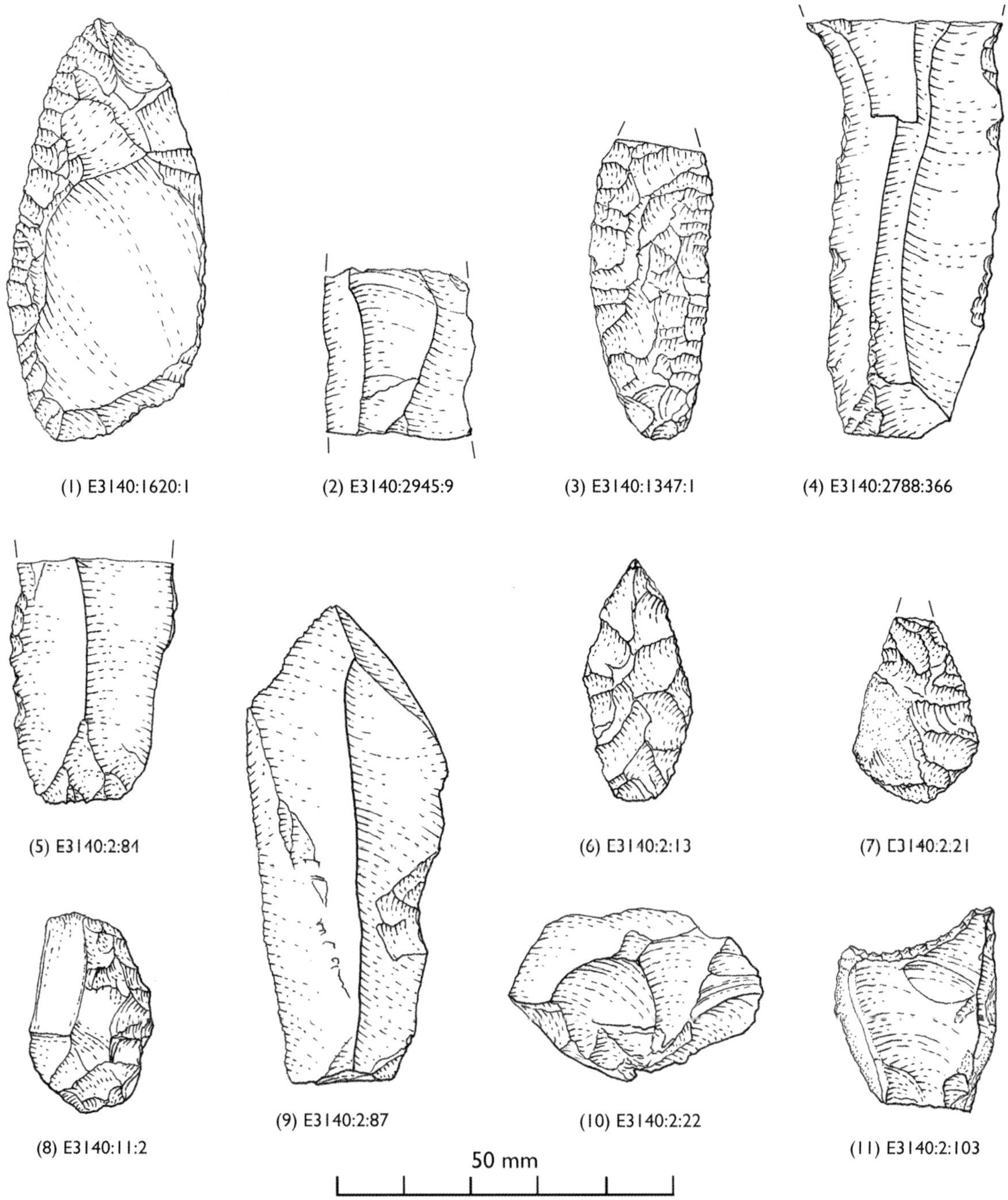

Illus. 4.11 Kilmainham 1C. Selected flint and chert artefacts. From top left: 1) Early Neolithic knife (flint); 2) Neolithic blade fragment (chert); 3) Early Neolithic plano-convex knife (flint); 4) Early Neolithic double-edged blade (chert); 5) Neolithic (?) edge-retouched blade; 6) and 7) Neolithic leaf-shaped arrowheads (flint); 8) Neolithic or Early Bronze Age unfinished arrowhead (flint); 9) Neolithic butt-trimmed flake (flint); 10) Early/Middle Neolithic biface laurel leaf (unfinished?) (flint); 11) Middle Neolithic hollow scraper (flint) (*Alva McGowan for IAC Ltd*).

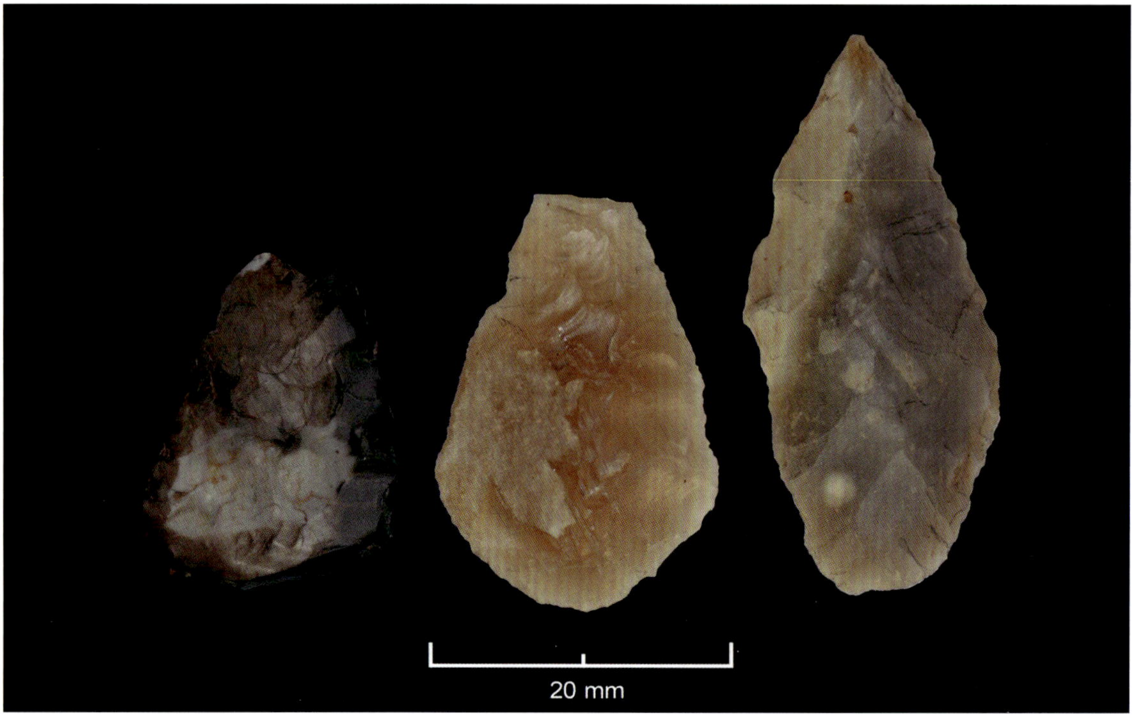

Illus. 4.12 Flint arrowheads from Kilmainham 1A (left, E3141:484:1) and Kilmainham 1C (centre, E3140:2:21, and right, E3140:2:13) (*Maeve Tobin*).

were unfinished or possibly broken during manufacture, but one of them was burnt and was missing its tip, so it is likely that it was used. This hints at pressure in a time of conflict, when projectile heads would have been needed quickly and were made without the usual respect for technique and form (Nelis 2011b). A chert arrowhead fragment was also found at Kilmainham 3.

More projectiles were found at Townparks 5, including the burnt tip of an arrowhead and a laurel leaf projectile head—a finely worked object made from chert (Illus. 4.13). It was recovered from the foundation trench of the western wall of the big rectangular house at Townparks 5. Laurel leaf projectiles are not typically associated with house sites, though one was reported at Ballynagilly, Co. Tyrone (ApSimon 1976). They are more frequently found on ritual sites like Donegore Hill and Lyles Hill, Co. Antrim, and court tombs such as Creggandevesky, Co. Tyrone, and Ballymarlagh, Co. Antrim (Mallory et al. 2011; Evans 1953; Foley 1988; Davies 1949). The presence of a laurel leaf projectile in a wall trench of the Townparks 5 house suggests either a ritual foundation deposit or simply the safe keeping of a valuable item (Nelis 2010).

Another very fine object from the Townparks 5 house is a small, lozenge-shaped pebble, perforated to form a bead or pendant (Illus. 4.14). This broadly resembles a bead from the Neolithic site of Thornhill, Co. Derry (Logue 2003, 154, fig. 17.6).

Two stone axeheads were found at Kilmainham 1A, both of them made from

Illus. 4.13 Chert 'laurel leaf' projectile head (E3151:24:1) from Townparks 5 (*Mark Moraghan*).

sedimentary stone resembling greywacke (Illus. 4.15). Two possible axe-polishing stones were also found at Kilmainham 1A, suggesting axe manufacture or repair and maintenance on this site. Previously, evidence for the working of stone axes has been recovered at Ballyharry, Co. Antrim (Crothers 1996; Moore 2003), and Cloghers, Co. Kerry (Kiely 2003) (cited in Smyth 2006, 240).

The most impressive of all the Early Neolithic artefacts recovered from the excavated sites on this road project was a small scraper made of quartz crystal (Illus. 4.16). This is an exceptional object, not only because of the unusual choice of material but also because the crystal is of such flawless clarity that it resembles glass. It was found in a spread of occupation soil on the floor of Structure 2 at Kilmainham 1A. There can be no doubt that this was a highly valued object. There is no visible evidence of wear or damage and it may have been made for display and not for everyday use (Nelis 2011b).

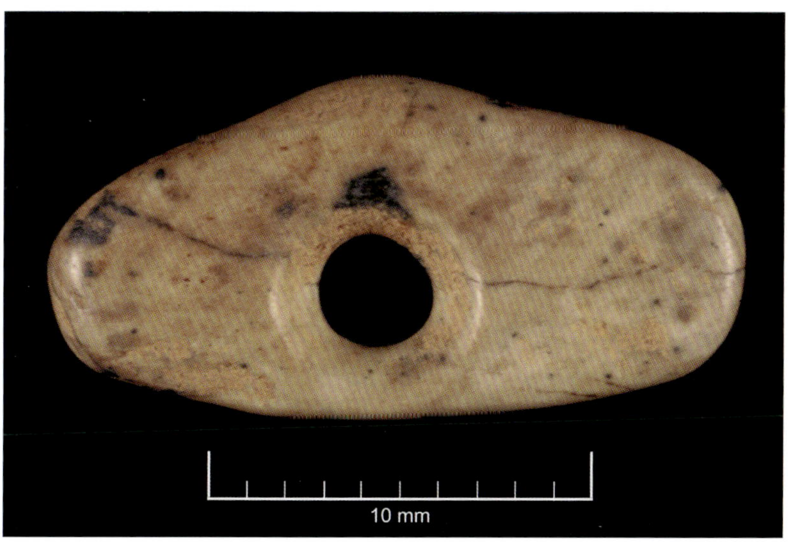

Illus. 4.14 Stone pebble bead or pendant (E3151:110:1) from Townparks 5 (*Mark Moraghan*).

Illus. 4.15 Stone axeheads from Grange 3 (centre, E3123:4:1) and Kilmainham 1A (left, E3141:1:5, and right, E3141:258:1) (*Mark Moraghan*).

Illus. 4.16 Rock crystal scraper from Kilmainham 1A (E3141:33:1) This exceptional artefact was found on an Early Neolithic house floor (Kilmainham 1A Structure 2). (*Mark Moraghan*).

For completeness we note hollow scrapers—possibly used in the production of arrow shafts—from Gardenrath 2, Nugentstown 1 and Kilmainham 1C (Illus. 4.11), and possible hollow scraper blanks from Nugentstown 1, though this is a classic Middle Neolithic tool.

An Early Neolithic farmstead at Townparks 5

Townparks 5 is the most complete Early Neolithic settlement recorded by our investigations. It invites us to draw a picture of daily life in the period. An artist's reconstruction by Dan Tietzsch-Tyler (Illus. 4.17) represents it as a well-managed farmstead. Much of the detail in this can be related to the excavated evidence from the site.

The larger of two buildings at Townparks 5 (Structure A) was no doubt the dwelling house and the main focus of daily life. The smaller house (Structure B) could also have been a dwelling, or possibly a utility building such as a barn or byre. The main house (Structure A) had a large floor area and was probably a tall building, with a steep roof. It has been observed that a typical Early Neolithic house in Ireland was similar in its ground dimensions to an early modern vernacular cottage (Rajic 2012). The ground-plan of the Townparks 5 house measured 9 m (east/west) by 7 m, which would make it comparable in area to many early Irish cottages. A thatched roof ideally has an incline of 50° or more to be weatherproof. In addition, a wide building with a steep roof plane necessarily has a high ridge or apex to the roof. So we can say with confidence that the Townparks 5 house was a spacious and impressive building.

The archaeological evidence for the house was a rectangular foundation trench lined with large, flat packing stones, which would have supported timber posts (structural timbers) and vertical planks (wall cladding) (Illus. 4.18). Gaps in the foundation trench in the east and south walls suggest one or more doorways. Inside the house, there is clear evidence for a large, central roof-support post in the form of a post-pad—a shallow pit with flat stones at its base. Other post-holes may represent supplementary roof-support posts or perhaps supports for a loft or for internal partitions. Otherwise, light wattle screens could have been used to divide the house internally, for sleeping quarters, cooking, storage, craftwork and perhaps animal stalls in wintertime. Oak was probably the wood used for the construction of the house. The roof would have been thatched.

The fills of the wall foundation trench, pits and post-holes became the accidental repositories of some of the raw materials of daily life in the house. They contained inclusions of burnt bone, pottery sherds, chipped stone tools and tool-making waste (debitage), and charred remains of cereal crops (emmer wheat and some wild taxa), hazelnut shells and wood charcoal. The ceramic sherds represent at least 11 carinated bowls—the classic vessel form of the Early Neolithic period in Ireland. The charcoals were mostly oak, with smaller amounts of ash, hazel, Pomoideae, birch and alder. Much of this represents fuel wood, no doubt, and indicates a variety of natural and semi-natural habitats within easy reach of the house.

Some post-holes set at a distance from the house on the eastern and southern sides hint at a fenced enclosure surrounding it. A pair of post-holes c. 10 m from the SSE angle of the house suggest a gateway. An enclosure around the house would have prevented damage by livestock, defined an area for daily household tasks like food preparation and provided a safe place for children to play. Other pits and post-holes in the immediate vicinity of the periphery of the house might be interpreted as the basis of hide preparation racks, refuse pits or even pig wallows. Beyond the domestic enclosure there would have been clearances for tillage and pasture, with fences or hedgerows to keep livestock from intruding on the crops. The margins between farmland and the forest would have been colonised by fruiting and nut-bearing trees and shrubs, offering welcome seasonal supplements to the produce of the farm.

Cattle were the main domestic animals. They would have been milked close to the house, or inside it, and were very likely to have been stalled in the house in winter. There is good evidence that dairy products were important. We know that the Early Neolithic carinated bowls from the Kilmainham excavations were used to store and/or heat milk, as analysis of residues on the pottery sherds identified animal fats (lipids) from dairying (Smyth & Evershed 2014). The wide, splayed rims of these bowls were perfectly suited to milking.

How did the members of this household engage with the wider community of the Kilmainham/Cookstown Great area? They probably moved freely through a mixed landscape of woodland and clearances along well-travelled footpaths that led to other farmsteads in the community. Many of their neighbours would have been relatives—extended family members. The bond between the households in this community was not based solely on blood ties but also on their shared outlook on life. They faced the same dangers—fears for the harvest, wild animals, threats from outsiders—and they needed each other's help to build and maintain their homes and to clear and work the land. The house was at the core of all of this. Houses were places for shelter, sleeping, storage and the innumerable tasks necessary for daily life, but they were also safe places for people from across the community to gather, make plans and tell stories.

Illus. 4.17 Townparks 5: artist's impression of the Early Neolithic farmstead (*Dan Tietzsch-Tyler*).

Illus. 4.18 Townparks 5: plan of the Early Neolithic buildings (Structures A and B) (top) and detailed plan of Structure 1 (below) (*IAC Ltd*).

Kilmainham/Cookstown Great in a regional context

The newly discovered Early Neolithic remains described above—with at least one major settlement core in the Kilmainham/Cookstown Great area—amount to a very significant addition to the previously known record of the period. Some clusters or groups of houses have been identified in this record—typically two or three together—but nothing on the scale that has been brought to light here. The scattered houses of the Kilmainham/Cookstown Great area represent a single rural community of permanent farmstead settlements. This interpretation is supported by the architectural evidence from the excavated sites, by high-quality radiocarbon dating of samples associated with the houses and by the uniform ceramic assemblage from the relevant sites.

There are several other Early Neolithic settlement and burial/ceremonial complexes in County Meath and adjoining counties. This is testament to a well-established population in the region, and especially from the Brú na Bóinne complex eastwards to the Irish Sea coast. Clusters of Neolithic settlement sites have been identified east of Brú na Bóinne at Sheephouse (Moore 2012) and Lagavooren (Moore & Walsh 2011), Co. Meath, and two rectangular Neolithic buildings were discovered at Coolfore, Co. Louth (Ó Drisceoil 2003). Locally, Neolithic settlements were also identified on other sections of the M3 Clonee to North of Kells motorway scheme. Building remains were recorded at Johnstown 1 just south of Dunshaughlin (Elder & Ginn 2009), and at Skreen 2 between Dunshaughlin and Navan (O'Neill & O'Hara 2009). The River Blackwater is a major tributary of the River Boyne and the Blackwater valley was probably an arterial routeway connecting Early Neolithic communities in the Kells district with the Boyne valley and the Irish Sea coast.

Although there is now plenty of evidence for the daily life of Early Neolithic communities in the Kells district, there is little evidence to date for burials and other aspects of their ritual life. To the north there are remains of court tombs at Cornaville North, Co. Meath, and Killeter, Co. Cavan, and a portal tomb to the east at Rathkenny—all within 20 km of Kells. Further east and north, at a distance of c. 40 km, there is a major complex of early funerary monuments, including 21 known court tombs and eight portal tombs, in the lowlands of the Mourne Mountains and the Carlingford district of south Down and north Louth. The general absence of megalithic tombs in the Kells district may simply be an effect of land clearance over many generations in the rich agricultural landscape of County Meath.

The 'big rectangular house' phase of the Early Neolithic period in Ireland was short-lived, perhaps lasting a few hundred years at most, and probably less than that (McSparron 2008; Smyth 2014, 41–50). This is reflected in the radiocarbon dates from the excavated house sites on the M3 Navan to Kells and N52 Kells Bypass project (Illus. 4.19). In the core Kilmainham/Cookstown Great area there is a distinct fall-off in settlement evidence in the Middle Neolithic period, with the exception of a small pottery assemblage from Townparks 5 and Phoenixtown 3, and a fragment of human skull, dated to 3086–2913 BC (UBA-12919), from a post-hole at Kilmainham 1C. This is a striking gap in settlement continuity in the

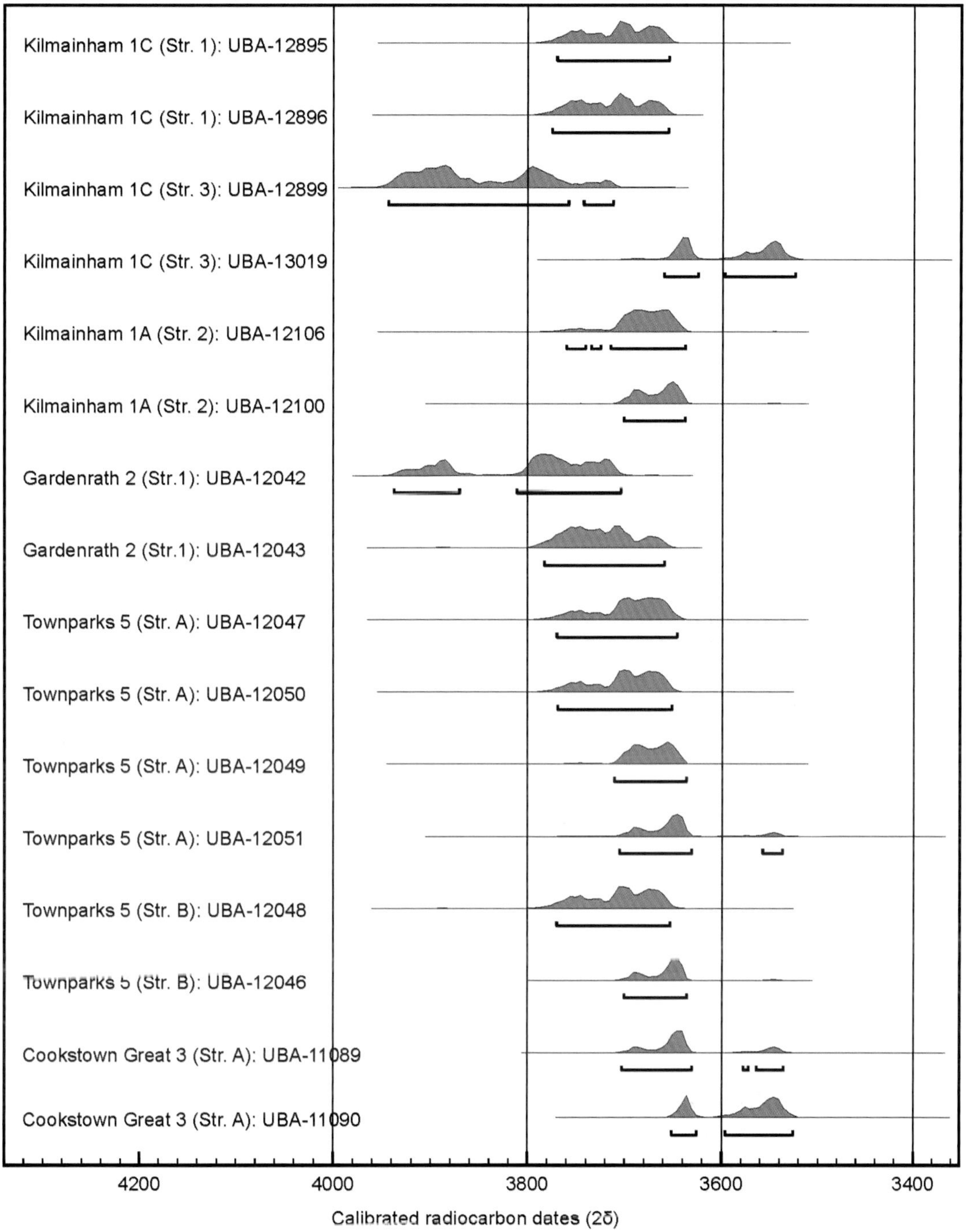

Illus. 4.19 Calibrated date ranges for the Early Neolithic houses and other buildings recorded on the M3 Navan to Kells and N52 Kells Bypass project (see also Table 4.1) (*IAC Ltd*).

area, which is not repeated until the Early Iron Age.

We can only speculate as to why this happened. There may have been a population decline in Ireland at this time. A model of changing population levels in Irish early history and prehistory, based on a database of over 8,000 radiocarbon dates, does show an extremely sharp decline in population at c. 3600 BC (Hannah & McLaughlin 2019, fig. 3), but this cannot have been a wholesale collapse leading to total depopulation. In our region, for instance, in the Middle Neolithic period, the passage tomb complexes of Lough Crew and Brú na Bóinne are evidence of an organised society capable of executing large-scale construction projects. It is possible that the population was not only smaller but was more locally concentrated in this period, in smaller territories focused on highly visible funerary monuments. This would have been a major change from the 'dispersed village' communities of the Early Neolithic period, represented on our project by the evidence from the Kilmainham/Cookstown Great area, where farmsteads with big rectangular houses were the focal points around which society was organised.

CHAPTER 5

Late Neolithic ritual monuments

Fintan Walsh

Late Neolithic ritual monuments

Almost a millennium has now passed since a dispersed community of Early Neolithic farmsteads flourished in the Kilmainham/ Cookstown Great area, to be followed by a long hiatus in the evidence for human activity in the landscape sampled by the road scheme, c. 3300–2900 BC. This is difficult to explain, though the demise of the 'big house' settlements of the Early Neolithic is a recognised pattern in the Irish archaeological record. Locally, it is possible that the population of the River Blackwater catchment around Kells migrated to some other territory in the Middle Neolithic period, perhaps becoming concentrated around the passage tomb cemeteries of Loughcrew and Brú na Bóinne.

Whatever the explanation, the tide of human life was flowing strongly again in the Late Neolithic period (c. 2900–2450 BC). Elsewhere in County Meath there are excavated sites of embanked ritual enclosures and timber circles at Knowth (Eogan & Roche 1997) and Newgrange (Stout 1991), both in the Brú na Bóinne complex; at Lagavooren 7 (Stafford 2012), south of the River Boyne in the eastern part of the county; and at Bettystown (Eogan 1998; 1999) on the coast. Grooved Ware pottery, which is the key artefact distinguishing this period, has been recovered from many sites in the region (Brindley 1999). Evidence for domestic settlement is relatively scarce in comparison to ritual or ceremonial sites.

On our road project, the Late Neolithic period is represented by evidence from three principal sites: a building at Phoenixtown 5; ritual activity at Kilmainham 1C; and a ceremonial complex featuring a timber circle at Kilmainham 3.

Building at Phoenixtown 5

A possible building was identified at Phoenixtown 5 from a collection of post-holes, a slot-trench and pits in an L-shaped arrangement suggesting an oblong ground-plan (c. 4.5 m SW–NE by 4 m SE–NW) (Illus. 5.1). The fills of these features contained charcoal (mostly oak), burnt animal bone (mostly indeterminate but with one sheep/ goat fragment), sherds of at least three Late Neolithic Grooved Ware vessels, flint cutting/wedge tools, scrapers (including a thumbnail scraper) and debitage. One of the pits contained fire-cracked stone. Sooting and a burnt, blackened accretion on one of the Grooved Ware vessels indicate that this pot, at least, was used for cooking. Hazel charcoal from a post-hole and from two pits within the putative building returned dates of 2867–2579 BC (UBA-12108), 2866–2580 BC (UBA-11105) and 2831–2487 BC (UBA-12109). Though Grooved Ware is often found on ritual or ceremonial sites, this diminutive structure is tentatively interpreted as a domestic building.

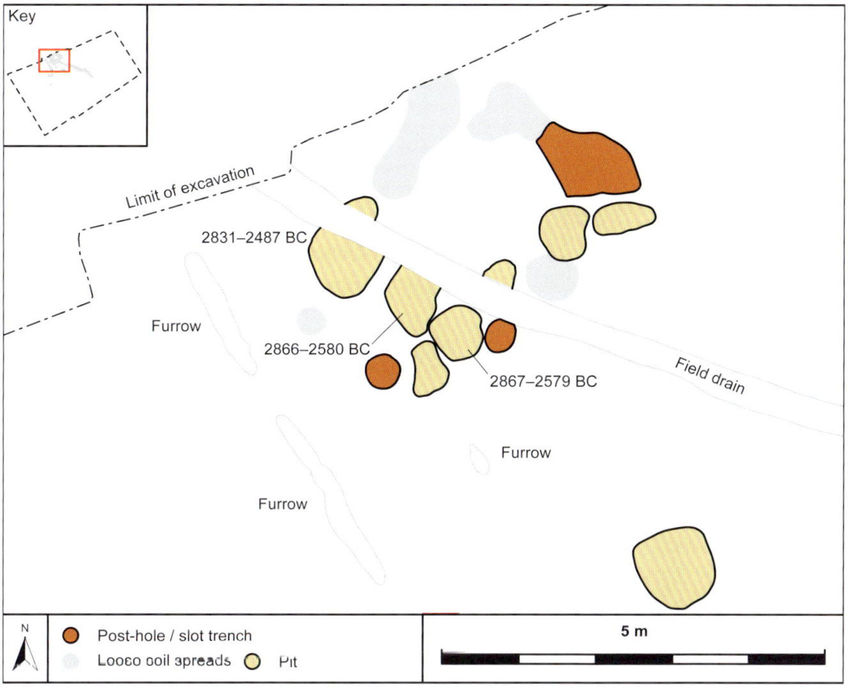

Illus. 5.1 Phoenixtown 5: plan of Late Neolithic features, possibly a domestic building (*IAC Ltd*).

Ritual site at Kilmainham 1C

The key element of this period at Kilmainham 1C was a rectangular 'four-post' arrangement, Structure VI. This was indicated by an arrangement of three post-holes, forming two sides of a rectangle that would have measured 6 m west–east by 2 m north–south (Illus. 5.2). There was probably a fourth post-hole at the north-west corner, but this appears to have been removed by a later pit. Young oak charcoal from a fill of one of the post-holes was dated to 2870–2490 BC (SUERC-29343). The same deposit also produced a single chert flake.

The structure was located at the centre of a large concentration of undated pits, post-holes and stake-holes. It is likely that some of these, at least, were contemporary with it. Notably, a curvilinear arc of several post-holes and stake-holes 9 m west of the structure may have been part of an enclosure or timber circle with a projected diameter of up to 20 m (max.). None of these was dated but they can be compared with the very clear evidence for a timber circle surrounding a central post-built structure at Kilmainham 3 (below).

Several metres west of Structure VI, on the arc of the putative timber circle, a Grooved Ware pot (Vessel 56; Illus. 5.3) had been placed upright into a scoop or hollow in soft sandy soil. (The surviving parts were the intact base and lower body, and some neck/rim sherds.) Similar pottery was recovered from two pits immediately south-west of Structure VI, one of which contained 17 sherds of Grooved Ware pottery and a piece of burnt flint. In addition to these, some residual Grooved Ware pottery was also recovered from features dated to later periods at Kilmainham 1C.

A large pit near the centre of the projected timber circle, and partly overlapping the footprint of Structure VI, contained a Beaker pot (Rockbarton type) from the Chalcolithic period. This is unlikely to be chance. The 'revisiting' or later introduction of Beaker pottery to Grooved Ware timber circle sites is mirrored at Paulstown, Co. Kilkenny (Elliot 2007; 2009; Grogan & Roche 2009), and Armalughey, Co. Tyrone (Dunlop & Barkley 2012, 38).

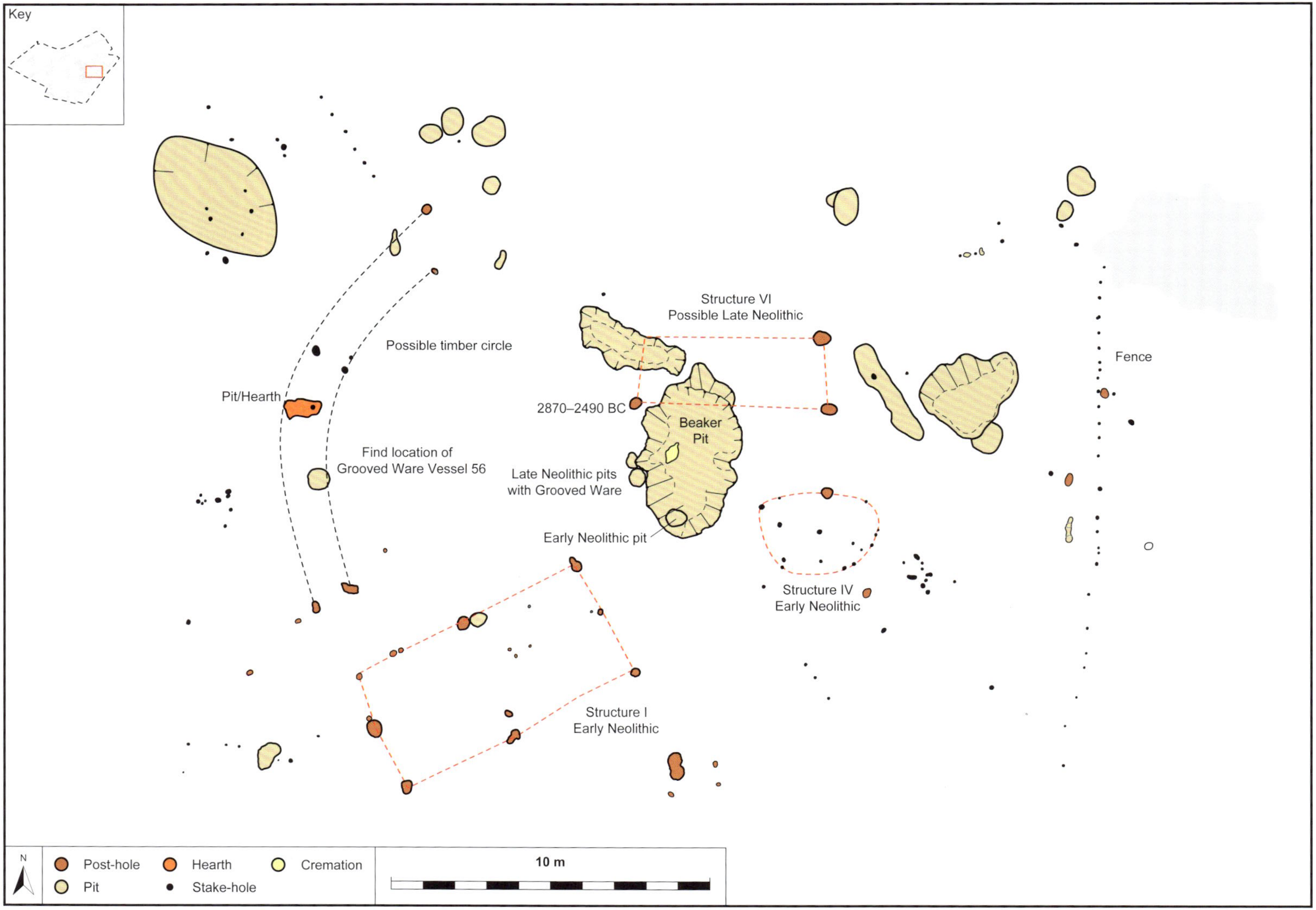

Illus. 5.2 Kilmainham 1C: excavated prehistoric features included a Late Neolithic four-post structure (Structure VI) within a possible timber circle and pits containing Grooved Ware (*IAC Ltd*).

Illus. 5.3 Kilmainham 1C: A near complete Grooved Ware pot (Vessel 56: base, lower body and some rim sherds) was found in a shallow pit forming part of the putative timber circle with a four-post structure (Structure VI) at the centre. Sherds of similar pottery were found in two other pits close to the four-post structure (*Maeve Tobin for IAC Ltd*).

Ceremonial complex at Kilmainham 3

The most impressive elements of the Late Neolithic period were found at Kilmainham 3. There was an impressive timber circle (Structure 2) with a subrectangular arrangement of pits and post-holes in the middle. The central pits had associated burnt bone and Grooved Ware pottery. Two substantial post-built structures (Structures 1 and 3) positioned NNW and SSE of the circle were contemporary with it, based on the evidence of radiocarbon dates (below) and associated Grooved Ware pottery. A group of possible cremation pits located north-east of the timber circle contained burnt bone but this could not be identified to species.

This ritual complex would have been a place of pilgrimage for the people of the district in the latter stages of the third millennium BC—a sacred place where communal ceremonies were performed and witnessed. Approximately 25 timber circles with associated Grooved Ware pottery have been identified to date in Ireland. Typically, they incorporate some or all of the following features: one or more enclosing rings of post-holes, an internal square setting of four large post-holes, and a south-east-facing entrance that often had a screen or façade of posts. The post-hole ring and central post-built structure on the present site are clearly from the same broad tradition but, taken altogether, the suite of Late Neolithic features at Kilmainham 3 has no direct parallels in Late Neolithic Ireland.

As an aside, we should note again that Kilmainham 3, like many other excavated sites along the road scheme, had a history of use in several periods. A small campsite was established here in the Early Neolithic period (3702–3638 BC, UBA-12080). Long after the Late Neolithic ritual phase represented by the timber circle complex, there was Bronze Age ritual activity associated with a ring-ditch and, later again, Iron Age pits. How can we explain this continuity? Perhaps extensive woodland clearances in earlier prehistory had a lasting impact on vegetation and land use, leaving a mosaic of regenerated woodland, scrub and open grassland areas that would have continued to attract people even in much later periods.

Timber circle (Structure 2)

The timber circle at Kilmainham 3 was identified as 40 post-holes in a subcircular arrangement measuring 18 m north/south by 16 m (Illus. 5.4 and 5.5). The southern half of the circle was defined by a regular arrangement of double post-holes, with pairs of posts set at intervals of 1.5 m. In the northern half there were only single post-holes, which were less evenly spaced. This suggests that the structure was more open to the north, in the direction of the River Blackwater. This arrangement of post-holes is most unlikely to represent a roofed building. Instead, we can imagine a defined space that contained a central structure of larger posts (described below), surrounded by a double ring of free-standing posts, and which was open to be viewed from the outside.

The post-holes were 0.1–0.43 m deep—clearly some were heavily truncated—and 0.1–0.32 m in diameter. The charcoal assemblage was dominated by oak and, as this was the most abundant wood available locally, the posts were probably of oak too. There is no evidence that the posts were burnt *in situ*, but deliberate charring to harden the buried ends and prevent decay might account for at least some of the charcoal. The post-hole fills contained small quantities of Grooved Ware pottery (from two post-holes) and 15 pieces of flint debitage (from a dozen post-holes, including one of the two with Grooved Ware).

Samples from the outer post-holes produced four very different radiocarbon dates, ranging across the Mesolithic, the Middle and Later Neolithic and the early medieval periods: 5620–5480 BC (SUERC-29340), 3637–3377 BC (UBA-12085), 2880–2580 BC (SUERC-29341) and AD 608–665 (UBA-12084). The Mesolithic date most probably represents a chance incorporation of much older, residual charcoal in a Late Neolithic post-hole. The Middle Neolithic date could represent material deliberately placed in one of the post-holes as part of a founding deposit or, again, simply chance incorporation of residual material. All three prehistoric dates were from hazel charcoal. The early medieval date was obtained from a single grain of barley, which was the only cereal grain found in the post-hole and which must be considered a random, intrusive item.

Central post-built structure

At the centre of the timber circle (Structure 2), a group of post-holes formed a subrectangular or trapezoidal arrangement (3.4 m north/south by 3.0 m). There were five post-holes in this arrangement, including

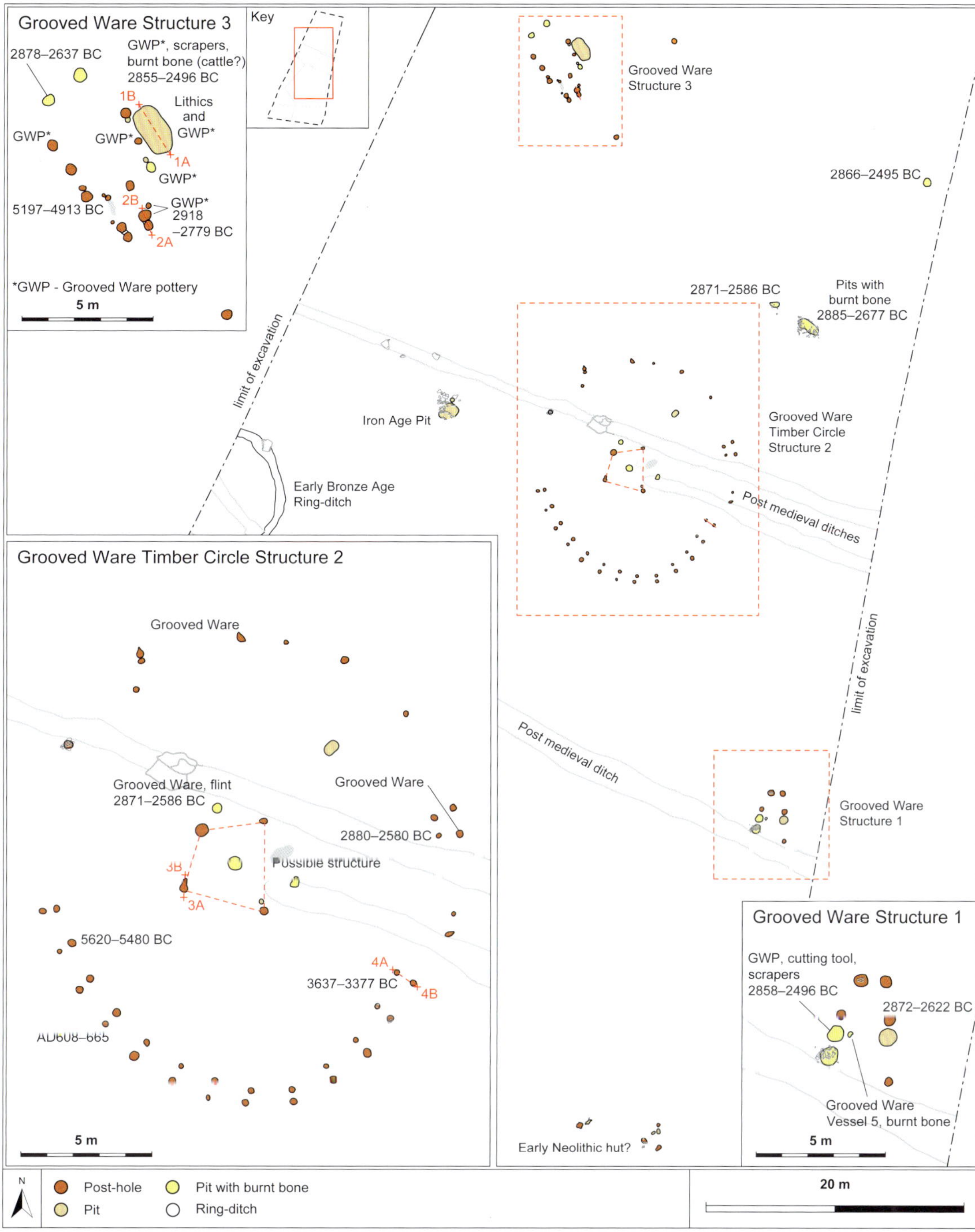

Illus. 5.4 Kilmainham 3: the Late Neolithic ceremonial complex featured a four-post structure in a timber circle (Structure 2), with smaller satellite structures (Structures 1 and 3) and pits containing burnt bone fragments (upper right) (*IAC Ltd*).

Illus. 5.5 Kilmainham 3: view from north of the four-post structure and timber circle (Structure 2). Note the double post-hole pairs in the southern sector of the circle (top) (*Hawkeye*).

two that were conjoined or intercut at the south-west corner, so that the group can be considered to represent a more typical four-post structure. The posts may have supported a platform but it is equally likely that they were simply free-standing uprights, defining a sacred space at the centre of the timber circle. The post-holes were variously 0.22–0.51 m wide and 0.08–0.46 m deep (Illus. 5.6). Clearly, a few of the posts were quite substantial and the structure may have been taller than the enclosing timber circle. Again, oak was the dominant charcoal from the post-hole fills. Flint debitage was found in all of the post-holes. One of them contained over 30 Grooved Ware sherds.

A shallow pit in the middle of this central post-built structure contained a small quantity of burnt bone. A few pieces could be identified as animal bone. Another pit, just north of the structure, also contained burnt bone fragments (unidentified), a single sherd of Grooved Ware and several pieces of worked flint. One flint flake fragment from the pit had been retouched after breaking and may have been a 'special' item, deliberately placed in the pit. A charred hazelnut shell from the pit was dated to 2871–2586 BC (UBA-12086).

Satellite structure at SSE (Structure 1)

Structure 1 stood SSE of the timber circle and was one of the two satellite structures within about 10 m of it. It comprised five post-holes and three other pits with burnt bone,

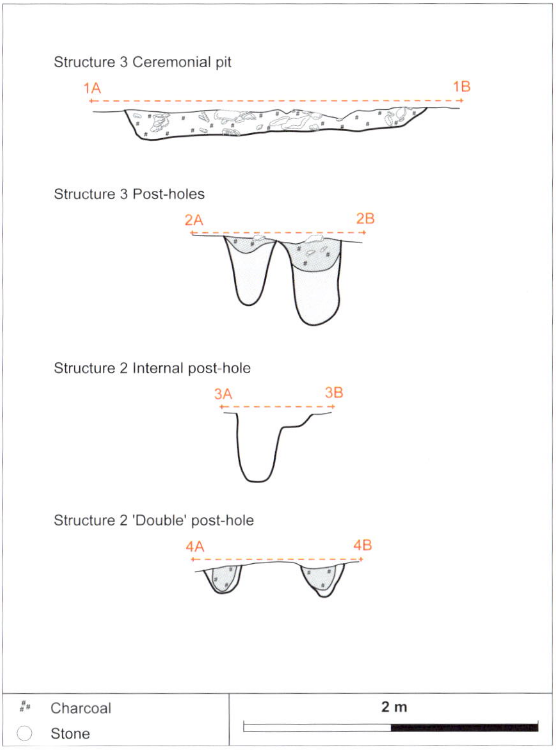

Illus. 5.6 Kilmainham 1C and Kilmainham 3: sample post-hole sections (Structures 2 and 3) and ceremonial pit with burnt animal bones, Grooved Ware and worked flint (Structure 3) (*IAC Ltd*).

possibly from cremations. These features combined to form a trapezoidal shape, narrowing from south to north (Illus. 5.4). The structure was 4.2 m long, 2.2 m wide at the southern end and 0.5 m wide at the northern end. The post-holes were variously 0.3–0.5 m wide by 0.23–0.38 m deep. A hazelnut shell from one of the post holes was dated to 2872–2622 BC (UBA-12081).

Together with the post-holes, three other pits completed the trapezoidal plan of Structure 1. These were partly stone-lined and contained small quantities of burnt bone. The contents of one of these pits were clearly 'structured'. It contained a sherd of Grooved Ware pot, some burnt bone, a flint cutting tool and two flint scrapers. The cutting tool was placed on a centrally positioned flat stone at the base of the pit. There was a charcoal-rich basal deposit of silty sand, sealed by a redeposited clay layer that lined the sides, and then another layer of black, silty sand, which contained a moderate amount of burnt bone. A hazelnut shell from the upper fill was dated to 2858–2496 BC (UBA-12082). Some of the bone from this pit was identified as animal. None of the bone from any of the three pits was identified as human.

A total of 40 pieces of worked flint was recovered from these stone-lined, burnt-bone pits. Mostly this was debitage but it included the cutting tool described above and a fine long scraper. The base of a Grooved Ware pot (Vessel 5) was found at the centre of this trapezoidal area, between bedrock ridges at the base of a small, shallow pit. Like the cutting tool in the stone-lined pit (above), it was also likely to have been deliberately placed in this position. This is mirrored at Lagavooren 7, Co. Meath, where the crushed remains of a Grooved Ware vessel were found in the north-west quadrant of the timber circle (Stafford 2012).

Satellite structure at NNW (Structure 3)

Structure 3 was located NNW of the timber circle. It was defined by a regular oblong arrangement of pits and post-holes, open at the north-west end and with a porch-like opening at the south-east end. The structure measured 5 m long by 3.4 m wide (max.); the 'porch' was 1.3 m wide (Illus. 5.4 and 5.7). Some of the post-holes were very deep, with a range of 0.16–0.40 m in width and 0.1–0.56 m in depth, suggesting that they supported large posts that may have been over 2 m in height (Illus. 5.6). The pits and post-holes were arranged in symmetrically opposing pairs along the central NW–SE axis, a design feature that is shared with some other timber circle sites. A large shallow pit immediately adjacent to the structure on its north-east side was perhaps a place for votive offerings.

There were two shallow pits at the open, north-western end of the structure, positioned c. 1.5 m beyond the last pair of post-holes. They had charcoal-rich fills with large amounts of burnt bone (66.7 g and 45.1 g). None of it could be identified to species but the relatively large quantities suggest that these features were cremation pits, though burnt animal bone can also occur in similar contexts in association with ritual structures. Oak charcoal was the main wood type from the pits. Oak is the most common charcoal type associated with cremation deposits in the Irish archaeological record: it can burn for a long time at a high temperature and was the preferred fuel for funerary pyres (O'Donnell 2007, 45–50).

There was a solitary post-hole c. 4.5 m south-east of the porched entrance to Structure 3, roughly aligned with its central long axis. The post-hole is undated but may have held a post that stood on a processional route between Structure 3 and the timber circle.

Radiocarbon-dated hazelnut shells from the pits and post-holes confirmed the Late Neolithic date of Structure 3, with date ranges of 2918–2779 BC (UBA-12092), 2878–2637 BC (UBA-12094) and 2855–2496 BC (UBA-12093). Unexpectedly, however, a hazelnut shell from one post-hole produced

Illus. 5.7 Kilmainham 3: view from east of the pits and post-holes forming Structure 3 (*Hawkeye*).

a Mesolithic date of 5197–4913 BC (UBA-12091): obviously, this was a random, residual inclusion in the fill of that feature.

The large, shallow pit on the eastern side of Structure 3 had a charcoal-rich fill with frequent pebbles, stones, burnt bone, pottery sherds and worked flint pieces. The burnt bone fragments that could be identified were from large mammals, most likely cattle. There were over 50 pottery sherds, all from a single large Grooved Ware vessel, decorated with lightly scored horizontal and oblique lines. There were over 100 worked flint pieces, mostly debitage and much of it burnt, but also six scrapers. Two of these were shaped, it seemed, so that they could be hafted. This volume of material, including burnt animal bone and a single decorated pot, suggests a ceremonial pit—perhaps a place where offerings were made as people passed through the structure, or where the debris of a ceremonial meal was ritually buried, along with other offerings, including the six scrapers.

Outlying pits with burnt bone

A few scattered pits in the area north-east of the timber circle contained burnt bone. One pit was lined with stone slabs and had a covering of four flat slabs. The fills contained burnt and charred material, including 2 g of burnt bone. The bone fragments could not be identified but may have been a token cremation deposit. Hazelnut shell from the pit was dated to 2866–2495 BC (UBA-12088). A larger quantity of burnt bone (150.8 g) was recovered from another pit (undated) east of Structure 3. Some of the bone was animal but most of it could not be identified. The two pits nearest the timber circle contained high volumes of wood charcoal. Hazelnut shells from these pits returned dates of 2871–2586 BC (UBA-12090) and 2885–2677 BC (UBA-12089). One of them contained sherds of pottery from a Grooved Ware vessel and a flint cutting tool, as well as nine other pieces of flint. A very small quantity of burnt bone (0.4 g) recovered from one pit was not identifiable to species.

Some of the burnt bone from these pits could be identified as animal. None of it was positively identified as human. The excavated examples were close to the limit of excavation on this eastern side of the site, so that there may be more of these features beyond the footprint of the road project.

The Kilmainham 3 ceremonial complex

The deposits of burnt bone, chipped stone and Grooved Ware associated with Structures 1 and 3 indicate that they were each used for ceremonial actions, but we may also view them as integral parts of a complex of elements that included the timber circle (Structure 2) and its central 'four-post' structure. It is easy to imagine that all these structures would have been interlinked by a complex series of ritual acts, performed in a prescribed sequence, which culminated in access to the core of the site, where the main ceremony of the day was played out within the timber circle. In this scenario we can interpret Structures 1 and 3 as 'portals' that channelled people towards the timber circle. Structure 1 was trapezoidal in plan, narrowing to the north, while Structure 3 was bottle-shaped, with its 'porched' entrance pointing south-east. A large post positioned several metres from this porched end of Structure 3 may have marked a point where people turned towards the timber circle, or away from it, as they followed a prescribed route around the monument in a processional ritual. As people passed through

A ceremony at Kilmainham

In writing about his work on the Stonehenge Riverside Project, Parker Pearson (2013, 77) described monuments like Stonehenge as 'monuments to the ancestors, constructed in stone to represent the eternity of life after death'. He contrasted them with wooden monuments, like the timber circles at nearby Durrington Walls, which he believes were 'monuments of the world of the living'. If wood was for the living and stone was for the dead, we should view the timber circle complex at Kilmainham 3 as a place for the celebration of life rather than a place of burial and mourning. With a little imagination we can form a picture of what might have happened here during a ceremony around 2800 BC (Illus. 5.8).

A ceremony at Kilmainham 3 would have been a special event, when the whole community gathered together, perhaps to participate in a key annual religious festival, or to celebrate a harvest, a marriage or rites of passage into adult life. It would have been an opportunity for the ordinary person to give thanks to the gods and to make a token offering of something personal—a stone tool or bone fragments from a family cremation. The elaborate organisation of the site, with its controlled way of approaching the inner circle, would have added to the sense of a special experience, helping to engrain memories of the event as something above the ordinary. The area enclosed by the timber circle, with central four-post structure, was no doubt an inner sanctum reserved for the most important participants—the religious leaders or celebrants. The openness of the whole structure would have allowed the community to observe the ceremonies in the timber circle while maintaining a defined boundary between the public area and the sacred space. Food was cooked and shared, adding to the sense of occasion.

Durrington Walls was linked to Stonehenge, over 3 km away, by avenues leading from the River Avon. These links between major monuments in Wiltshire open the possibility of similar links in the prehistoric landscape around Kells, and it is entirely possible that the River Blackwater was important, as a practical and spiritual route, for the people who visited Kilmainham 3. Perhaps, like the Avon in Wiltshire, it offered a ceremonial route between major monuments representing the realms of life and death. At the very least we can assume that some people journeyed to Kilmainham along the river, and perhaps the final stage of their journey, from the river to the timber circle site, was important to the ceremonies of the day.

the portals (Structures 1 and 3), offerings of special items were made, including worked flint objects, pottery or token amounts of cremated bone.

The primary focus of ceremonies would have been within the area defined by the timber circle and especially the 'four-post' structure at its centre. The posts forming the timber circle were widely spaced at intervals of 1.5 m or greater, so whatever ritual was performed at the central four-post structure was also a spectacle to be witnessed by crowds of people standing outside the circle. Thus the timber circle had a practical purpose in organising and dividing the site, but also a metaphysical purpose in separating the mundane world outside the circle, and the people inhabiting that world, from the sacred space inside the circle, where their priests or shamans communicated with the gods.

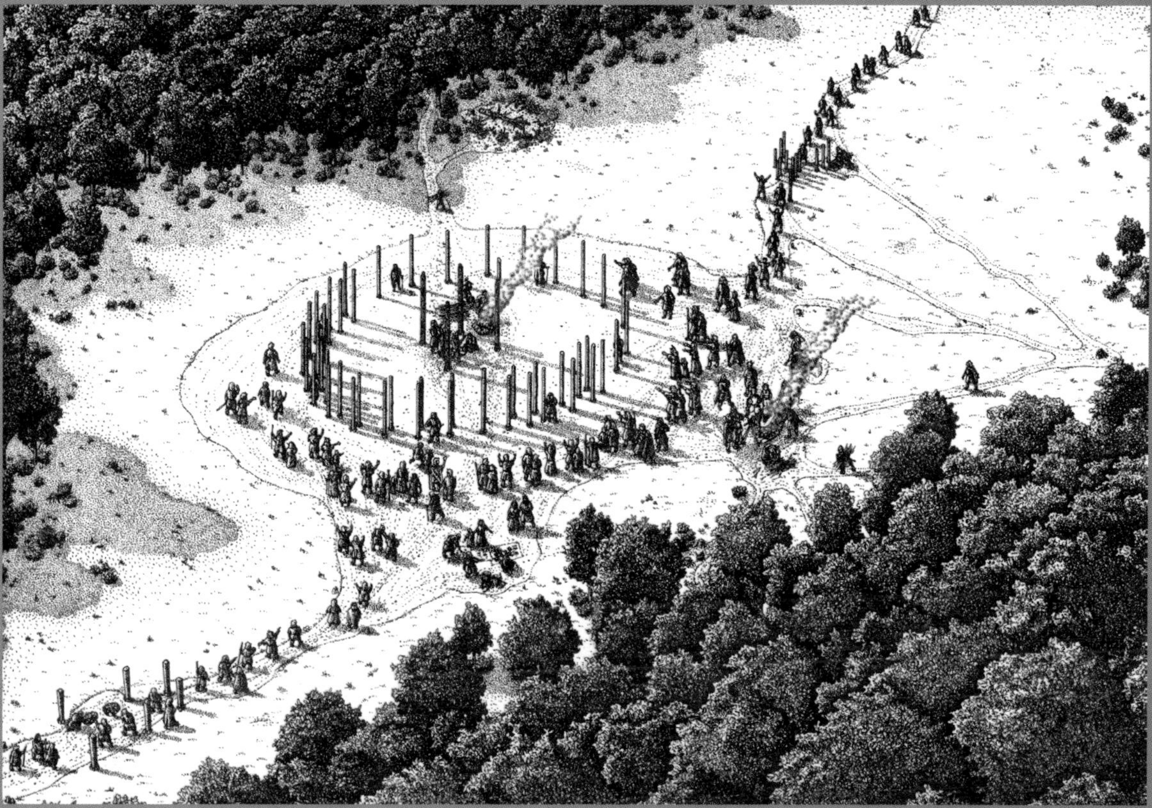

Illus. 5.8 Kilmainham 3: artist's impression of proceedings at the Late Neolithic ceremonial complex, showing the four-post structure and timber circle (centre) and satellite structures (Structure 1, bottom left; Structure 3, top right) framing the approaches to the central area (*Dan Tietzsch-Tyler for IAC Ltd*).

The timber circle tradition

There are several Irish Late Neolithic ceremonial sites that can be compared with Kilmainham 3, though none offers a direct parallel. They include Grooved Ware timber circle sites such as Knowth (Eogan & Roche 1997), Bettystown (Eogan 1998; 1999) and Lagavooren 7 (Stafford 2012), Co. Meath; Balgatheran, Co. Louth (Ó Drisceoil 2009); Paulstown, Co. Kilkenny (Elliot 2007; 2009; Grogan & Roche 2009); Ballynahatty, Co. Down (Hartwell 1998; 2002) (Illus.5.9); and Armalughey, Co. Tyrone (Dunlop & Barkley 2012). Kilmainham 3 shares some components with these sites, such as the internal four-post arrangement, but it does not have their regular symmetry. The only comparison for the double (paired) post-hole arrangement along the southern portion of the Kilmainham 3 timber circle is the timber circle at Armalughey (not illus.), where close-set groups of four posts formed the outer circle and entrance.

As a complex of several structures, Kilmainham 3 can be compared with the

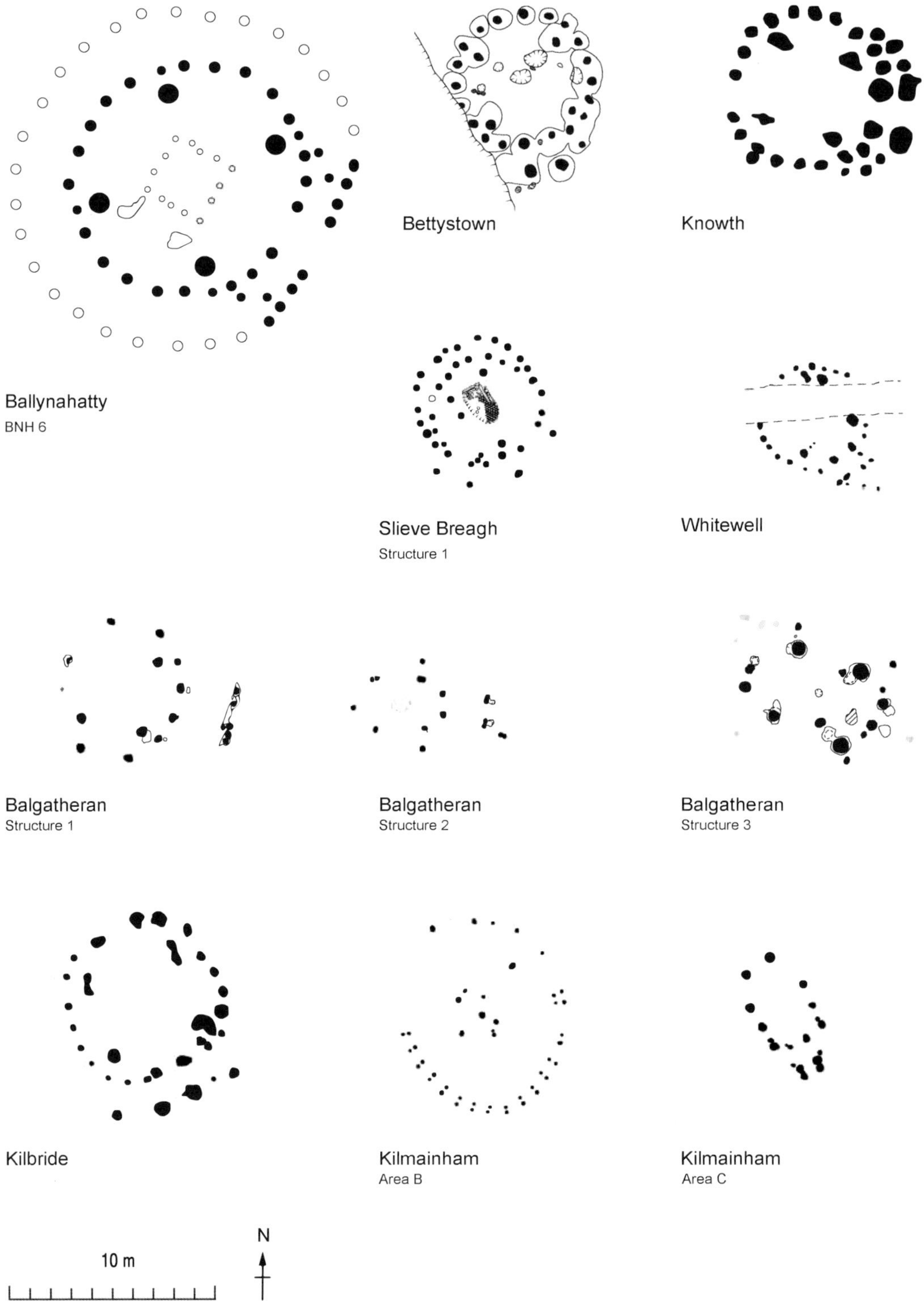

Illus. 5.9 Some Neolithic post-built structures associated with Grooved Ware in Ireland, including parts of the Kilmainham 3 complex (*after Smyth 2014, 88, fig. 5.13*).

much larger and more elaborate Late Neolithic ceremonial complex at Ballynahatty (Hartwell 1998; 2002), principally in the control of access to the central area. The principal upstanding remains at Ballynahatty are a huge, embanked enclosure with a passage tomb at its centre. Adjacent excavated features include the remains of an elaborate, multi-phase timber circle (Illus. 5.9). The timber circle began as a single ring of posts, 11 m in diameter, which enclosed a four-post arrangement (BNH 6). This early phase would have mirrored the ground-plan of simple timber circles at Lagavooren 7, Knowth and Paulstown. The next phase resulted in all of the original posts being replaced by much bigger ones, now encircled by a second, larger ring of posts, measuring 16 m in diameter—the same diameter as Kilmainham 3. This was then encircled by a large oval enclosure (BNH 5) consisting of a double ring of posts, with a post-built corridor leading out from this to an entrance within an elaborate annexe. Hartwell (2002, 253) believes that the complex arrangement of posts at Ballynahatty formed passageways designed to choreograph movement and control access to the central timber circle. Another example of this controlled access, although simpler and on a smaller scale, can perhaps be seen in the funnel-shaped entrance feature leading into the timber circle at Armalughey. In Britain formal access corridors are well documented. The classic example is the avenue of posts leading from an outer façade into the Northern Circle at Durrington Walls, Wiltshire (Wainwright & Longworth 1971).

The Kilmainham 3 timber circle is missing one common component of these other Late Neolithic timber circle sites—a recognised front and entrance or monumental façade. Perhaps the intention of having access points via satellite structures at Kilmainham 3 (i.e. via Structures 1 and 3) was to allow for a more open public space around the timber circle. Evidently there was a shared architectural vocabulary in the Late Neolithic timber circle tradition but also freedom to combine and adapt the components in different ways, suitable to the requirements of individual communities.

The pattern of deposition or deliberately placed inclusions in the Kilmainham 3 pits also has parallels with other sites in the timber circle tradition. The pits forming the four-post structure at the centre of the timber circle contained quantities of worked flint, as well as Grooved Ware. Ritual deposition of worked flint is documented at other timber circle sites, including Ballynahatty and Knowth. More particularly, ritual deposition at portal or entrance features—Structures 1 and 3 at Kilmainham 3—is mirrored at Ballynahatty, where pits containing burnt bone flanked the lines of access to the central enclosed area.

There were burnt bone fragments in many of the post-holes and pits forming the ritual structures at Kilmainham 3, and also in the scattered group of pits east of the timber circle. Some of this was identified as animal bone but none could be identified as human. The large quantities of animal bone (mostly pig), with minimal breakage patterns, recovered at Durrington Walls were interpreted as evidence of large-scale feasting (Parker Pearson et al. 2006, 234). There is an echo of this at Kilmainham 3 in the large mammal bones (probably cattle) from the large pit by Structure 3, and communal feasting would certainly be compatible with our interpretation of the monument as an 'open' group of structures designed for the celebration of life events.

CHAPTER 6

Beaker pits and pottery

Fintan Walsh

Beaker pits and pottery

The transition period from the end of the Stone Age (Late Neolithic period) to the start of the Bronze Age proper is known in archaeological writing as the Chalcolithic period (c. 2450–2200 BC). This is signalled in the archaeological record by a suite of new artefacts, including highly decorated and distinctive pottery forms (Beakers), barbed-and-tanged arrowheads, and stone wrist-guards used by archers. Traditionally these objects were attributed to a 'Beaker culture' but archaeologists no longer believe that they represent the arrival in Ireland of an invading 'Beaker people' (Carlin 2018, 25–6) (Illus. 6.1). The Chalcolithic period is more especially characterised by the first use of metals. Copper was used to make simple axes and daggers. Gold was used for personal ornaments. Bronze, which is an alloy of copper and tin, would become the dominant metal from c. 2200 BC, marking the end of this transitional period.

The excavated sites of the Chalcolithic period in Ireland are mostly domestic in character, in contrast to the Late Neolithic period, which is mostly represented in the record by public ceremonial monuments, as we saw in the previous

Illus. 6.1 Beaker vessel and cremated human bone from Knowth, Co. Meath. The Chalcolithic period is signalled in the archaeological record by a suite of new artefacts traditionally identified with 'Beaker culture' and a gradual shift from communal burial monuments to individual burials in cists and pits (*Ken Williams*).

chapter. Some old customs persisted, such as the revisiting of ancestral places to make offerings and the votive deposition of objects in buildings. The wedge tombs of this period represent a last flowering of megalithic funerary monuments in Ireland. Individual burials in cists and pits would become common by the Bronze Age—suggesting the increasing importance of the individual and perhaps belief in an afterlife—but to date there is only very limited Irish evidence for individual cist and pit burials in the Chalcolithic period (Mount 2012).

On the Navan to Kells and N52 Kells Bypass section of the M3 motorway scheme, the excavated evidence for the Chalcolithic period was generally found on archaeological sites that also featured earlier periods. They mostly occurred in the Kilmainham/Cookstown Great area, with only occasional discoveries elsewhere along the road corridor. The evidence from Kilmainham/Cookstown Great is typical of the Irish material as a whole: it is characterised by Beaker pottery and other domestic material occurring in small pit groups and isolated pits and soil spreads. In addition, one of the earliest burnt mounds on the road scheme was dated to this period at Townparks/Commons of Lloyd 1 (Burnt Mound 2) (2462–2212 BC, UBA-11124).

Chalcolithic evidence from Kilmainham/Cookstown Great

At Kilmainham 1C a large pit, located on the site of a former Late Neolithic four-post structure (Chapter 5), contained the partial remains of a Rockbarton Beaker vessel (Illus. 6.2) and sherds from at least nine other Beaker vessels, flint objects and a polished stone. This constituted most of the Beaker pottery from this site. Few of the vessels from the pit were complete—most were represented by fewer

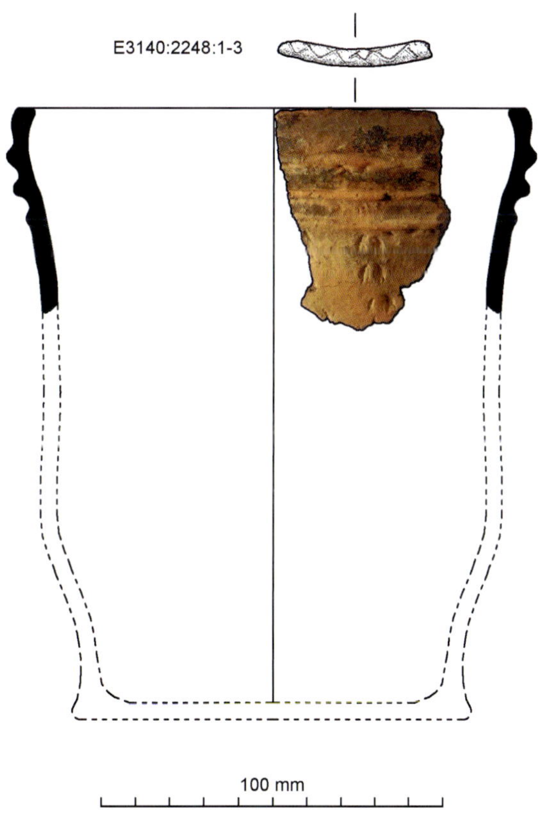

Illus. 6.2 Kilmainham 1C: conjectural reconstruction of a Rockbarton Beaker pot (Vessel 49) (Finds Nos E3140:2284:1–3). Two sherds were recovered from a large pit that also contained sherds from at least nine other Beaker vessels, flint objects and a polished stone (*Johnny Ryan and Alva MacGowan for IAC Ltd*).

than 10 sherds. The sherds themselves were not fresh, suggesting that they were collected together, perhaps from a midden, before being thrown into the pit. The pit was 5.5 m long, 3.5 m wide and 0.7 m deep. A smaller pit cut into its base contained burnt bone fragments. These could not be identified but, in this context, we must consider the possibility that they were cremated human remains. The pottery and other objects were deposited in the primary, charcoal-rich fills of the pit. These were sealed in turn by sterile clays and gravel, which appear to have been quickly and deliberately backfilled, perhaps immediately or soon after the pit was used and the objects were deposited. In effect, the pit was 'closed' by these upper clay and gravel deposits.

Burnt organic material on the inner surface of the Rockbarton Beaker vessel was radiocarbon-dated to 2287–2051 BC (UBA-14139). This date range is at the very end of the Beaker period and is comparable with a date from hazel charcoal (2350–2130 BC) for a pit containing Rockbarton pottery from Lismullin, Co. Meath (O'Connell 2009), further south-east on the M3.

Elsewhere at Kilmainham 1C, another large pit (3 m wide by 0.6 m deep) was partly sealed by an Early Bronze Age metalled platform (Platform A). It had a similar fill sequence to the Rockbarton pit on the same site (above), but sherds from just one Beaker vessel were recovered from its charcoal-rich fill.

At Kilmainham 1B, an adjacent site on the present sector of the M3, not far to the south, a Beaker pot was also deliberately deposited in a large/shallow pit (Illus. 6.3 and 6.4). This was an almost complete 'S-shaped' Beaker vessel, placed carefully towards the base of the pit.

A Chalcolithic domestic building at Kilmainham 1C?

The features recorded as Structure 6 at Kilmainham 1C offered rare evidence of a possible Chalcolithic building. A group of 29 stake-holes, two hearths, nine pits and a metalled surface extended over an area roughly 5 m in diameter (Illus. 6.5). The post-holes and stake-holes did not form a clear plan but were obviously grouped around a central hearth, located on the edge of the

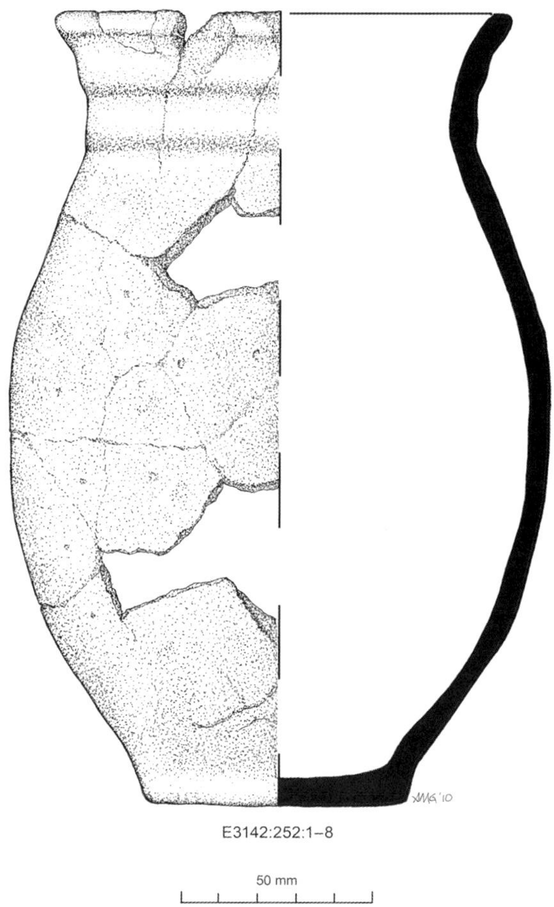

Illus. 6.3 Kilmainham 1B: 'S-shaped' Beaker vessel (Vessel 2) (Finds Nos E3142:252:1–8) (*Alva McGowan for IAC Ltd*).

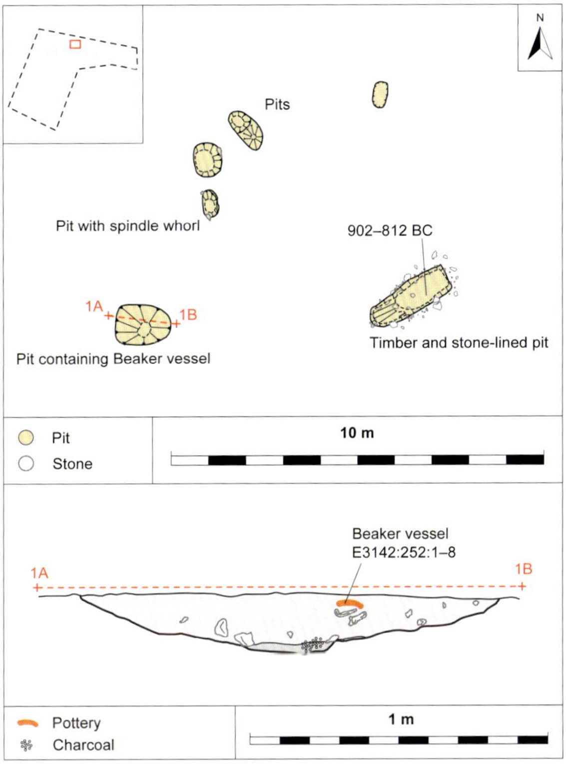

Illus. 6.4 Kilmainham 1B: plan and section of a pit that contained an almost complete 'S-shaped' Beaker vessel (*IAC Ltd*).

metalled area. North of the building there were some large spreads of occupation soil containing sherds of domestic Beaker ware. Structure V, a possible animal pen or corral (below), stood a short distance to the east.

The building plan of Structure 6 was not clearly defined by the evidence, but this is not unusual in an Irish context. Although domestic activity dominates the archaeological record of this period, good evidence for buildings is rare. Where buildings have been identified, the evidence often survives as clusters of stake-holes and post-holes, with associated pits and hearths, lacking any clear pattern. It seems likely that houses of this period had only very slight foundations, unlike, for instance, the big rectangular houses of the Early Neolithic, with their deep foundation trenches. Consequently, Chalcolithic houses typically leave few traces in the ground. Despite these difficulties, several houses of the period have been tentatively identified elsewhere in County Meath, at Newgrange (Cooney & Grogan 1994, 79–81). Nationally, Carlin (2018, 55–9) recently reviewed the evidence from several sites where Chalcolithic houses have been proposed by the excavators—including Roughan Hill on the Burren, Co. Clare (Jones 1998), and Ross Island, Co. Kerry (O'Brien 2004, 173–215)—but was not persuaded by these examples and concluded that Graigueshoneen, Co. Waterford, is 'the least ambiguous example of a Beaker-associated structure' (Carlin 2018, 59). This structure was 7.6 m in diameter and was represented by three concentric rings of stake-holes, with internal pits and a hearth (Tierney et al. 2008).

Two radiocarbon date ranges for charcoal samples from Structure 6 at Kilmainham fit well within the Chalcolithic time-frame. Alder from a possible post-hole was dated to 2433–2148 BC (UBA-12920), and hazel from the central hearth was dated to 2287–2061 BC (UBA-13021). The latter date range is closely comparable with the date from the charred accretions on the Beaker Rockbarton pot, described above.

Animal pen or corral at Kilmainham 1C

A short distance to the east of Structure 6 at Kilmainham 1C, a group of eight post-holes was recorded as Structure V (Illus. 6.5). All of the features were very shallow, probably truncated, and had no surviving evidence of stone packing or of post-pipes (i.e. the humic soil traces of decayed timbers). They were, however, arranged in a regular subrectangular

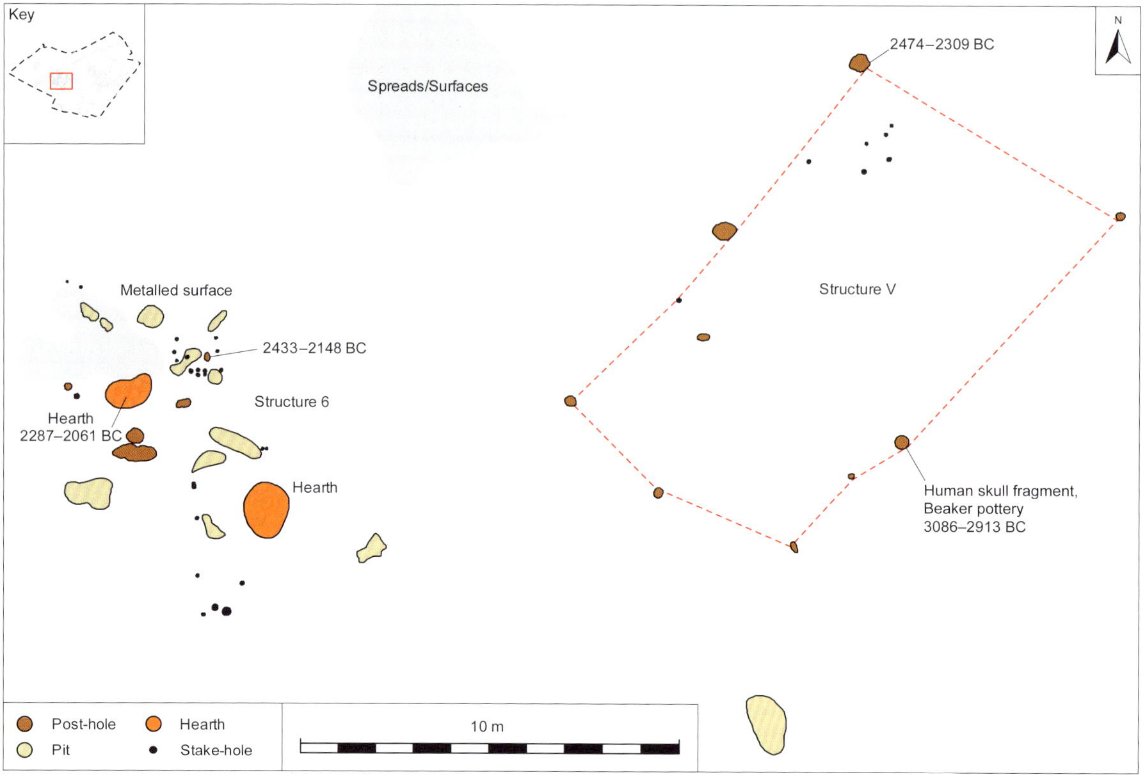

Illus. 6.5 Kilmainham 1C: plan of a possible Chalcolithic-period house (Structure 6, left) and animal corral (Structure V, right) (*IAC Ltd*).

fashion, 13 m long by 7.75 m wide. If these features did form a single structure, this is more likely to have been an animal pen or corral than a domestic, roofed building. A young oak charcoal from one post-hole was dated to 2474–2309 BC (UBA-15480). A small sherd of Beaker pottery was found in another post-hole. A burnt bone fragment (possibly from a human skull) from this feature was dated to 3086–2913 BC (UBA-12919). The latter date is Middle Neolithic and, obviously, does not correspond with the Beaker pottery from the same feature or the Chalcolithic-period date from another feature in this structure. It is not impossible that an ancient skull fragment was discovered and was retained as a valued object, to be buried again at the construction of a building or animal pen. A simpler explanation is that the skull fragment is a residual object, which lay in the soil until it was accidentally incorporated into a later post-hole.

Other Chalcolithic sites in Kilmainham/ Cookstown Great

Although most of the evidence for this period on our project was from Kilmainham, there was evidence of at least small-scale, sporadic activity in other townlands in this part of the road corridor. At Gardenrath 1, oak charcoal from a hearth with associated pits was dated to 2473–2301 BC (UBA-12935). At Gardenrath 2, burnt bone (unidentified) from a pit, with an associated hearth and pit, was dated to 2457–2202 BC (UBA-12936). The

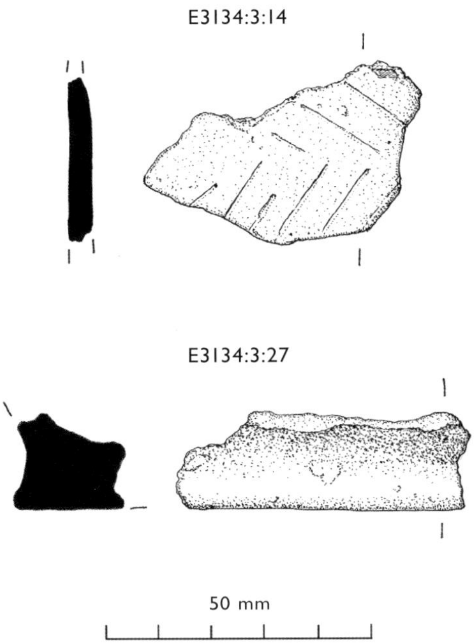

Illus. 6.6 Nugentstown 3: 32 domestic Beaker sherds from a pit represented at least five vessels. They were all abraded and may have lain on the surface for some time before being gathered and buried. These examples are from Vessel 2 (Finds Nos E3134:3:14 (top) and E3134:3:27) (*Alva MacGowan for IAC Ltd*).

hearth contained a Beaker neck sherd. These last features were found at the same location as the Gardenrath Early Neolithic house (Chapter 4). A spread of charcoal-rich soil that partly sealed the remains of that house contained 11 sherds from another Beaker vessel—thus one of two from the site.

At Cookstown Great 2, hazel charcoal from a small, isolated cooking pit, containing heat-fractured stones in its fill, was dated to 2337–2144 BC (UBA-11083).

A pit containing domestic Beaker sherds (Illus. 6.6) and a thumbnail scraper was recorded at Nugentstown 3. There were 32 sherds from at least five vessels. The pottery was all abraded, suggesting that the sherds had lain in the open for some time before being gathered up and placed in the pit. Alder charcoal from the pit was dated to 1915–1759 BC (UBA-12068), in the Early Bronze Age, representing a gap of at least 300 years from the end of the Chalcolithic period. One explanation is that the Beaker pottery and scraper may have been recovered, curated and deposited within the pit centuries after they were made. This would indicate a focus of repeated activity at this small site over a long period of time and suggests that the people of the Early Bronze Age had an active interest in their ancestors or, at least, in the cultural relics occurring in their ancestral landscape. This curation and deposition of already ancient objects is mirrored in the deposition of Beaker objects at Late Neolithic monuments (Chapter 5 and above).

Chalcolithic evidence from Grange/Phoenixtown

The Grange/Phoenixtown area yielded only small-scale evidence for activity throughout the Neolithic period. Prehistoric settlement did not reach its zenith here until the Bronze Age (see Chapter 7), when important settlements were established at Grange 3 and Phoenixtown 3. In our transitional Chalcolithic period, on a site at Phoenixtown 1 with a Middle Bronze Age burnt mound, charcoals of alder and ash from two pits were dated to 2559–2300 BC (UBA-11103) and 2457–2205 BC (UBA-11104). A classic artefact of the Chalcolithic period—a barbed-and-tanged arrowhead—was found close by at Phoenixtown 6 (Illus. 6.7). At Grange 3, oak charcoal from a cereal-drying kiln (a figure-of-eight pit) was dated to 2460–2210

Illus. 6.7 Phoenixtown 6: this barbed-and-tanged flint arrowhead is a classic artefact of the Chalcolithic period (Finds No. E3127:6:2) (*Mark Moraghan*).

BC (UBA-12059). The post-holes of a small structure at Grange 4 (not illustrated) contained a mixture of material, including Early Neolithic pottery, but charred hazelnut shell from one of the pits was dated to 2574–2474 BC (UBA-11128), at the threshold of the Chalcolithic period.

A Chalcolithic landscape

The evidence from the Kilmainham/Cookstown Great area represents a previously undiscovered node of Chalcolithic/Beaker activity in the north Leinster area. A similar, newly discovered concentration of activity has been identified in areas around the Hill of Tara, including Berrilstown, Ardsallagh, Lismullin and Blundelstown (Grogan 2013).

The greatest concentration of Chalcolithic/Beaker activity in this region—and, indeed, in the entire country—is in the catchment of the lower Boyne. Here there are large artefact assemblages from the passage tomb complexes of Knowth (Eogan 1984; Eogan & Roche 1997) and Newgrange (Cleary 1983), and from the embanked enclosure at Monknewtown (Sweetman 1976), all in County Meath. Large assemblages of Beaker pottery have also been reported from excavations in advance of the Platin–Oldbridge section of the M1 Drogheda Bypass, on the eastern fringes of the Brú na Bóinne complex. One of the largest Beaker assemblages in Ireland was recovered from pits at Rathmullan 6 (Bolger 2011), Rathmullan 9 (D Nelis 2011) and Rathmullan 10 (Bolger 2012), Co. Meath. The objects were all found in pits and soil spreads on these sites. The assemblage from Rathmullan 10 represented at least 37 and as many as 110 Beaker vessels, including at least four polypod bowls. A red siltstone wrist-guard was recovered from a spread of occupation soil, associated with Beaker pottery, which was radiocarbon-dated to 2460–2200 BC by means of a bone sample. Four polypod vessels and a handled Beaker were recovered from

Rathmullan 6. Although polypod vessels are a recognised part of the Beaker assemblage and are associated with the Wessex/Middle Rhine group of Beaker wares, they are still considered to be a very rare occurrence on Beaker sites.

Not far north of Rathmullan, and north of the Boyne, c. 500 Beaker sherds, including part of a polypod bowl, were found in occupation deposits at Water Under, Mell, Co. Louth (McQuade 2005). Quantities of Beaker sherds and a barbed-and-tanged arrowhead were found in pits at the Hill of Rath, Co. Louth (Duffy 2000). Further north in County Louth, near Dundalk, pits on a possible Chalcolithic habitation site at Newtownbalregan 2 produced 156 sherds of Beaker pottery from at least 10 vessels and an almost complete polypod bowl (Delaney et al. 2020, 44–9).

Structured deposition

Beaker pottery is found in a variety of contexts in Ireland, including Chalcolithic and older funerary monuments (especially wedge tombs, as well as court tombs), burnt mounds, Late Neolithic (former) timber circle sites, and natural contexts such as bogs and lakes. Overwhelmingly, however, Beaker pottery is found in pits, post-holes and soil spreads on sites that are usually interpreted as settlements, and where it often occurs with burnt bone, chipped stone and especially stone-working debris or 'debitage'. A straightforward interpretation of this pattern is that it simply represents the incidental disposal of domestic waste. As many of these deposits seem to be structured, selective and deliberate, however, rubbish disposal alone is unlikely to be the whole explanation. Carlin (2018, 91–2) gives full and nuanced consideration to this question in a recent study that we can only quote here briefly:

> 'It is clear from the complex treatment of Beaker-associated occupational debris that it was considered a highly significant and meaningful cultural material that fulfilled numerous important social roles ... These depositional acts may have represented an important occasion for local groups, during which the life stories of the people and the places associated with these settlement deposits may have been remembered and celebrated.'

Beaker pottery sherds were recovered on the present project from a variety of contexts, including pits and spreads of occupation soil. The deliberate deposition of Beaker pots or pot sherds in pits at Kilmainham 1B and Kilmainham 1C certainly seems to reflect a ritual intent. This is mirrored on a larger scale in the evidence from Brú na Bóinne, where a range of ritual practices were taking place at both Knowth and Newgrange, associated with the use of Grooved Ware and then Beaker pottery, in the period from around 2900 BC until after 2500 BC (Cooney 2000, 30). This long time-span suggests that the Beaker pottery we found in pits on our road project, at sites in Kilmainham, was part of a tradition of ritual deposition that was already much older than the Beaker phenomenon.

CHAPTER 7

Bronze Age settlement, burnt mounds and burials

Fintan Walsh

Bronze Age settlement, burnt mounds and burials

Towards the end of the third millennium BC the archaeological record of the M3 Navan to Kells and N52 Kells Bypass project shows an intensification of human activity in the River Blackwater valley. There is increasing evidence for habitations and burials along the road corridor, especially in the Kilmainham/Cookstown Great and Phoenixtown/Grange areas. By the Middle Bronze Age the settlement evidence reaches its zenith, most notably with a number of large, impressive round-houses (Illus. 7.1). This is a marked contrast with the Chalcolithic period (Chapter 6) and Early Bronze Age, when domestic buildings seemed to be smaller and flimsier, typically leaving only slight archaeological remains.

Burnt mounds (*fulachtaí fia*) are the commonest expression of human activity in the landscape in this period—though here,

Illus. 7.1 Grange 3: excavation and recording of a Middle Bronze Age round-house (Structure 1), viewed from south (*IAC Ltd*).

as elsewhere in Ireland, they occur from the Late Neolithic period right through to the Late Bronze Age/Iron Age transition. Many of the burnt mounds recorded on this project were found in marginal land, close to streams or wetlands. Nonetheless, they should be seen as part of a mosaic of settlement features in an occupied, organised landscape and not only as isolated features in marginal settings.

The hallmark of the Bronze Age was, of course, the use of metal for tools, weapons and personal ornaments. Some of the most impressive gold and bronze objects in the national collections were made in this period. In our region, bronze clothing-fasteners, hair-rings and bracelets have been found (Waddell 2010, 232–77). No Bronze Age metal artefacts were recovered by our own investigations on the road scheme, although we did find some evidence for metalworking. Clay mould fragments from Cakestown Glebe 2 were probably used to cast a metal blade. A rectangular stone- and timber-lined (oak) pit at Kilmainham 1B contained clay mould fragments and remnants of furnace lining. A fragment of burnt bone from the pit was dated to 902–812 BC (UBA-12934), in the Late Bronze Age. The pit may have been used, among other things, as a water trough for quenching objects during the metalworking process.

Among other artefact types, important assemblages of Early, Middle and Late Bronze Age pottery were recovered, which is significant, as they extend the known distribution of this material in the north Leinster area and include a unique Late Bronze Age broad-rimmed vessel from Cakestown Glebe 2 (Grogan & Roche 2011). Chipped and polished stone tools were still made in this period and were used widely for mundane work, but no longer included finely crafted, prestige objects.

The Bronze Age saw the first clear evidence for human burials in our investigations on the road scheme. By now the dominant burial tradition had changed from collective burials in megalithic tombs to individual cist or pit burials, which occurred in isolation or in cemeteries. There were simple cremation pits on excavated sites in the Kilmainham/Cookstown Great and Phoenixtown/Grange areas. Ring-ditches and barrows were also used as funerary monuments at Kilmainham and Grange.

The climate of Ireland, and of western Europe generally, was wetter in the Bronze Age than in previous periods. Fossil pollen records show an increase in the growth of blanket bogs. Higher rainfall caused leaching, with a corresponding loss of soil fertility, and this was exacerbated by human pressure on the land, which probably included overgrazing (Waddell 2010, 113). In the wood charcoal assemblage from our project (Chapter 2) there is significantly less oak (*Quercus*) by the Early/Middle Bronze Age transition but increasing amounts of ash (*Fraxinus*) (O'Donnell, Chapter 2), which represents large-scale woodland clearance. This is also indicated by the presence of more plantain (*Plantago lanceolata*), which is a characteristic weed of pasturelands and does not grow under closed-canopy woodlands (Gearey et al. 2011, 58; see also Chapter 2).

Taken all together, the archaeological and palaeoenvironmental evidence from the M3 Navan to Kells and N52 Kells Bypass project indicates a population boom in the area in the Bronze Age. We can speculate from the abundance of settlement evidence, in particular, that this peaked in the Middle Bronze Age (1700–1200 BC). As in earlier periods, the 'core' areas at Kilmainham/Cookstown Great and Phoenixtown/Grange remain important, but we now see

Bronze Age burnt mounds, habitation sites, burial monuments and/or isolated pits throughout the entire length of the road scheme. This reflects a national pattern in the archaeological record across the island of Ireland, where a Bronze Age population boom is already well attested.

What were the consequences of a growing population, pressure on land and the limited availability of prestige objects manufactured by highly specialised metalworkers? These elements combined to drive major change towards a more hierarchical and territorial society. The great hillforts of the Late Bronze Age represent the emergence of powerful élites or chiefdoms. There were examples near Kells that probably date from this period, at Commons of Lloyd and Faughan Hill (Chapter 1). By now, however, the remarkable expansion of human society that began in the Middle Bronze Age had already passed its peak and the following generations would see a decline in population, from around the end of the second millennium—a pattern that is seen in the archaeological record throughout Atlantic Europe. Whether this was caused principally by a downturn in climate and consequent food shortages or by social factors, including competition, conflict and disruption of communities, remains a moot point in the archaeological literature (e.g. Raftery 1994; Tipping et al. 2008; Armit et al. 2014).

House and home

The Early Bronze Age evidence from the road scheme includes buildings that were typically small and outlined in plan by irregular arrangements of post-holes, stake-holes and pits (Illus. 7.2). In the Middle Bronze Age there was a marked change in the style and size of domestic buildings. From about 1500 BC we begin to see evidence for bigger buildings, up to 12 m in diameter, circular in plan and footed on regular arrangements of post-holes. Typically, there is evidence for a porched entrance and sometimes internal screens represented by clusters or lines of stake-holes. These features represent big, thatched round-houses that were more impressive and probably more durable than the smaller and less substantial buildings of the Early Bronze Age. There were good examples on the present road scheme at Kilmainham 1A, Grange 3 and Phoenixtown 3 (Illus. 7.3). The appearance of bigger houses from the mid-second millennium BC corresponds with a widespread trend observed throughout Ireland in Bronze Age settlement studies (Doody 2000; 2008; McQuade et al. 2009; Ginn & Plunkett 2020, 48).

Changes in domestic architecture invariably correspond to changes in society. Once again in the Middle Bronze Age—as we saw in Early Neolithic times (Chapter 4)—a big, permanent and imposing building seems to have become central to family and community life. The practice of placing 'special' objects within the foundations of these buildings, or within associated features, re-emerges, for example, at Grange 3 (Structure 1), where a stone axe, a saddle quern and a hammerstone were deposited within an internal pit. The practice of making offerings in these buildings emphasises the strong attachment to their houses felt by the people who built and occupied them.

It is not unusual to find these houses in pairs or in small groups, as occurred on our project at Grange 3. This is primary evidence for households of extended families—or similarly affiliated small social groups—living and working side by side. Village settlements, of much larger groups of houses, do not seem to have been part of the cultural and demographic landscape in the Irish Bronze Age. There is one remarkable exception, which was a discovery of international importance, at Corrstown, Co. Derry. On this Bronze Age village site there were altogether 76 buildings of different phases, including 74 round-houses, arranged in rows, with a cobbled road and metalled paths (Ginn & Rathbone 2012). The village at Corrstown flourished for at least 200 years in the Middle Bronze Age, so it cannot simply be dismissed as a failed social experiment. Yet we cannot explain why no other, similarly large, concentrated settlements dating from this period have been found elsewhere in Ireland, and smaller clusters of two or three round-houses remain the norm in the archaeological record.

The circular building design that dominated domestic architecture in the Middle Bronze Age continued in use into the Late Bronze Age and Iron Age in many other parts of Ireland. On our project, however, some of the Late Bronze Age buildings seem to revert to a simpler type, similar to those of the Early Bronze Age—as seen in the evidence for smaller and possibly slighter buildings at Cakestown Glebe 2. A completely different type was recorded at Townparks 3, in the form of a rectangular building. These buildings and other evidence for Bronze Age occupation along the road project corridor are described in more detail below.

Early Bronze Age buildings

Kilmainham 1C (Structures 2 and 4; Structure VII)

The most likely evidence for buildings at Kilmainham 1C consisted of the irregular arrangements of post-holes recorded as Structure 2 and Structure 4. The footprints of the two post-hole groups measured 2.4 m by 1.5 m and 2.7 m by 2.3 m (Illus. 7.2). In Structure 2 some of the post-holes were substantial, with depths of up to 0.45 m indicating a sturdy structure despite its small size. In both buildings it is likely that the posts were roof supports, for one or more phases of construction, rather than wall members. In this scenario the walls may have been supported by slighter posts that did not leave an archaeological trace or perhaps were built with sod. Either way, if the post-holes were internal roof supports then the total floor area of the buildings would have been larger than indicated by their archaeological footprints. Ash charcoal from a post-hole in Structure 2 was dated to 1953–1774 BC (UBA-12898) and charred hazelnut shell from a post-hole in Structure 4 was dated to 2128–1926 BC (UBA-13020).

There was also one tentatively identified Early–Middle Bronze Age building at Kilmainham 1C, recorded as Structure VII (Illus. 7.2). This was represented by post-holes irregularly dispersed along a projected circle c. 9 m in diameter. Charred hazelnut from one of the post-holes was dated to 1880–1530 BC (SUERC-29342).

Kilmainham 1B

At Kilmainham 1B, immediately south of Kilmainham 1C, there were groups of pits, post-holes and hearths dispersed across the site, some containing sherds of Early Bronze Age vase urn pottery. There was no clear-cut evidence for buildings, however, and these may have been located outside the excavated area.

Cookstown Great 3 (Structures C and D)

At Cookstown Great 3, south-west of Kilmainham, two small Early Bronze Age buildings were recorded as Structure C and

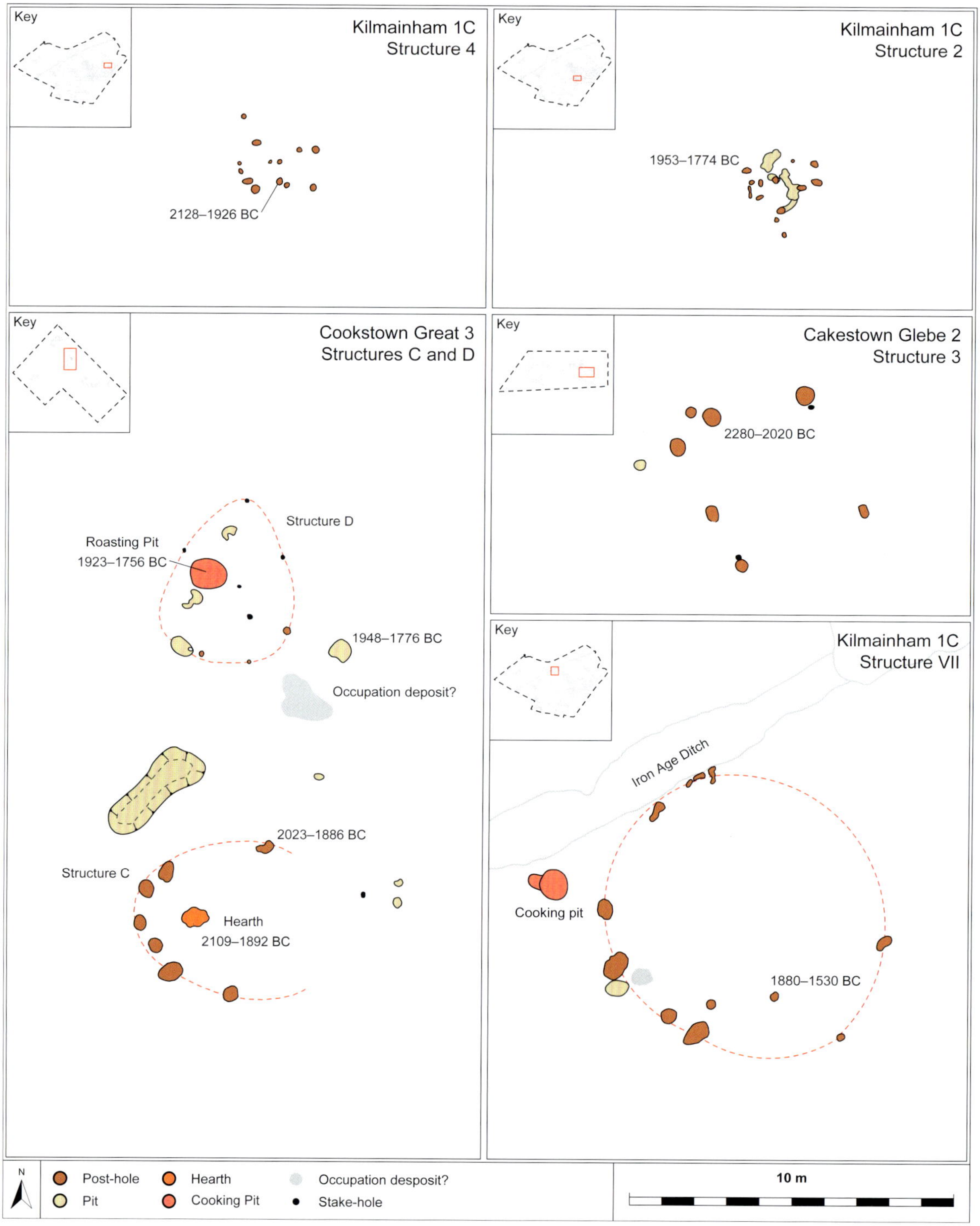

Illus. 7.2 Plans of Early–Middle Bronze Age buildings recorded on the M3 Navan to Kells and N52 Kells Bypass project (*IAC Ltd*).

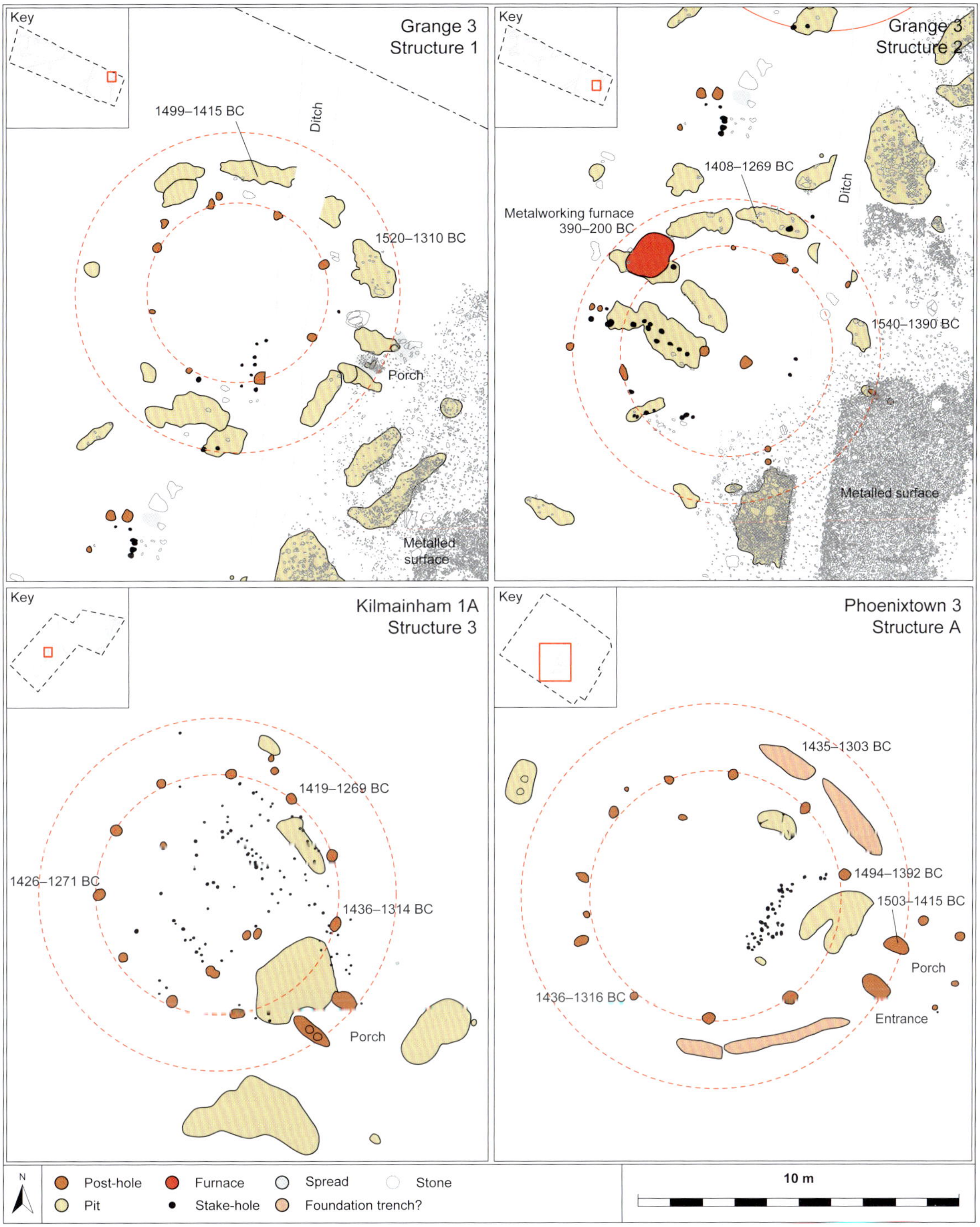

Illus. 7.3 Plans of Middle Bronze Age buildings recorded on the M3 Navan to Kells and N52 Kells Bypass project (*IAC Ltd*).

Structure D (Illus. 7.2). They stood within 10 m of each other and both were roughly D-shaped.

Structure C, c. 4 m in diameter, was represented by seven post-holes, indicating the wall line, and an internal hearth. The archaeological footprint of this building was heavily truncated and, consequently, the features were shallow, with the post-holes measuring as little as 0.05 m in depth. One of them contained a rim sherd from an Early Bronze Age food vessel. Alder charcoals from one of the post-holes and from the hearth were dated to 2023–1886 BC (UBA-11093) and 2109–1892 BC (UBA-11094) respectively.

The second building, Structure D, was again c. 4 m in diameter. It was defined by 12 stake-holes and post-holes grouped around a large circular hearth or roasting-pit (1.14 m wide by 0.92 m deep) with a basal fill of heat-affected stones and scorched, oxidised sides. Alder charcoal from the pit was dated to 1923–1756 BC (UBA-11096). None of the stake-holes or post-holes was dated but ash charcoal from a nearby pit was dated to 1948–1776 BC (UBA-11095). In addition, the roasting-pit was similar to some circular pits associated with a burnt mound (Cookstown Great 3: Burnt Mound B, below) that was found a short distance to the north-west and which was dated to 1912–1742 BC (UBA-11097). Together, these other dates broadly corroborate the date from the roasting-pit as evidence of activity in and around the building at this time.

Were these two small buildings flimsy domestic huts? Or could they have been saunas or sweat-houses? In the case of Structure D, in particular, we can easily imagine a wicker-framed hut, clad in hide, filled with steam from water splashed onto hot stones in the roasting-pit. Sweat-houses, steam baths and sauna baths using hot stones are documented across Europe from classical times to the modern era and may already have been in use long before they were first recorded in historical sources. For instance, Herodotus, writing in the fifth century BC, describes how the Scythians took steam baths using hot stones in simple tripod structures covered by felted wool, which he compared to the vapour baths of the Spartans (Rawlinson 1910, Book 4, 73). In the early 10th century, the Persian historian and geographer Ibn Rustan described semi-subterranean hot-stone saunas, with sod roofs supported on wooden poles, used by the Saqāliba (Slavs) to sustain them in the extreme cold of northern European winters, and which were built by 'the head of the family … for his family and relatives' (Lunde & Stone 2011, 125).

Cakestown Glebe 2 (Structure 3)

Structure 3 at Cakestown Glebe 2 was a small hut or house represented by seven post-holes and two stake-holes forming a roughly square structure, 4.4 m by 4.6 m in plan (Illus. 7.2). Oak (sapwood) charcoal from a post-hole was dated to 2280–2020 BC (SUERC-29338). We have already described Early Bronze Age buildings as typically smaller and less substantial than domestic buildings of the Middle Bronze Age (below), but this example at Cakestown Glebe 2 is a reminder that any building supported on stout posts could be robust and durable, regardless of its size.

Middle Bronze Age round-houses

From the Middle Bronze Age, commencing c. 1500 BC, there was a distinct change in domestic architecture. The houses of this period left an impressive archaeological footprint formed by circular arrangements of post-holes, pits and slot-trenches (Illus. 7.3). These buildings were bigger and doubtless more imposing than those of the preceding period. Four of them were identified on our road project: two at Grange 3, one at Phoenixtown 3 and one at Kilmainham 1A. All four were built around a circle of post-holes or 'post-ring'. Three of them—at Grange 3 Structure 1, Kilmainham 1A and Phoenixtown 3—had a porch in the south-east quadrant. Taken all together, the radiocarbon dates from these buildings have a wide range, broadly spanning the period c. 1500–1300 BC. The houses at Grange and Phoenixtown may have been built and occupied before 1400 BC, with the house at Kilmainham 1A possibly somewhat later in the series (Appendix 1).

A ring of post-holes, variously 5.6–8 m in diameter, is the main defining feature of these buildings. This can be interpreted in two ways. Either the posts were internal roof supports, with an outer wall of slighter construction, or they had a double function as wall posts that also provided structural support for the roof. These are not merely technical differences. The first interpretation allows for a much bigger house, both in floor area and in height, and we can assume a correspondingly greater diversity of household activities and social interactions.

We favour the first interpretation and believe that the post-rings recorded in the Middle Bronze Age houses at Grange 3, Kilmainham 1A and Phoenixtown 3 were internal features, providing the main structural support for the roof, while the walls stood some distance outside the post-ring and were of slighter construction, bearing little or no weight and leaving no archaeological footprint. Such walls could have been built with blocks of sod or light wattled panels and would probably have been protected from the elements by the low, overhanging eaves of a thatched conical roof.

How big were these houses? If the post-ring was an internal feature that did not define the outer wall line, how do we know the full diameter and floor area of the buildings? And how was the extra space outside the post-ring used? The intermittent series of large, shallow pits lying outside the post-rings of the Grange 3 houses recall Middle Bronze Age 'ring-ditch' houses of upland northern Britain. These typically have pitted, worn and gullied areas in the outer part of the floor which have been interpreted as wear or erosion features caused by stalling livestock indoors, in the space between the post-ring and the outer wall, and by seasonally mucking out their dung and straw (Feachem 1965; Jobey & Tait 1966; Reynolds 1982). In a recent review of Bronze Age houses in northern Britain, Pope (2015, 180) observed that 'Middle Bronze Age ring-ditches tend to be restricted to one half of the house, often to the right of the entrance, and may suggest the stalling of just a few milk animals'. This corresponds nicely with our examples and especially with the houses at Grange 3, where the outer pitting is mostly on the northern and eastern sides of the post-rings. Whether or not these features represent livestock stalling in our houses, they at least indicate a peripheral floor area, outside the post-ring, that was intensively used for some sort of household activity.

As to the size of the houses, the telling evidence here is provided by the porches. Three of our houses have porches represented by pairs of elongated pits or post-holes in the south-east quadrants of the buildings—at Grange 3 (Structure 1), Kilmainham 1A and Phoenixtown 3. If these 'porches' were in fact internal features, leading from the doorway into the main domestic space defined

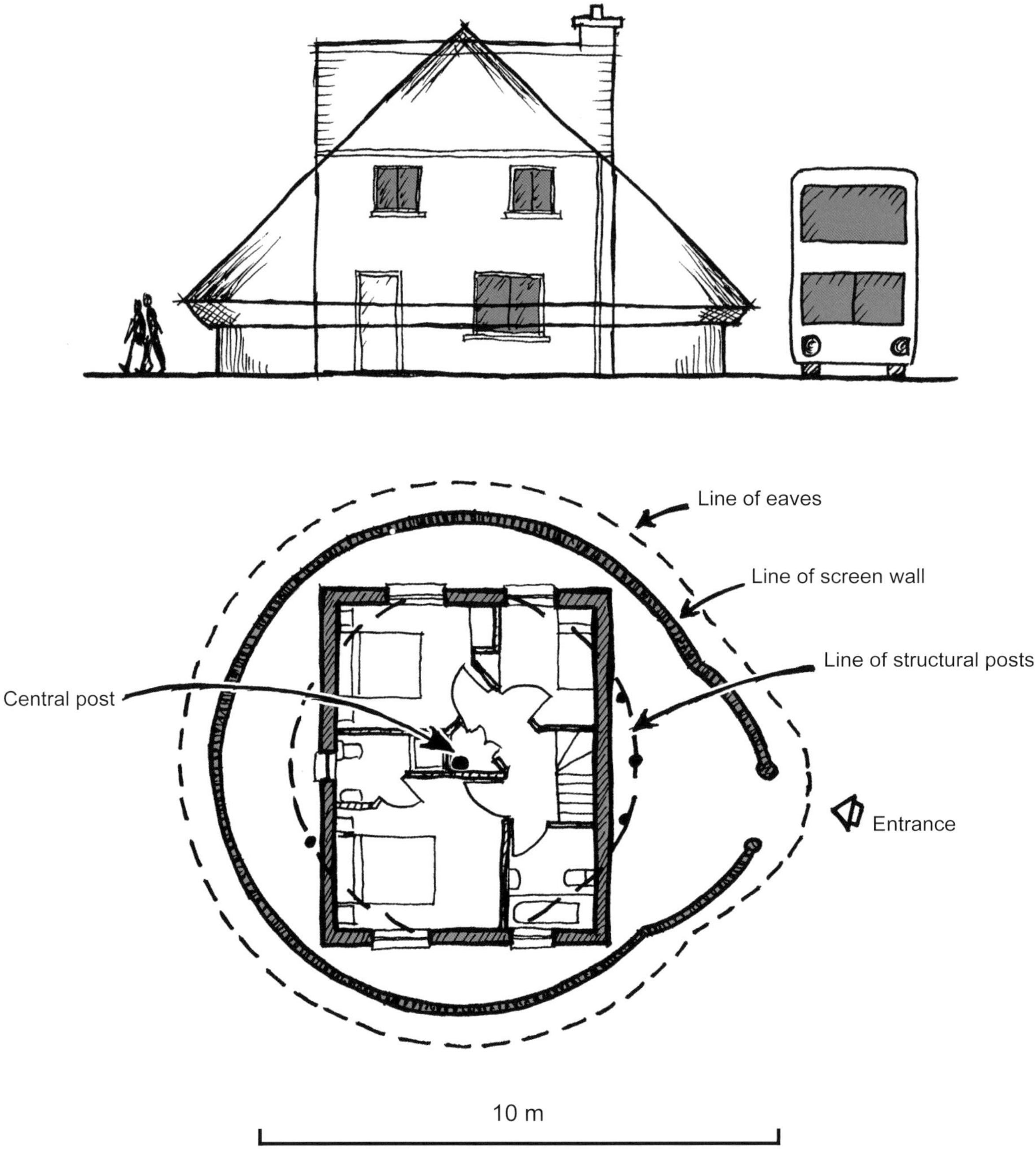

Illus. 7.4 Architect's drawings comparing a Late Bronze Age house from Tober, Co. Offaly, with a modern townhouse (*Allman 2009*). The Bronze Age round-house was larger and at least as impressive as the townhouse and would have provided room for sleeping quarters, storage, craftwork, cooking and the social gatherings of an extended family.

by the post-ring, their outer ends would correspond with the positions of doorways in the walls. From this we can project wall lines, concentric with the internal post-rings, with diameters of up to 12 m in the largest example (Phoenixtown 3).

Taken together, these two pieces of evidence—the outer perimeter of pits and gullies and the length of the porches—suggest that the wall lines of the houses were between 1.5 m and 2 m outside the post-rings, resulting in diameters of c. 9–12 m and corresponding floor areas of 64–113 m^2. Our interpretation, therefore, is that these were quite large houses, suitable for the needs of an extended family, with plenty of room for sleeping quarters, storage, craftwork, cooking areas and social gatherings, and perhaps for bringing livestock indoors for the winter.

Allman (2009) examined similar evidence with an architect's eye in reconstruction drawings that compare a Late Bronze Age round-house from Tober, Co. Offaly, with a modern three-bedroomed townhouse. The house at Tober was 10 m in overall diameter. It was defined by an inner ring of post-holes that supported the roof, and an outer ring of much slighter post-holes that supported the wall (Walsh 2011b; 2011c). It was thus broadly similar in size and in design to our houses at Grange 3, Kilmainham 1A and Phoenixtown 3. As Allman's drawings show with graphic clarity, these Middle Bronze Age buildings were all more commodious and, arguably, more impressive than a modern two-storey townhouse (Illus. 7.4).

Grange 3 (Structures 1 and 2)

Two Middle Bronze Age round-houses were recorded at Grange 3 (Illus. 7.3, 7.5 and 7.8). Structure 1 was defined by a circle of 10 post-holes forming an internal post-ring, surrounded by a series of elongated, irregular pits. The overall diameter of the house is estimated as 9.6 m. The entrance opened to ESE and was indicated by a series of pits and post-holes that formed a 'porch'. There was localised metalling within the porch and a much larger metalled surface or 'yard' outside it. A cluster of stake-holes in the southern quadrant of the interior may represent some sort of household furniture or a screen. Burnt bone (unidentified) and hazel charcoal from two of the shallow pits at the perimeter were dated to 1499–1415 BC (UBA-12937) and 1520–1310 BC (SUERC-29331) respectively.

There were signs of intense burning in the perimeter pits in Structure 1. They contained burnt clay and charcoals of alder, ash, hazel, Maloideae and *Prunus* sp.; small amounts of charred hazelnut shells, barley, oats and wheat; burnt bone fragments, including sheep/goat; sherds of Middle and Late Bronze Age pottery; and several chipped stone pieces. Stone implements recovered from the pits included a large stone axe (which had possibly been reused as a hammer), a saddle quern, stone mortar and a hammerstone (Illus. 7.6). A similar hammerstone was found in an outlying, charcoal-rich pit. These artefacts could just be household waste, left behind when the inhabitants moved on, but Brück (1999) argued that saddle querns and hammerstones found in unusual contexts (i.e. in the corners or terminals of ditches) represent deliberate deposits for ritual purposes. The stone objects in our house may therefore have been deposited at the construction or abandonment of the house or on some important occasion(s) during its occupation. This deliberate deposition of 'special' objects was clearly evident in the remarkably well-

A Bronze Age homestead at Grange 3

Grange 3 offers the most complete glimpse of Bronze Age life as recorded on the road project. It was the homestead of an extended family who farmed the surrounding land and buried their dead close by, sometime between the 15th and 13th centuries BC. The evidence included two large round-houses with a metalled yard (Illus. 7.5); boundary ditches; and an impressive funerary monument in the form of a barrow.

There was evidence from other periods, too (Illus. 7.7 and 7.8). In the Iron Age, people smelted metal here, in small bowl furnaces. Later still, an early medieval community dug a large, rectangular, ditched enclosure and farmed the fields around it, processing their barley, oats and wheat in cereal-drying kilns found on the site. There was a small burial-ground, too, from the Iron Age/early medieval transition period, but the most coherent evidence of human activity from this site was from the Bronze Age.

The Bronze Age round-houses were big, impressive buildings with plenty of room for sleeping quarters, storage areas, craftwork, cooking and social gatherings. Both buildings fronted onto a metalled yard, though it is not clear that the two buildings were occupied at the same time. (Radiocarbon dates from the buildings are ambivalent in this regard.) Most of the chipped stone from the site was waste flint and chert found in and around the yard, and one of several quern-stones from the site formed part of its metalled surface. We can easily envisage

Illus. 7.5 Grange 3: artist's impression of life on a Middle Bronze Age farmstead (*Dan Tietzsch-Tyler*).

people using this space for making stone tools and preparing food. All of the pottery from the site—as many as 21 vessels—was domestic and most of it was found in association with the buildings. A stone axe in a pit in the floor of the bigger round-house may have been a family heirloom. The pit also contained a saddle quern and a hammerstone. These objects may have been offerings to the house. We do not know whether they were buried at the construction of the house, during its use or at its abandonment. In any case, such offerings reflect the importance of domestic buildings in the lives of their occupants and the spiritual relationship that made houses into homes.

The barrow was only 170 m from the houses. During ceremonies at the monument the community ate pork, mutton and venison, and threw their food waste (animal bones) into the open ditch. The barrow continued to be used for many centuries after the houses were abandoned and would, in time, be separated from the habitation area by a pair of linear field ditches. Perhaps there were other, later Bronze Age houses in this area—waiting to be discovered outside the limits of our excavations for the road project. Immediately adjacent to the barrow we discovered a small Iron Age/early medieval burial-plot (Grange 2). It may be that this particular spot was always known as a sacred place, remembered for many centuries, prompting the people of the fifth century AD to bury their dead here too.

Illus. 7.6 Grange 3: a stone mortar (E3123:3:1) and a hammerstone (E3123:4:3) were among the finds from a Middle Bronze Age house (Structure 1) (*Maeve Tobin for IAC Ltd*).

Illus. 7.7 Grange 3: aerial view from south, showing the Bronze Age round-houses and boundary ditches (right), barrow monument (left) and early medieval enclosure (*Studio Lab*).

preserved, stone-built Bronze Age house at Ballyprior Beg, Islandmagee, Co. Antrim (Suddaby 2003). Here there was evidence of both 'foundation' and 'closing' deposits in the form, respectively, of a stone axe and a broken bronze palstave (Cleary 2006, 18).

Structure 2 at Grange 3 was a slightly smaller house, with a similar but less well-defined archaeological footprint than Structure 1. Again, the main structural feature was an internal ring of post-holes and, again, there were some elongated, irregular pits in a peripheral area outside the post-ring. Unfortunately, part of the eastern quadrant of the house, where evidence of a porch might have occurred, was truncated by a later ditch. Nonetheless, the overall diameter can be estimated as (max.) 9 m. A linear cluster of stake-holes in the south-west quadrant might represent household furniture or a screen partition. The pits on the periphery contained charcoals of ash, alder, wild/bird cherry, hazel, holly and Maloideae, sherds of Middle to Late Bronze Age pottery and chipped stone pieces, including a flint core. Charcoals of ash (brushwood) and hazel from two of the peripheral pits were dated to 1408–1269 BC (UBA-12058) and 1540–1390 BC (SUERC-29332) respectively.

The two houses were fronted on the eastern side by a large, metalled yard that extended north–south over an area of about 150 m^2 (25 m by 6 m). Two quern-stones were found here, one of them incorporated within the stones forming the surface of the yard. A clay spread overlying the metalled surface contained numerous sherds of Middle Bronze Age cordoned urn pottery and pieces of worked flint and chert. There was a particular concentration of these materials in the yard to the front of Structure 2, including 80 sherds of Middle–Late Bronze Age domestic pottery, 45 pieces

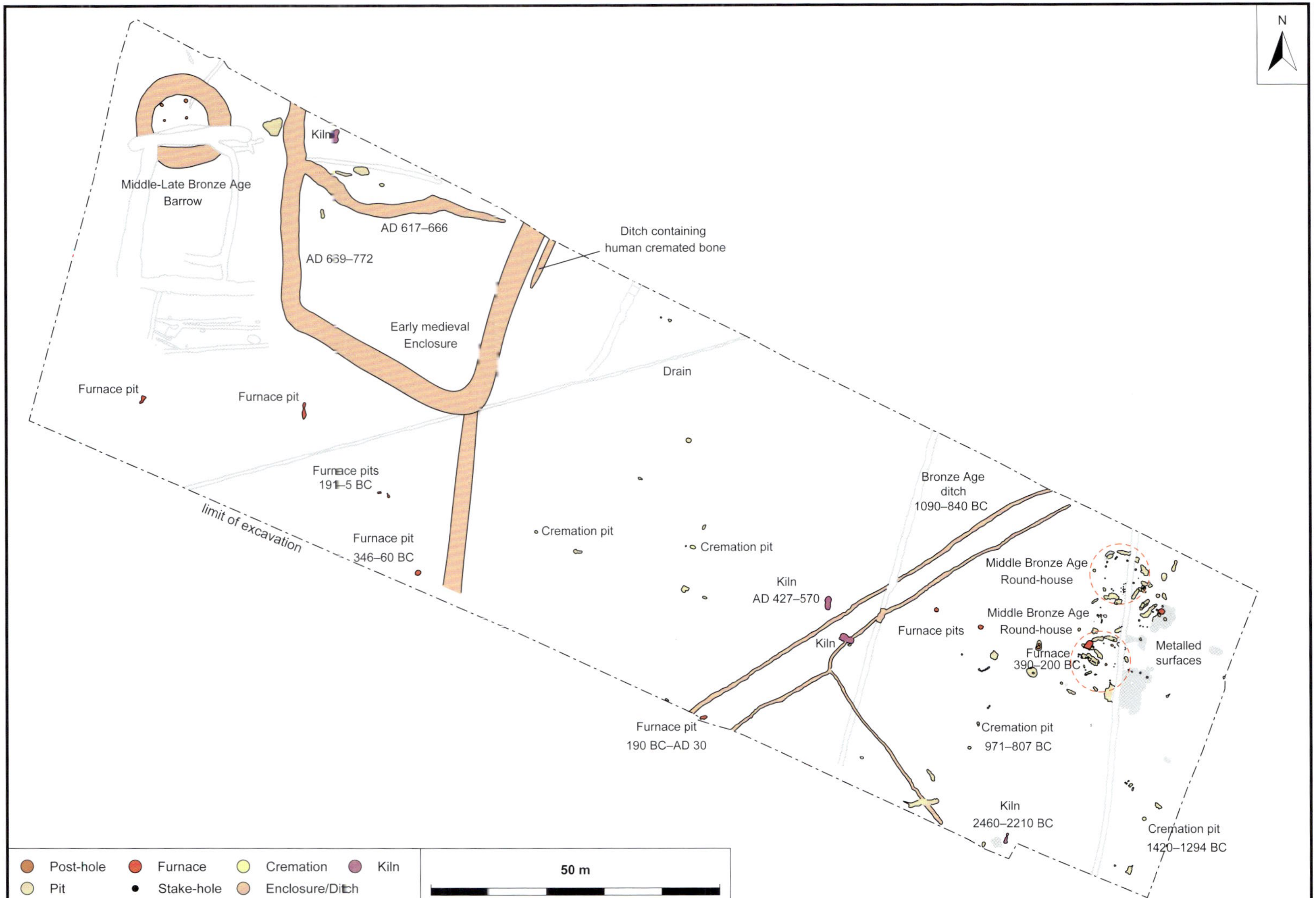

Illus. 7.8 Grange 3: plan of the excavated features, showing the Bronze Age round-houses and boundary ditches (right), barrow monument (left) and early medieval enclosure (*IAC Ltd*).

of chert and 32 pieces of flint. The metalled surface forming the yard sealed a number of small pits. One of them contained a stone with a central perforation and deep grooves scored along one edge, which was interpreted as a spindle-whorl (O'Brien 2010a).

Phoenixtown 3 (Structure A)

Structure A at Phoenixtown 3 was defined by a circular arrangement of 10 post-holes with two larger post-holes extending from the circle at the south-east, indicating a porched entrance (Illus. 7.3 and 7.9). Structure A is the largest of the four Middle Bronze Age houses recorded on the road project, with an overall estimated diameter of 12 m. On the east side of the building there were long, narrow pits outside the post-hole circle, on either side of the entrance. The long narrow pits north of the entrance had stony metalled bases. Those south of the entrance were distinctly different and may in fact have been footing trenches for a wall. An L-shaped arrangement of four small post-holes outside the entrance, opening to the south, probably supported a weather-screen for the doorway. A dense, linear cluster of stake-holes inside the entrance suggests an internal screen. A large pit between the entrance porch and this internal screen contained a hollowed stone, possibly a mortar, though there were no signs of use. Other artefacts included sherds of domestic ware and some chipped stone pieces. Charcoals from pits and post-holes in the building included ash, alder, wild/

Illus. 7.9 Phoenixtown 3: ranging rods mark the positions of post-holes in the internal post-ring of a Middle Bronze Age house and the porched entrance (foreground). The excavation team fits comfortably within the floor area of the building. View from south-east (*IAC Ltd*).

bird cherry, hazel, oak and Maloideae. There were also a few grains of wheat, some burnt bone fragments and a burnt hazelnut shell. Charcoal samples from post-holes and from the peripheral shallow pits in this building were dated to 1503-1415 BC (UBA-11112), 1494-1392 BC (UBA-11111), 1436-1316 BC (UBA-11113) and 1435-1303 BC (UBA 11114).

A small number of post-holes and pits (not illustrated) to the north-east and south-east of the house may represent animal pens or working areas. One of these pits produced some 30 pieces of flint debitage. There was a long, irregular pit (14 m long, 2.5 m wide and 0.6 m deep) c. 11 m south-east of the house, directly opposite the entrance. This contained a quantity of Middle Bronze Age pottery sherds, representing at least seven vessels. The pottery was a domestic variant of the Cordoned Urn Tradition and at least one vessel bore evidence of cooking (Illus. 7.10). Charcoals of alder and ash from the pit fills were dated to 1607–1451 BC (UBA-12941) and 1515–1428 BC (UBA-12111) respectively, so that the feature could have been contemporary with the house.

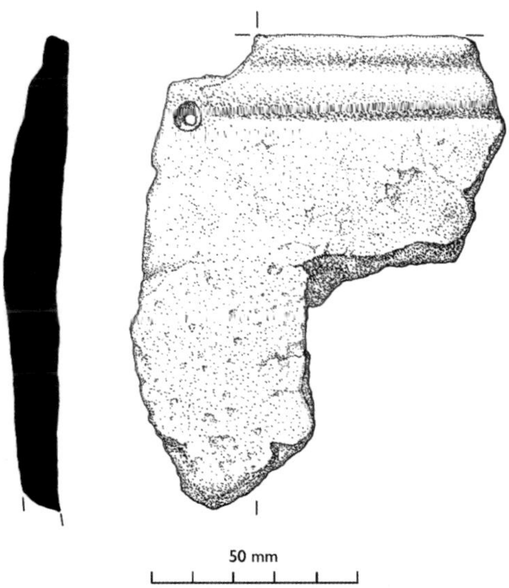

Illus. 7.10 Phoenixtown 3: a sherd of Middle Bronze Age pottery from a domestic variant of the Cordoned Urn Tradition (Vessel 6, E3130:1194:1 and 9) (*Alva MacGowan for IAC Ltd*).

Kilmainham 1A (Structure 3)

Structure 3 at Kilmainham 1A was similar to the house at Phoenixtown 3 and was possibly contemporary with it. Again, the main structural elements in the footprint of the building were 10 post-holes representing an internal post-ring and a pair of elongated pits in the south-east quadrant, indicating a porched entrance (Illus. 7.3). There were linear clusters of stake-holes and post-holes in the interior and, as at Phoenixtown 3, one of these clusters suggests a fixed partition screening the entrance area from the interior. Other stake-hole clusters combined to delineate a roughly square area in the centre of the house. There were remnants of an irregular stone floor (not illustrated). Charcoals from pits and post-holes in the building included alder, ash, hazel, Maloideae and oak.

There was a large, shallow pit immediately inside the entrance to Structure 3. A compact stony 'metalled' layer in the base of the pit contained a saddle quern fragment, but the pit fills included a single sherd of Early Neolithic carinated ware and charcoal (alder/birch) from an upper fill of the pit was dated to 3791–3659 BC (UBA–12098). In view of this ambiguous evidence, we cannot say that the pit was related to Structure 3.

Charcoals of hazel and alder (from three post-holes in Structure 3 were dated to 1436–1314 BC (UBA-12099), 1426–1271 BC (UBA–12102) and 1419–1269 BC (UBA–12103). A charcoal sample (*Prunus* sp.) from a meandering gully or shallow ditch, c. 20 m north-east of the house, was dated to 1497–1415 BC (UBA–12097). This was possibly the footing trench for a palisade.

Kilmainham 1C (Structure 1)

At Kilmainham 1C a circular arrangement of post-holes and stake-holes (Structure 1), with a diameter of 8 m, is more likely to have been an animal pen than a building, as the posts and stakes would all have been rather light and there was no other evidence for domestic use. For completeness we note also groups of pits and post-holes in the southern part of the site (Illus. 1.9) which contained domestic pottery of Middle–Late Bronze Age date. This could be domestic refuse on a habitation site, although, again, there was no clear evidence for buildings.

Late Bronze Age buildings and habitation evidence

Cakestown Glebe 2 (Structures 1 and 2)

The key site for evidence of Late Bronze Age settlement was Cakestown Glebe 2, where two buildings (Structures 1 and 2), possibly contemporary, were positioned side by side within 5 m of each other. The archaeological footprint of the buildings consisted of two dense, irregular clusters of post-holes, stake-holes, pits and hearths (Illus. 7.11–7.13). These features did not compose a coherent ground-plan for either building. Late Bronze Age houses were most likely to have been circular buildings with internal roof-support posts, similar to those of the Middle Bronze Age. If these were buildings, then on present evidence we can only suggest that Structure 1 was at least 8 m in diameter and Structure 2 was possibly smaller.

In Structure 1 an occupation layer of charcoal-rich soil contained flint flakes and blades. One of several pits within this floor area contained a large quantity of Late Bronze Age pottery—including several sherds from a unique vessel (i.e. for which there are no readily identifiable parallels in the Irish archaeological record). A clay mould found in one of the post-holes would have been used to cast a plain, straight-sided blade (Grogan & Roche 2011). No other metalworking evidence was found here, so the mould may have been brought from elsewhere. Charcoal (Maloideae sp.) and fragments of human bone from two hearths in this building were dated to 1122–939 BC (UBA-12071) and 993–838 BC (UBA-12943).

The post-holes identifying Structure 2 suggest a post-ring c. 5 m in diameter, which would have been the main structural element in a larger house with an outer wall that has left no archaeological trace. The overall diameter of the building can thus be estimated as 6–7 m at least. Hazel charcoal from one of the smaller post-holes was dated to 1251–1013 BC (UBA-12072). An outlying group of post-holes and stake-holes south-east of Structure 2 may be remnants of a porch or perhaps part of another, unrelated building.

Kilmainham 2 (Structure 1)

There was tentative evidence for another Late Bronze Age structure at Kilmainham 2 in a rectilinear arrangement of four post-holes measuring 8 m (ENE–WSW) by 6 m (Illus. 7.13). Associated pits contained a small quantity of domestic pottery sherds, burnt animal bone, carbonised wheat and barley grains, and a stone ammonite bead resembling beads found in Neolithic passage tombs (O'Brien 2010b). Hazel charcoal from one of the post-holes was dated to 1112–921 BC (UBA-12066).

Kilmainham 1C (Structure 7)

Another arrangement of four post-holes was recorded at Kilmainham 1C. These

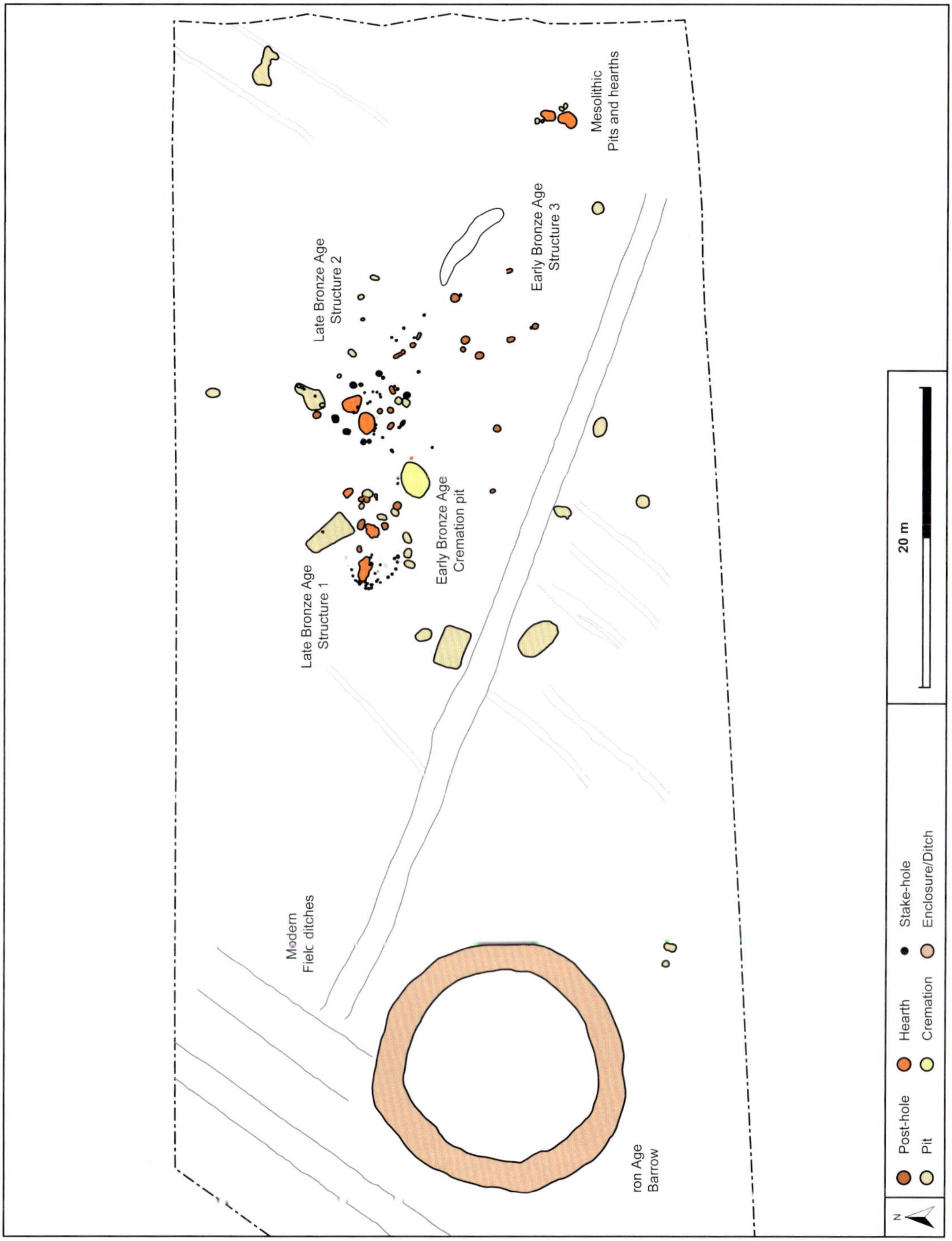

Illus. 7.11 Cakestown Glebe 2: p an of the excavated features, including Bronze Age buildings Structures 1, 2 and 3 (*IAC Ltd*).

Illus. 7.12 Cakestown Glebe 2: post-holes, stake-holes, hearths and pits represent two small buildings located with 5 m of each other (*Hawkeye*).

represented a much smaller structure measuring 2.4 m (NW–SE) by 2.3 m (Illus. 7.13). This 'four-poster' might have been the base for an elevated grain silo, designed to keep the grain dry and safe from vermin and other animals. A mixed charcoal sample of hazel and alder from one of the post-holes was dated to 1119–932 BC (UBA-12914). Nearby pits contained sherds of Middle–Late Bronze Age pottery.

Townparks 3 (Structure 1)

At nearby Townparks 3 a rectangular structure was represented by a regular arrangement of nine post-holes forming a ground-plan measuring 8 m (ENE–WSW) by 2.5 m (Illus. 7.13). If this was a roofed building, the post-holes would have held the main weight-bearing members and possibly carried horizontal beams (wall-plates) that in turn supported the rafters. Middle Bronze Age pottery fragments from large, bucket-shaped pots were found in the post-holes. Traces of sooting and blackened accretions on sherds from two vessels suggest that they were used in cooking. Holly charcoal from one of the post-holes was dated to 1019–906 BC (UBA-12115). Late Bronze Age buildings of rectangular plan are rare in Ireland but are not unknown. An example was recently recorded at Rathwilladoon, Co. Galway, on the route of the M18 motorway (Lyne 2012, 43–5).

Nugentstown 1 (Structure 3)

Finally, another small and unusual Late Bronze Age structure was identified at Nugentstown 1. Structure 3 was represented by three narrow trenches

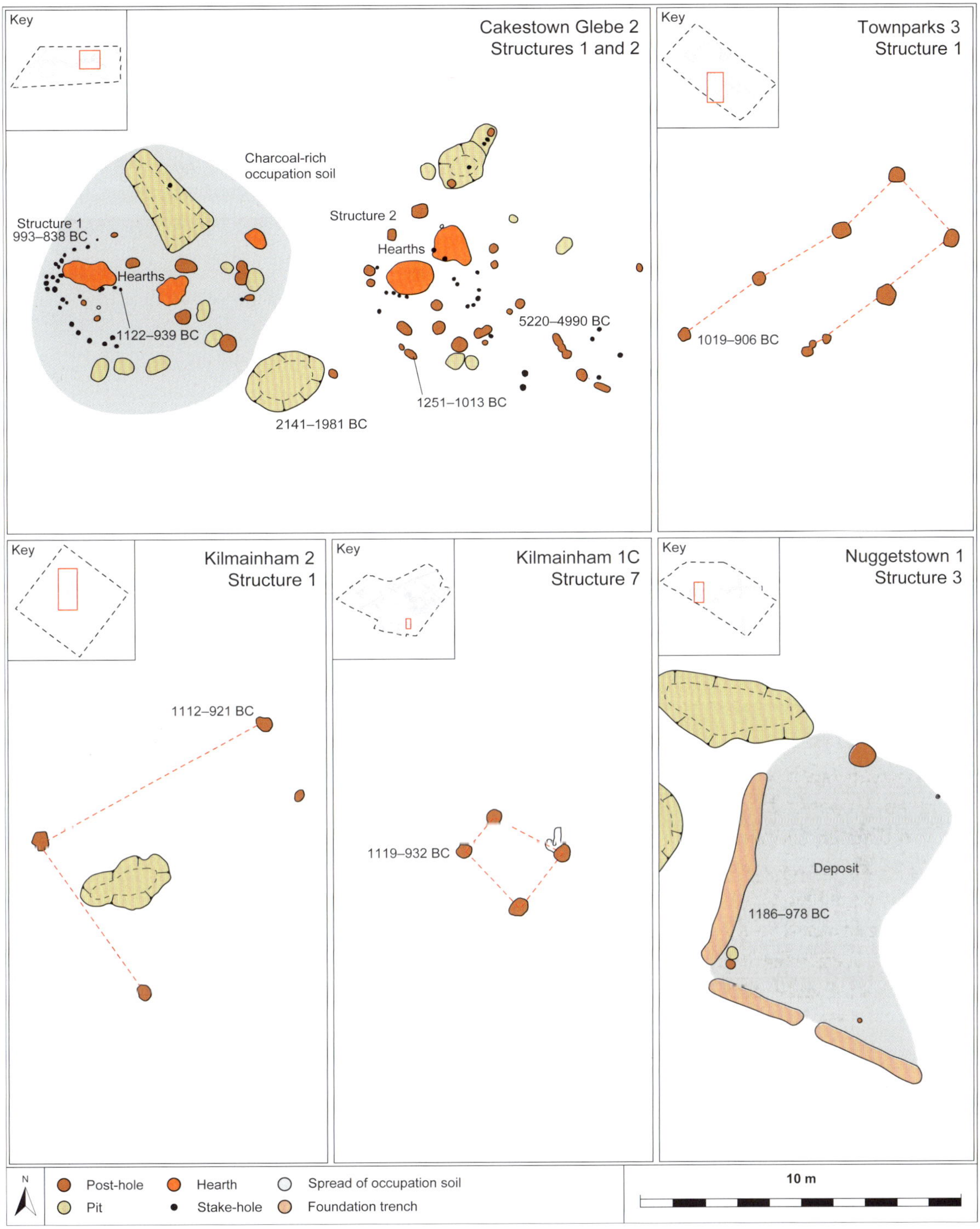

Illus. 7.13 Plans of Late Bronze Age buildings recorded on the M3 Navan to Kells and N52 Kells Bypass project (*IAC Ltd*).

Farming and manufacturing at Kilmainham

Excavations in Kilmainham townland recorded at least half a dozen Bronze Age buildings, including some that were certainly dwelling houses and others that may have been farm buildings or workshops. In the environs of the buildings there were many other features representing aspects of Bronze Age life. Segmented ditches at Kilmainham 1A and 1C indicate organised land divisions for agriculture and grazing (Illus. 4.8 and 1.9). Carbonised grains of barley, wheat, oats and rye were found in several different features and attest to crop-processing near the fields and houses. Cremations were found in peripheral areas at both Kilmainham 1A and 1C (below)—evidence that the people who lived here buried their dead within view of their homes. A seasonal pond at Kilmainham 1C, in a low-lying part of the site, supplied water for an adjacent burnt mound. These features were not all contemporary and are dated, variously, to the Early, Middle and Later Bronze Age but, taken all together, they portray a busy and productive landscape throughout the period.

One of the more unusual features at Kilmainham 1C was a metalled platform (Platform A) positioned on the eastern face of a gently rising gravel ridge (Illus. 7.14). The platform was built up in accumulated layers of small stones, each layer in turn compacted to form an even surface. Early Bronze Age cinerary urn pottery and flint debitage were recovered from the lowest levels, and charcoal (ash) from one of the earliest deposits was dated to 1896–1752 BC (UBA-12922). Pits, post- and stake-holes were cut through successive levels of the platform, especially around the periphery, including one especially dense cluster of post-holes on the north-west margin of the platform and linear groups of stake-holes south of it. These features do not seem to represent roofed buildings and are more likely to be remnants of makeshift structures associated with craftwork—such as drying frames and windbreaks. The upper levels of the platform were covered by a charcoal-rich deposit that contained chipped stone objects and debitage, including an unfinished arrowhead, an arrowhead blank and a pressure-flaked arrowhead—all of leaf-shaped form. A sample of charcoal (ash) from this deposit was dated to 1906–1683 BC (UBA-12923), in the Early Bronze Age. This is at odds with the conventional date for the arrowheads, as the leaf-shaped form is a Neolithic type. The arrowheads might simply have been residual objects, from disturbed contexts relating to some earlier episode on the same site, or perhaps our Bronze Age flint-knappers at Kilmainham 1C were simply experimenting with this less familiar form.

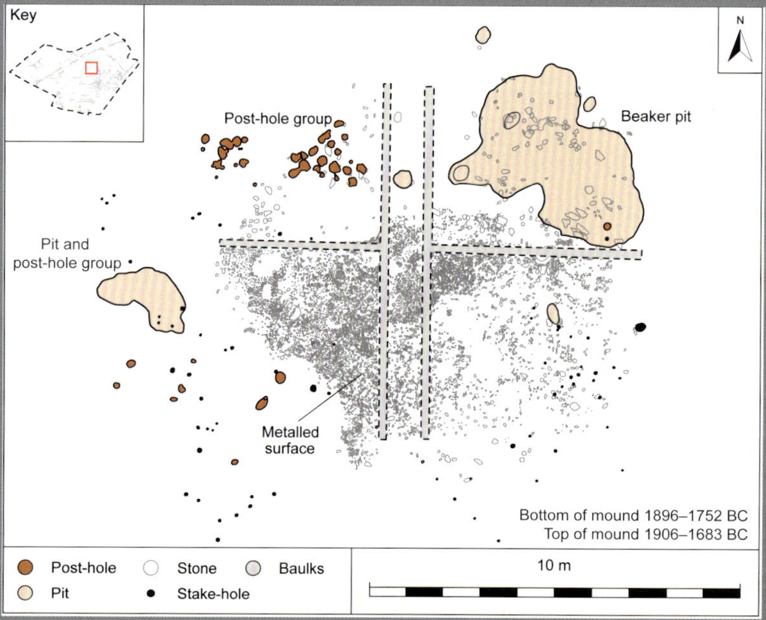

Illus. 7.14 Kilmainham 1C: a metalled platform built up in successive layers of small stones was littered with flint debitage and three arrowheads in a charcoal-rich spread of occupation soil (*IAC Ltd*).

(possibly footing trenches for wooden walls) defining two sides of a subrectangular building measuring at least 8 m (NE–SW) by 9 m (Illus. 7.13). There was a clay floor layer in the interior, with three post-holes, a pit and a stake-hole scattered about the periphery of the building. Unusually, no pottery or chipped stone was found in association with this structure. Its interpretation as a domestic building is tentative at best. Alder and/or hazel charcoal from one of the slot-trenches was dated to 1186–978 BC (UBA-12060).

Boundaries

There is clear evidence from Kilmainham 1A, Kilmainham 1C and Grange 3 that the space around some of the Bronze Age domestic buildings was divided by assorted stake-built barriers and field ditches. The ditches were generally shallow and could have been supplemented by hedgerows. Charcoal samples from the fills of these features produced radiocarbon dates in the Middle and Late Bronze Age (Appendix 1). A meandering gully at Kilmainham 1A could have been the footing trench for a wooden palisade (Illus. 4.8). A charcoal sample (*Prunus* sp.) from the fill was dated to 1497–1415 BC (UBA-12097). At Kilmainham 1C there were continuous ditches, segmented ditches and wooden fences indicated by lines of stake-holes. Two long, straight, boundary ditches were set at right angles to one another, giving a glimpse within the excavation site of large-scale land divisions that no doubt extended out into the surrounding farmland (Illus. 1.9). Charcoal samples from one ditch (*Prunus* sp.) and an upper fill of the other (hazel) were dated, respectively, to 1440–1316 BC (UBA-12917), in the Middle Bronze Age, and 1128–977 BC (UBA-12916), in the Late Bronze Age.

The only other evidence of Bronze Age land management from the excavated sites was at Grange 3, where two parallel ditches (4 m apart)—possibly a droveway—traversed the site NE/SW, with a third, conjoined ditch extending away at a right angle to the south-east (Illus. 7.7 and 7.8). A charcoal sample (Maloideae) from one of the parallel ditches was dated to 1090–840 BC (SUERC-29329), in the Late Bronze Age. In addition, the ditches were slighted by a group of Iron Age/early medieval cereal-drying kilns (Chapter 8), which establishes a broad *terminus ante quem* for the features. A large barrow was located less than 200 m west of the ditches, and the Middle Bronze Age round-houses described above (Structures 1 and 2) were located a short distance to the east of them.

Burnt mounds

Burnt mounds or *fulachtaí fia* are present throughout the whole of Ireland and are one of the commonest site types discovered by large-scale field investigations in advance of development. Dated examples are mostly Bronze Age, but Neolithic, Iron Age and even early medieval examples have also been recorded. On the M3 Navan to Kells and N52 Kells Bypass project there were 20 examples, on 15 excavation sites, making an important addition to the record of this landscape in the Bronze Age (Appendix 2).

Burnt mounds are commonly identified as mounds or spreads (i.e. flattened mounds) of heat-fractured stone and charcoal-rich sediment. On further investigation, the mounds and spreads are often found to be associated with earth-cut troughs—sometimes lined with wood, clay or stone—and with

Illus. 7.15 Ballybeg 1: some of the excavated burnt mound sites on the M3 Navan to Kells and N52 Kells Bypass project were located near water; this example was close to a stream. View from north (*Studio Lab*).

pits, hearths and wells. Occasionally there is also evidence for small buildings and water-management features. As to the location of burnt mounds in the landscape, access to water is the essential factor, so they are typically found in low-lying, poorly drained places with high water-tables—like Ballybeg 1 (Illus. 7.15) on our project, which was close to a stream, or one of the mounds at Kilmainham 1C (Burnt Mound 1), which was close to a seasonal pond (Illus. 7.16). Many of the burnt mounds on our project did not, however, have an obvious, natural water supply at hand, and some of them—e.g. Cookstown Great 2 and 3, Townparks 1 and perhaps Newrath Little 2—relied on pits or wells dug down into the subsoil for access to local groundwater.

Hot stones immersed in the water filling the troughs could quickly cause it to boil. Cleaning and reuse of the troughs eventually resulted in the quantities of discarded heat-shattered stone and charcoal-rich sediment that form the main identifying feature of these sites. But how was the heated water and/or steam used? Over the years a wide range of activities have been proposed in the archaeological literature, including cooking, bathing and saunas, textile-processing, leather-working and brewing. Some commentators (Delaney et al. 2012, 60; Quinn & Moore 2009, 53) have described burnt mounds as 'the kitchen sinks of the Bronze Age', capable of generating large volumes of hot water for a variety of uses, but cooking was especially favoured in a recent review of the Irish evidence by Hawkes (2018, 155), who concluded that burnt mound sites were communal feasting places, used on festive

Illus. 7.16 Kilmainham 1C: one of two burnt mounds on this site was located close to a seasonal pond. Two other major features that are visible in this view are an Iron Age ditch and a low, rounded gravel ridge. View from south-west (*Studio Lab*).

occasions to share hospitality and reinforce relationships.

On our road project we found two distinct clusters of burnt mounds, associated with the two main areas of prehistoric settlement along the road corridor: Phoenixtown/Grange towards the south-eastern end of the corridor, and Kilmainham/Cookstown Great towards the opposite, north-western end. Early, Middle and Late Bronze Age burnt mounds were recorded in both areas, although there were more late burnt mounds in the Kilmainham/Cookstown Great area, which corresponds with the higher incidence of Late Bronze Age domestic activity recorded there.

Burnt mounds in Phoenixtown/Grange and environs

Five burnt mounds (Illus. 7.17) were found in this area. Four of them, at Phoenixtown 1 and 6 and Ballybeg 1 and 3, formed a distinct group. The fifth, at Ardbraccan 1, might appear to be an isolated site at the south-eastern end of our project but in fact is an outlier of a cluster of burnt mounds excavated in Ardbraccan and Boyerstown, on the adjoining M3 Navan Bypass project (e.g. Mossop et al. 2009; Clarke 2008). The number of burnt mounds, spanning the entire Bronze Age period, in the wider Phoenixtown/Grange landscape is testimony to a major Bronze Age population.

The sites in the Phoenixtown/Grange area were all located on relatively flat or gently

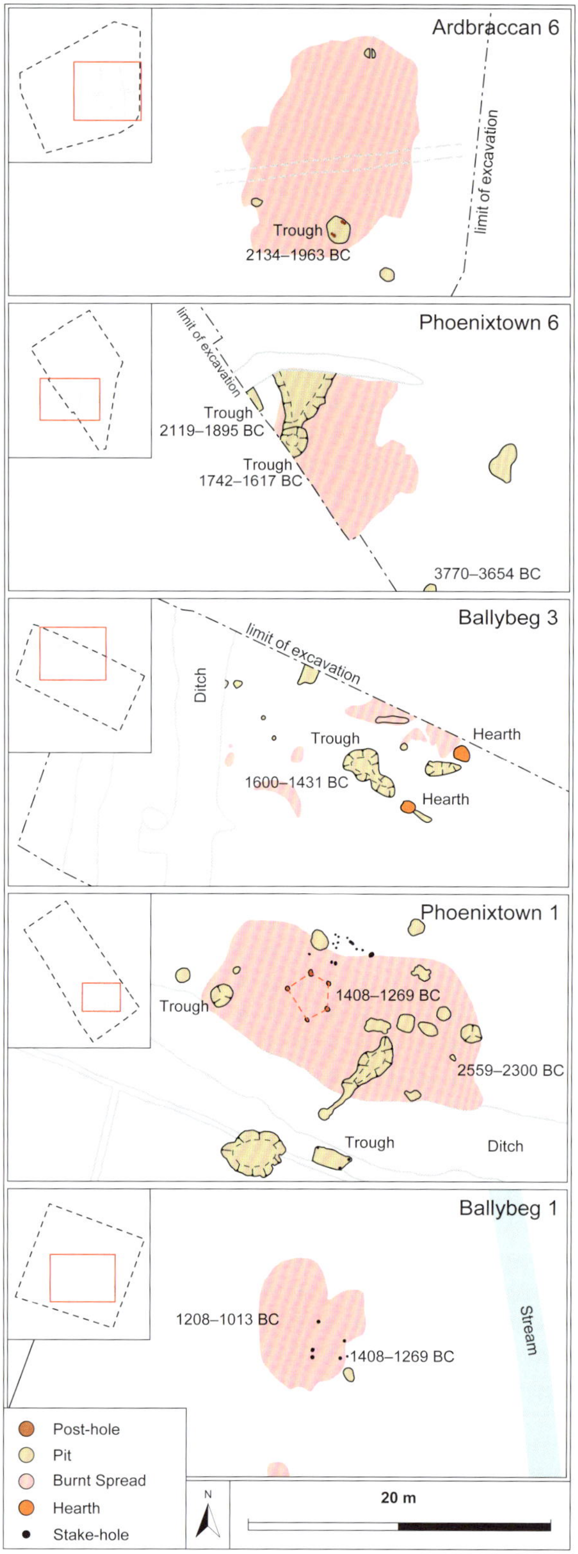

undulating farmland. Ardbraccan 1 was in boggy land, adjacent to a stream. Phoenixtown 1 and 3 were on flat land, dotted with pools or ponds. Ballybeg 1 was located by a stream, while Ballybeg 3 had no obvious water source.

The sites were relatively simple—other than Phoenixtown 1 (below)—and mostly had one or two central troughs, some associated pits and a shallow burnt mound deposit. Only Ballybeg 3 had surviving evidence of a hearth. At Ardbraccan 1, some of the wooden lining of a circular trough was preserved *in situ* in the form of four sharpened alder and ash stakes.

In spite of their general simplicity, the wide range of radiocarbon dates from these sites indicates multiple episodes of use. For example, charcoal (ash) from a rectangular trough at Phoenixtown 6 was dated to 2119–1895 BC (UBA-11108), but charcoal (ash) from a later, circular, trough on the same site was dated to 1742–1617 BC (UBA-11106).

Phoenixtown 1 was the largest and most complex burnt mound in this group, and the only one with remains of an associated wooden structure. The mound was centred on a number of troughs and pits and also overlay a circular arrangement of five stake-holes and post-holes, c. 3 m in diameter,

Illus. 7.17 (Left) Plans of burnt mounds in Ardbraccan, Ballybeg and Phoenixtown on the M3 Navan to Kells and N52 Kells Bypass project (*IAC Ltd*).

Illus. 7.18 (Opposite) Plans of burnt mounds in Kilmainham/Cookstown Great and some neighbouring townlands on the M3 Navan to Kells and N52 Kells Bypass project (*IAC Ltd*).

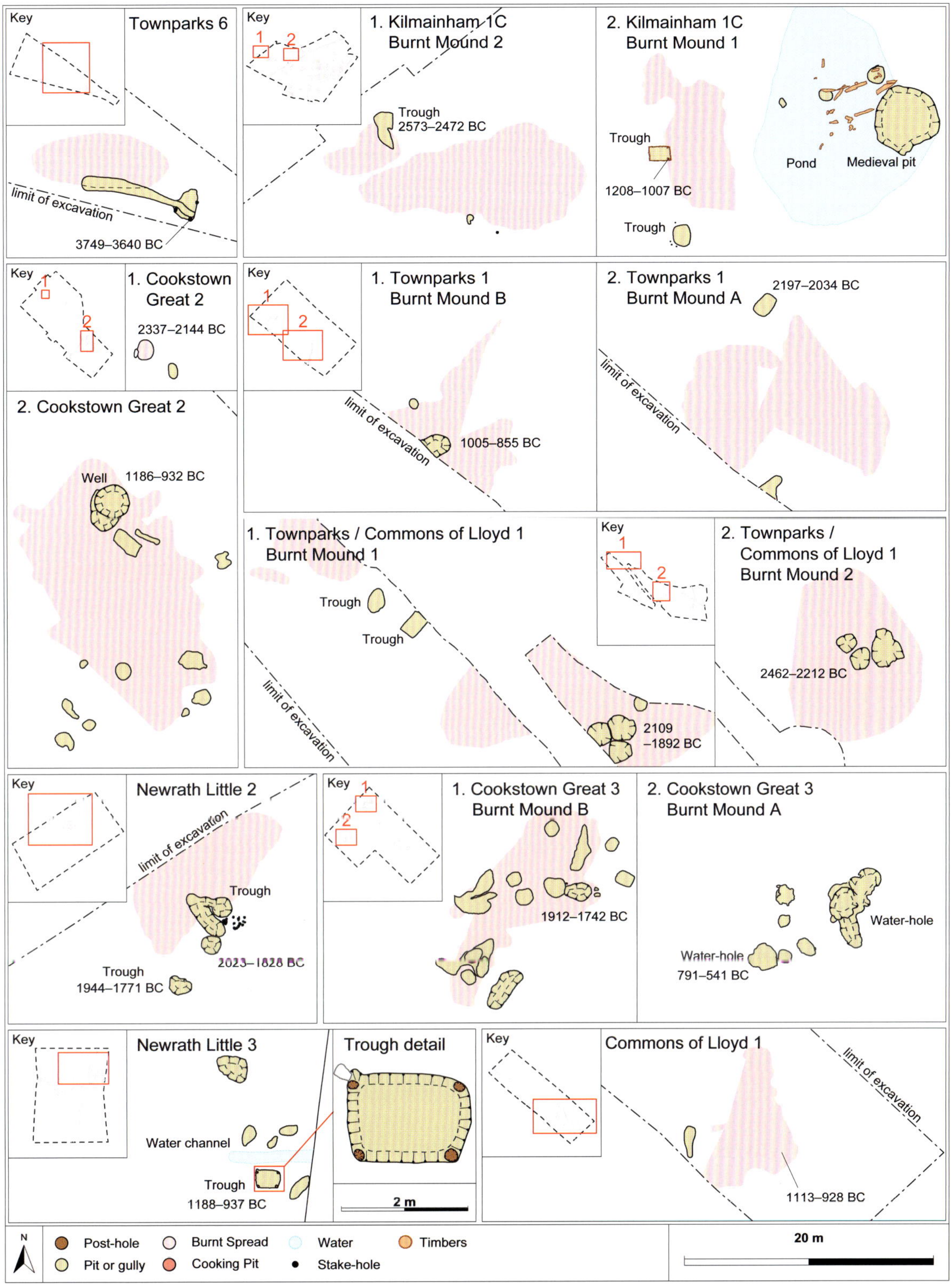
Key
Townparks 6
limit of excavation
3749–3640 BC
Key
1. Kilmainham 1C
Burnt Mound 2
Trough
2573–2472 BC
2. Kilmainham 1C
Burnt Mound 1
Trough
1208–1007 BC
Trough
Pond
Medieval pit
Key
1. Cookstown
Great 2
2337–2144 BC
2. Cookstown Great 2
Well
1186–932 BC
Key
1. Townparks 1
Burnt Mound B
limit of excavation
1005–855 BC
2. Townparks 1
Burnt Mound A
2197–2034 BC
limit of excavation
1. Townparks / Commons of Lloyd 1
Burnt Mound 1
Trough
Trough
limit of excavation
2109
–1892 BC
Key
2. Townparks /
Commons of Lloyd 1
Burnt Mound 2
2462–2212 BC
Key
Newrath Little 2
limit of excavation
Trough
2023–1828 BC
Trough
1944–1771 BC
Key
1. Cookstown Great 3
Burnt Mound B
1912–1742 BC
2. Cookstown Great 3
Burnt Mound A
Water-hole
Water-hole
791–541 BC
Key
Newrath Little 3
Water channel
Trough
1188–937 BC
Trough detail
2 m
Key
Commons of Lloyd 1
limit of excavation
1113–928 BC
N
Post-hole
Pit or gully
Burnt Spread
Cooking Pit
Water
Stake-hole
Timbers
20 m

A seasonal pond at Kilmainham

A natural hollow in a low-lying part of the Kilmainham 1C excavation site was found to be infilled with peaty, organic sediments. Radiocarbon dates from a monolith sample (i.e. a column of sediment) indicate that the peaty deposits started to accumulate in the Early Bronze Age and were still accumulating in the Middle–Late Bronze Age (Beta-235626 and Beta 235627; Appendix 1). The hollow is likely to have been a seasonal pond, as it filled naturally with water in the wetter months during excavation in the course of the M3 archaeology project.

A number of timbers were found in the pond, including worked pieces of hazel, alder and oak (Illus. 7.19 and 7.20). Some of this was lying randomly within the peaty sediments but there was also a structured group of larger timbers. This consisted of several large oak posts driven into the base of the pond, associated with several split oak planks lying horizontally within the peat. These oak timbers are interpreted as remnants of a wooden platform built to give better access to the water. The platform would have been up to 5 m long and 2 m wide. Distinctive cut marks (jam curves) on the timbers indicate that they were worked with Bronze Age axes (O Carroll 2011), which agrees well with the radiocarbon dates for peat accumulation in the pond. However, one oak post with typical Bronze Age axe marks (jam curves) was dated much earlier than this at 6745–6599 BC (UBA-13961), and another oak post was dated to 3800–3640 BC (SUERC-29348). Other than date error, the only explanation for these anomalously early dates is that the posts were made with already ancient timbers that had been preserved in peat, elsewhere in the environs.

Pollen evidence from the pond sediments (Gearey et al., Chapter 2) indicates a mixed landscape of woodland, grass pasture and possibly tillage in the environs. Insect analysis suggests that the pond was—for some of the time at least—a shallow, still body of water in shaded conditions (Allison et al. 2011). It was probably used to water livestock and to supply water to nearby burnt mound troughs. The accumulation of sediments in the pond would have been accelerated by disturbance or trampling by humans and animals.

Illus. 7.19 Kilmainham 1C: alder log with axe marks from the base of the pond. Other worked timbers, including stakes and planks, suggest a platform built to give convenient access to the water (*IAC Ltd*).

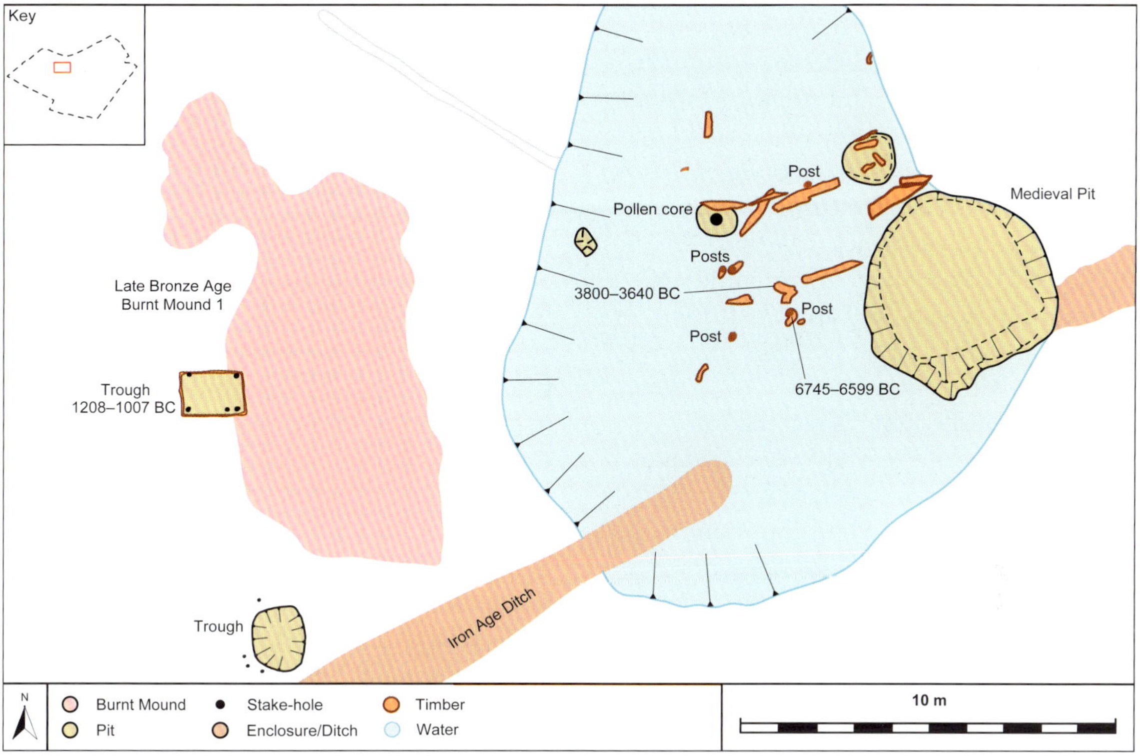

Illus. 7.20 Kilmainham 1C: plan of the Bronze Age pond and adjacent burnt mound. Preserved timbers in the pond included the remnants of a platform made with oak posts and planks (*IAC Ltd*).

which may have been a shelter, a store hut or a sauna hut. Charcoal (hazel) from one of the post-holes was dated to 1408–1269 BC (UBA-11102). Charcoal (alder) from another pit sealed by the mound was dated to 2559–2300 BC (UBA-11103), in the Chalcolithic period, and perhaps represents some much earlier and unrelated activity on the site.

Burnt mounds in Kilmainham/Cookstown Great and environs

A second concentration of burnt mounds, in the Kilmainham/Cookstown Great area, corresponded to the abundant evidence of later prehistoric settlement in the environs. The burnt mounds were recorded at 10 sites—Commons of Lloyd 1; Cookstown Great 2 and 3; Kilmainham 1C; Newrath Little 2 and 3; Townparks 1, 5 and 6; and Townparks 1/Commons of Lloyd 1. They exhibited considerable variety in their size and complexity (Illus. 7.18).

An early example (Burnt Mound 2) at Kilmainham 1C was identified as a group of pits and a thin spread of burnt sediment. Charcoal (alder) from the fill of one of the pits was dated to 2573–2472 BC (UBA-12925), in the Chalcolithic period. A second and later example (Burnt Mound 1) at this site had a rectangular trough with hazel rods in each corner supporting a poorly preserved wooden lining, of alder and ash. Charcoal (alder) from an associated stake-hole was dated to 1208–1007 BC (UBA-12924). This mound was adjacent to a seasonal pond that gradually infilled with peaty organic deposits (see text box).

At Townparks 6, charcoal (twig oak) from a post-hole associated with the burnt mound site produced a very early date of 3749–3640 BC (UBA-11101). Given the proximity of the burnt mound to an Early Neolithic settlement on the same site, this date must be treated with caution.

The two burnt mounds recorded at Cookstown Great 3 also had associated pits and troughs but were different from other examples in this area in one important respect. They both depended on large, deep pits/wells dug into the subsoil for access to local groundwater. Charcoal (alder) from the trough of Burnt Mound B was dated to 1912–1742 BC (UBA-11097), in the Early Bronze Age, but a bone sample from the well associated with Burnt Mound A returned a much later date of 791–541 BC (UBA-11092), in the Early Iron Age. This shows again, as with several of the other burnt mound sites of this landscape, that some locations could be repeatedly favoured for the same activities but at different times in prehistory––in this case to extract large volumes of groundwater for boiling in troughs.

The three burnt mounds at Townparks/Commons of Lloyd 1 had multiple troughs and/or pits beneath burnt spreads. Two of the troughs in Burnt Mound 1 had remnants of timber lining. One of three large pits beneath Burnt Mound 2 had a collection of large, flat stones placed in its base, which could have been heated for roasting rather than boiling.

Petrology, finds and fauna of the burnt mounds

Heated stones

The type of stone selected for use in the burnt mounds of this landscape was restricted by local geology. In all cases it was identified as sandstone and/or dolerite (Mandal 2011). Sandstone is the stone of choice for use in burnt mounds, as it has a high resistance to cracking when heated and is chemically stable (unlike limestone, which produces calcium hydroxide when roasted and boiled), so that it can be heated more than once.

Pottery and chipped stone

Some Bronze Age pottery was found in features close to the burnt mounds at Cookstown Great 2 and Phoenixtown 1, but it is our interpretation that these relate to other phases of activity, unrelated to the mounds.

On the other hand, a small assemblage of chipped stone was recovered from features directly associated with the burnt mounds. These include an impressive barbed-and-tanged flint arrowhead from Phoenixtown 6 and a (burnt) flint knife from the earlier, Chalcolithic-period burnt mound at Kilmainham 1C.

Animal bones

In spite of the long-standing hypothesis that burnt mound sites were used to cook food and especially large meat joints, there is an almost complete absence of animal bones from the burnt mound sites on our project. The exceptions are a horse molar and a cow molar from Cookstown Great 3 and Ballybeg 3 respectively. It is possible that meat joints cooked at burnt mound sites were taken away to be consumed elsewhere, in drier and less cluttered surroundings.

Ceremony and burial

Human remains dating from the Early, Middle and Late Bronze Age were recorded at five sites on the road project. As none of the burnt bone from earlier periods could be positively identified as human, these were our first confirmed encounters with the people who occupied this landscape in prehistory. The evidence was primarily in the form of cremations, found in small pits or ring-ditches. Although there were dozens of other Bronze Age pits with inclusions of charcoal and burnt bone in the fills, they are not considered here as cremations because the bone could not be identified as human or because, in some cases, it was identified as animal.

Early Bronze Age funerary evidence

Kilmainham 3 ring-ditch

The only funerary monument of the Early Bronze Age found on the road project was a small ring-ditch at Kilmainham 3. A third of the monument was excavated; the rest extended beyond the limits of the road project and was not disturbed (Illus. 7.21). In contrast to the much larger barrow monument at Grange 3 (below), the ditch was a slight feature (0.6 m wide by 0.24 m deep) with a projected external diameter of 9 m. There was only light charcoal flecking in the ditch fills and no burnt bone was recovered from the excavated part of the site. Charred hazelnut shell from the ditch fill was dated to 2137–1965 BC (UBA-12083).

The absence of burnt human bone is not unusual for these monuments and was recorded also in some of the seven ring-ditches in a Middle Bronze Age cemetery at Garretstown 2, near Dunshaughlin, Co. Meath (Rathbone 2009). In our example, cremated human remains may have been inserted into the unexcavated part of the ditch, outside the road project site, or in an earthen mound raised inside the ring-ditch but long since ploughed away. This sort of attrition is seen locally in a cluster of ring-ditches and barrows north of the road project in Kilmainham and adjoining Headfort townland. Only one of these monuments (RMP ME017:020) has a substantial surviving barrow mound (diameter 17 m) inside its ditch. The others have all been levelled and are visible now only as cropmarks in aerial photographs.

Kilmainham 1C cremation pit

One definite cremation burial was identified at Kilmainham 1C. This was deposited in a

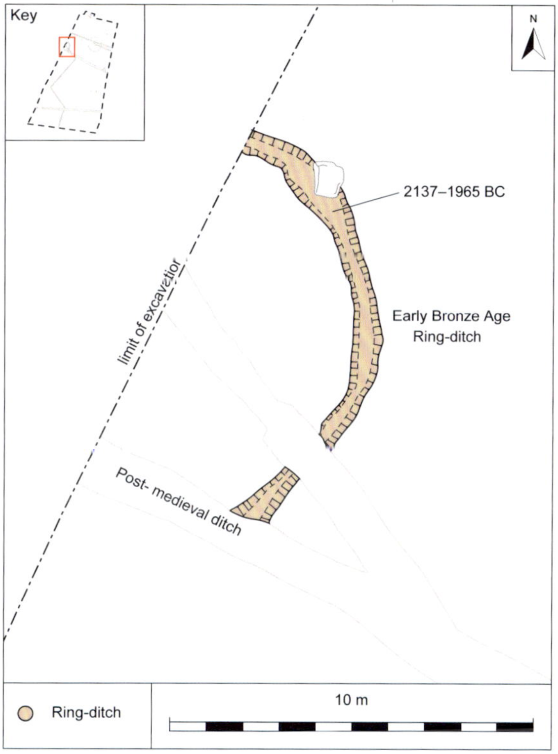

Illus. 7.21 Kilmainham 3: plan of a partly excavated Early Bronze Age ring-ditch discovered at the western limit of the road project site (*IAC Ltd*).

shallow circular pit (0.5 m wide by 0.22 m deep) (not illustrated). The bone fragments were from a single individual, probably an adult, but it was not possible to determine the sex. A bone fragment was dated to 1885–1749 BC (UBA-12909). The charcoals in the pit were mostly alder, though oak was most often used for cremation pyres. Charred grains of wheat and barley in this and in an adjacent pit may represent some aspect of the funerary rites. The cremation pit was located 15 m north of a large pit that contained the fragmented remains of a cordoned urn (a type of pottery widely dated to c. 1700 BC). It is possible that this was a second, disturbed burial, though no cremated human remains were recorded.

Cakestown Glebe 2 cremation pit

At Cakestown Glebe 2, a small cremation pit (0.4 m wide by 0.3 m deep) (not illustrated) was cut into the backfilled deposits of a much larger, undated pit. The cremation pit contained a large quantity of human bone that had been burnt at a high temperature (the fragments were fully oxidised). There were recognisable body parts from at least one individual, including fragments of skull, mandible, vertebrae, rib and pelvis. A bone fragment was dated to 2141–1981 BC (UBA-12944), which is broadly contemporary with the Early Bronze Age building recorded on this same site (Structure 3) and described above.

The cremations of this period included a range of skeletal elements—at both

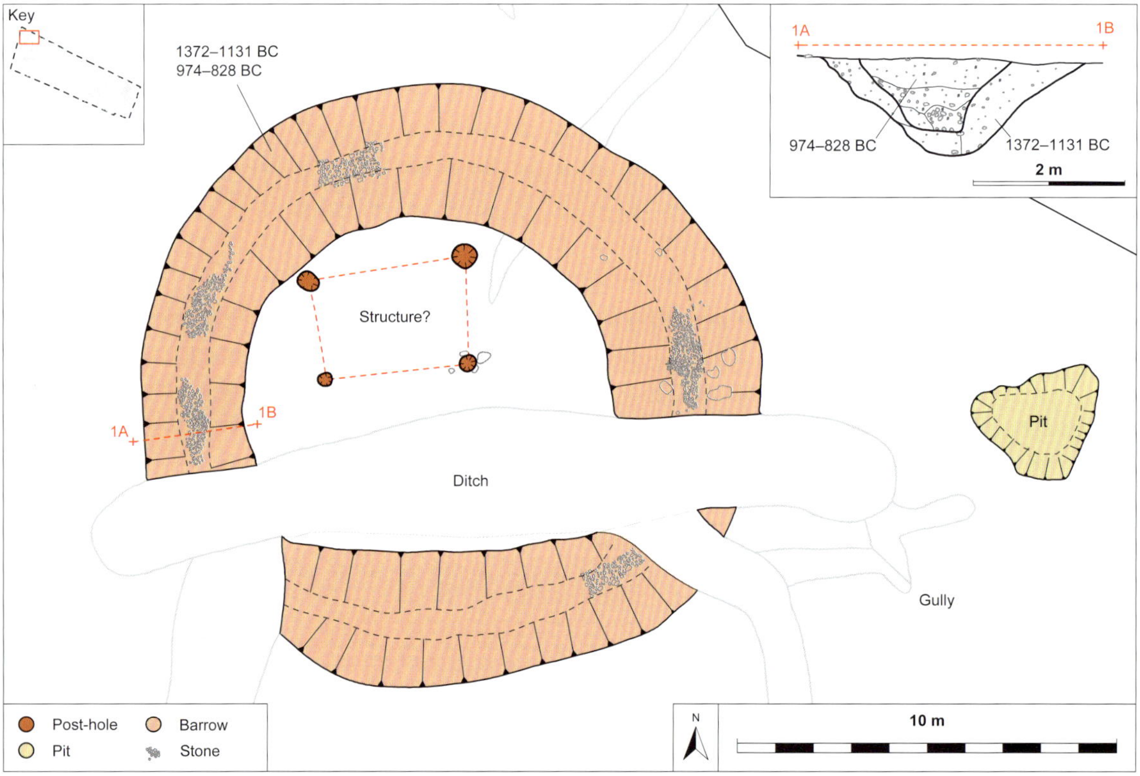

Illus. 7.22 Grange 3: plan and section of a Late Bronze Age barrow monument with an internal four-post structure. The ditch fills contained chipped stone and animal bones but no human bone (*IAC Ltd*).

Kilmainham 1C and Cakestown Glebe 2. No part of the body was excluded from burial. This is especially noticeable in the cremation from Cakestown Glebe 2, where small bones of the hands and feet were present. This suggests careful and deliberate deposition of the complete cremation, in contrast to the evidence from the Middle–Late Bronze Age cremations (below).

Middle and Late Bronze Age funerary evidence

Kilmainham 1A cremation pits

Three cremation pits at Kilmainham 1A were found within a large rock outcrop at the south of the site (not illustrated). This is depicted as a 'quarry' on early Ordnance Survey mapping (e.g. the first-edition six-inch map, 1837), so it is surprising that the cremations

Illus. 7.23 Grange 3: excavation in progress on the site of the Late Bronze Age barrow monument, with partly excavated ditch fills, viewed from west (*Hawkeye*).

survived at all. The outcrop was still visible prior to our excavations. As a prominent and permanent feature in the landscape it would have offered a natural 'monumental' setting for the cremations, offsetting the need for any other physical marker, such as a ring-ditch or barrow mound. Charcoals from the cremation pits included mixed alder, ash and oak. Hazelnut shell from one cremation pit and human bone from another were dated to 1619–1458 BC (UBA-12107) and 975–830 BC (UBA-12945) respectively.

Grange 3 barrow monument

The major burial monument of this period on the road project was a barrow at Grange 3 (Illus. 7.22 and 7.23). This had an external diameter of 16.5 m, with a ditch up to 4 m wide and 1.3 m deep. The internal diameter was 9.5–10 m. There was a subrectangular arrangement of four post-holes in the interior, marking an area measuring 3.5 m east/west by 2.5 m. Sherds of Middle–Late Bronze Age pottery were recovered from one of the post-holes. The ditch fills were recut, indicating two distinct phases of use. The lower or primary ditch fills contained chert, flint and a large quantity of animal bone, including remains of cattle, sheep/goat, pig and red deer. Red deer dominated the assemblage and included fragments of antler, scapula and tibia—some with butchery marks. These earlier fills were sealed by a stony layer in the base of the recut ditch. The stony layer contained a large quantity of very weathered and eroded animal bone—mostly cattle, with some horse. The cattle bones indicated local slaughter. There was also a small amount of burnt bone in the ditch fills but none of it was identified as human. A charcoal sample (alder, hazel) from the lower fills was dated to 1372–1131 BC (UBA-12054). A horse bone from the upper fill was dated to 974–828 BC (UBA-12053).

Again, the absence of human remains from this monument is hard to explain but is not unprecedented. The bone could have been buried elsewhere, or kept by the family of the deceased, or shared among friends and relatives. In this scenario the barrow was built as a cenotaph rather than a grave-marker. This was also the interpretation of barrows at Mitchelstowndown West (Barrows 55 and 61), Co. Limerick (Daly & Grogan 1993). A more prosaic explanation for the absence of human remains at our site is that an internal bank or mound containing burials was levelled or ploughed away. In fact, some human bones from a nearby boundary ditch were the only human remains from this site. They included cremated fragments of a skull, teeth and upper and lower limbs. They could have come from a disturbed burial in the barrow.

The animal bone in the ditch fills is likely to derive from feasting during the funerary rites. Animal bones have been recovered from fills of other ring-ditches and barrow ditches. An example at Raynestown 1, south of Dunshaughlin, Co. Meath, had burnt bones of cattle, sheep/goat, pig and horse, as well as cremated human bone (Elder et al. 2009).

The four-post structure at the centre of the barrow suggests that it may have had an external bank rather than a central mound. An external bank and deep ditch surrounding the interior would have been an impressive physical marker dividing public from ritual space. Four free-standing posts may have marked a kind of inner sanctum where only the principal celebrant was allowed. Alternatively, the posts may have supported a platform or mortuary house in which bodies were stored for a period of time before being cremated.

The Middle Bronze Age round-houses at Grange 3 would have stood about 170 m west of the barrow. Radiocarbon dating evidence indicates that they probably pre-dated it, but there may have been other dwelling houses in the vicinity when the barrow was constructed and used for funerary rituals. Cleary (2005) observed that ring-ditches and barrows are sometimes found in close proximity to Bronze Age houses but are not always contemporary with the buildings. She suggests that the burial monuments can be interpreted as boundary-markers on the edges of settlements, and this may have been the case at Grange 3.

Isolated pits and other features

Numerous isolated features or small groups of features were recorded outside of the main settlement sites or on the fringes of the main sites. This sort of 'isolated' Bronze Age activity occurred most often in the form of single pits or pit groups.

In the Grange/Phoenixtown area, for instance, at Grange 1, Grange 4 and Grange 5 there were pits and post-holes radiocarbon-dated to the Chalcolithic period and Middle Bronze Age on sites that otherwise had features of Iron Age/early medieval date (Appendix 1).

In the Kilmainham/Cookstown Great area a cluster or pits and post-holes at Nugentstown 3 (not illustrated) produced dates in the Early and Middle Bronze Age: charcoals of alder and ash were dated to 1915–1759 BC (UBA-12068) and 1664–1522 BC (UBA-11132) respectively. The pit that produced the earlier date also contained worn, abraded sherds of Chalcolithic (Beaker) pottery, which may have been carefully curated for ritual deposition. At the western extremity of this site a small spread of occupation soil contained remains of an Early Bronze Age food vessel. Although a small quantity of burnt bone (unidentifiable) was also found here, external sooting and a blackened accretion on the inner surface of the vessel suggest that it was used in a domestic context and was not from a burial. There was a hearth close by, at Nugentstown 1, flanked by two charcoal-rich pits. Charcoal (alder) from one of the pits was dated to 1657–1506 BC (UBA-12061), in the Middle Bronze Age. An adjacent line of post-holes, pits and a stake-hole may represent a screen or shelter.

Elsewhere in the Kilmainham/Cookstown Great area there was a diverse range of Bronze Age features in the vicinity of domestic buildings and burnt mounds. At Cookstown Great 2, charcoal (hazel) from a small cooking pit with heat-affected stone was dated to 2337–2144 BC (UBA-11083), in the Chalcolithic period or Early Bronze Age. Another pit contained sherds from a cordoned urn, a flint blade, burnt animal bone and charred wheat and barley grains. Charcoal (hazel) from the pit was dated to 1607–1450 BC (UBA-11088), in the Middle Bronze Age.

We cannot say what all of these scattered minor features represent but, collectively, they provide good evidence that the whole district was occupied and exploited in some form, and by a large population, throughout the Bronze Age.

CHAPTER 8

From Iron Age to early medieval times

Fintan Walsh

From Iron Age to early medieval times

The Early Iron Age (c. 800–400 BC) is often described as a 'dark age' in Irish archaeology. There is little evidence for settlement in the archaeological record for this period and, with some exceptions, the known sites have only slight remains. This national trend is mirrored in our investigations on the M3 Navan to Kells and N52 Kells Bypass project, where the recorded features from the Early Iron Age consisted of a few isolated pits at Kilmainham 1C and Cookstown Great 1, a burnt mound at Cookstown Great 3 and a cereal-drying kiln at Kilmainham 2. Further afield, on another sector of the M3, an Early Iron Age post-built structure, possibly a round-house, was excavated at Derver 4, c. 8.5 km north-west of Kells (Gallagher & Ginn 2008). No Iron Age domestic occupation sites were identified on our sector, however, and there was certainly no evidence for the sort of large, permanent houses that were built in the Early Neolithic period and

Illus. 8.1 View from Faughan Hill, looking north-west over a barrow towards the Hill of Lloyd. There were late prehistoric ceremonial centres on both hilltops. The paucity of Iron Age settlement evidence in their hinterland is puzzling but is consistent with a national pattern (*Faith Bailey for IAC Ltd*).

Middle Bronze Age. This is puzzling because, as we have seen already (Chapter 1), there were major late prehistoric settlement and ritual sites in the district at the Hill of Lloyd, Faughan Hill (Illus. 8.1) and possibly Teltown too. Emerging into the Middle Iron Age (c. 400 BC–AD 100), we begin to see numbers of cereal-drying kilns on our project, along with the first evidence of iron metalworking, and ritual monuments, including a large barrow at Cakestown Glebe 2. By the Late Iron Age/early medieval transition period (c. AD 400–500), there is increasing evidence for agricultural activity and metalworking. The first inhumation burials are found on the project, at Kilmainham 1C, and seem to be associated with a rectangular ceremonial enclosure.

Agriculture and cereal-drying kilns

The most commonly recorded features of the Late Iron Age/early medieval transition period on our project were cereal-drying kilns. These are common features in the rich arable landscapes of north Leinster. Similar kilns were recorded at several locations on other sectors of the M3, with a notable group of 13 kilns in Lismullin, 24 km south-east of Kells (O'Connell 2009; 2013, 115–21). In our sector, on the M3 Navan to Kells and N52 Kells Bypass project, 22 cereal-drying kilns were excavated: one in Gardenrath, three in Grange and 18 in Kilmainham (for details of individual kilns see Appendix 3).

The kilns were used to dry and harden cereal grain. This was especially important after a damp harvest and/or a short growing season. Grain that was processed in this way could be stored for a longer time without sprouting, rotting or being fouled by fungal infestation, and was easier to grind into flour. Simple cereal-drying kilns dating from the Late Iron Age to medieval times are found throughout Ireland. Their origins can be traced to Roman Britain, where similar kilns are found throughout the fertile lowlands in the south (Monk & Power 2012).

The early kilns found in Ireland have a

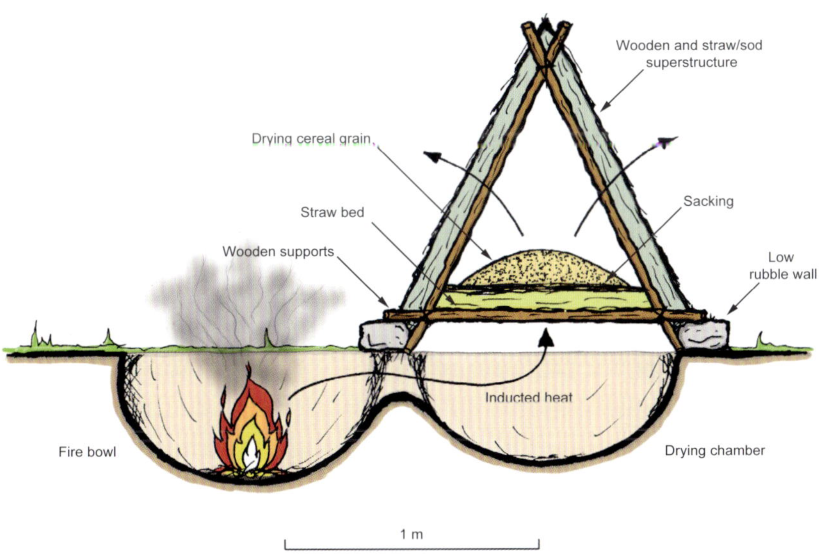

Illus. 8.2 Schematic representation of a simple figure-of-eight cereal-drying kiln. Typically, only the earth-cut or below-ground elements are found on Irish archaeological sites. Accidents seem to have been common and burnt grain is often found in the drying chambers (*Hugh Kavanagh*).

distinct archaeological footprint—most commonly a figure-of-eight or keyhole-shaped pit, sometimes lined with stone (Monk & Kelleher 2005, 77–84). Grain was heaped in the drying chamber on a rack of some sort, probably covered with a bed of sacking or straw. Heat was inducted into the drying chamber from a hearth or fire bowl via the flue. The fire bowl, flue and drying chamber are the earth-cut parts of a kiln that commonly survive in the archaeological record. The drying chamber would have been covered by some sort of superstructure—perhaps a dome of sticks and sods footed on a low wall or bank of rubble (Illus. 8.2)—but the evidence for this seldom survives.

Charcoals are commonly found in kilns, representing fuel wood or a superstructure destroyed by fire. Charred cereal grain found in drying chambers most probably represents accidental conflagrations, but it is sometimes found in the fire bowl too, as surplus grain could be used as fuel. Either way, charred grain from kilns is an excellent source of evidence for agriculture and diet.

Most of the 22 kilns recorded on our project were figure-of-eight-shaped, with the fire bowl towards the north or north-west (Illus. 8.3 and 8.4). In terms of dating, there are some outliers early and late in the series but samples from 15 of the kilns returned radiocarbon date ranges spanning the period from the early fifth to the mid-sixth century AD, and 14 of these were in Kilmainham and neighbouring Gardenrath. This extraordinary concentration of kilns in one area suggests a well-managed agricultural landscape with organised crop-processing on a large scale. The absence of associated habitation evidence is no puzzle. Kilns could be operated most efficiently when they were built close to the crops and to convenient sources of fuel. Here, therefore, we can envisage a working agricultural landscape, where wreaths of smoke rising from cereal kilns in early autumn represented the end of another seasonal crop cycle.

Kilmainham and Gardenrath

Early kiln at Kilmainham 2

The earliest kiln on the project was recorded at Kilmainham 2 (Kiln C33). It was a simple, figure-of-eight-shaped example. A barley grain from the kiln was dated to 510–387 BC (UBA-12065).[1] No other cereal type was identified. Kilns of this early date are rare in the Irish archaeological record.

Kiln group at Kilmainham 1C

There were 12 kilns at Kilmainham 1C. Most of them were located on a broad, low, well-drained gravel ridge, which was flanked on its south-eastern side by a ditch (2 m wide and 0.5 m deep) that extended across the entire length of the site. A charcoal deposit (holly) from the base of the ditch was dated to 203–51 BC (UBA-12915). This is significantly earlier than date ranges from any of the kilns on the same site. Nonetheless, a boundary ditch can have a long lifespan in the countryside and this one may have continued to divide areas of agricultural land in the Late Iron Age/early medieval transition period.

Most of the Kilmainham 1C kilns were figure-of-eight-shaped. There was one simpler kiln (C81), roughly oval in plan. This was also the earliest example on this site, dating from AD 27–127 (UBA-12927). There were two other relatively early kilns (C13 and C689),

1 Barley grains provided the radiocarbon-dating sample material from the kilns in all but two cases (Kilns C144 and C606), when hazel or hazelnut charcoal was used.

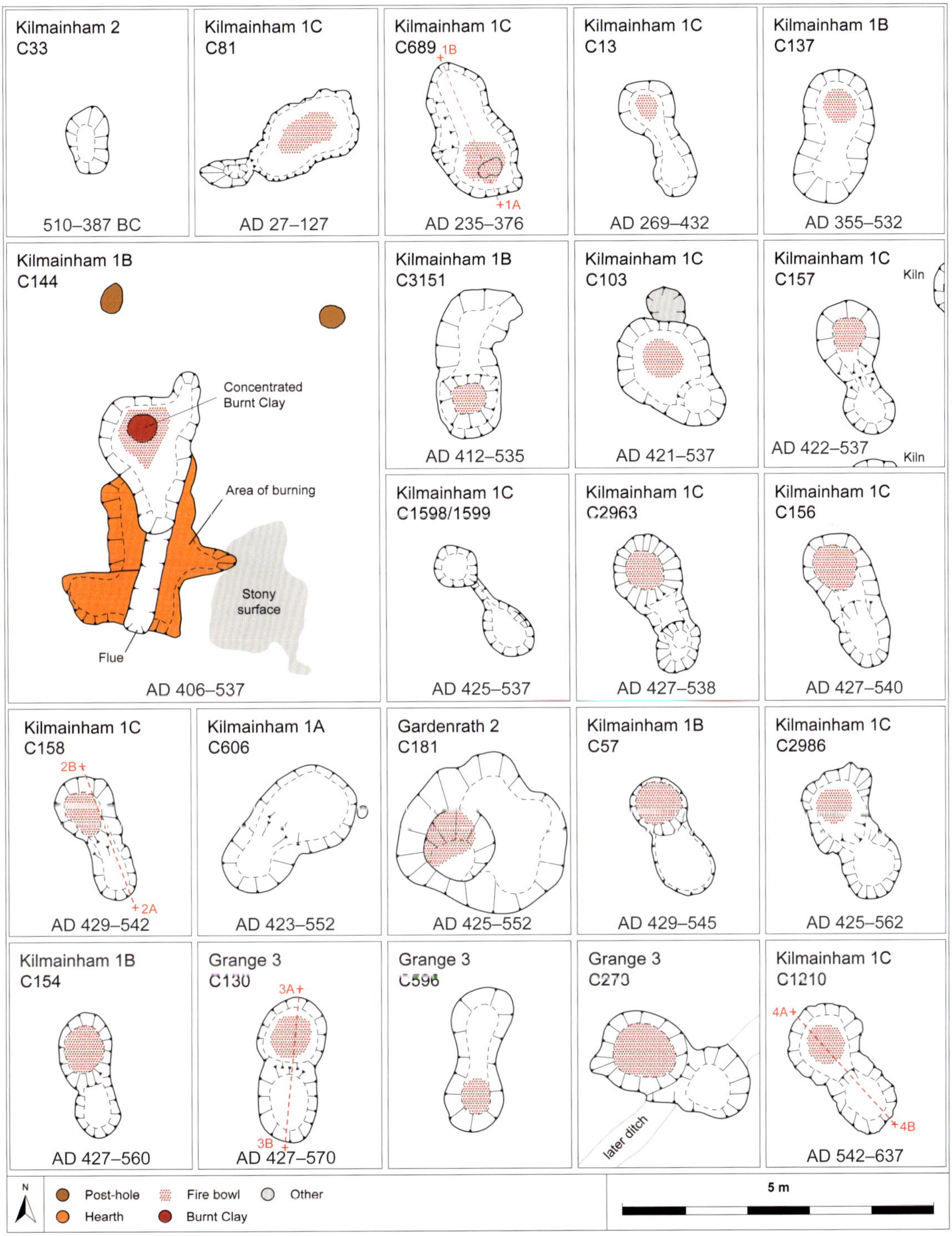

Illus. 8.3 Plans of cereal-drying kilns recorded on the M3 Navan to Kells and N52 Kells Bypass project. The kilns were generally figure-of-eight-shaped, with the fire bowl towards the north or north-west, and most of them were dated to a period between the early fifth and mid-sixth centuries AD (*IAC Ltd*).

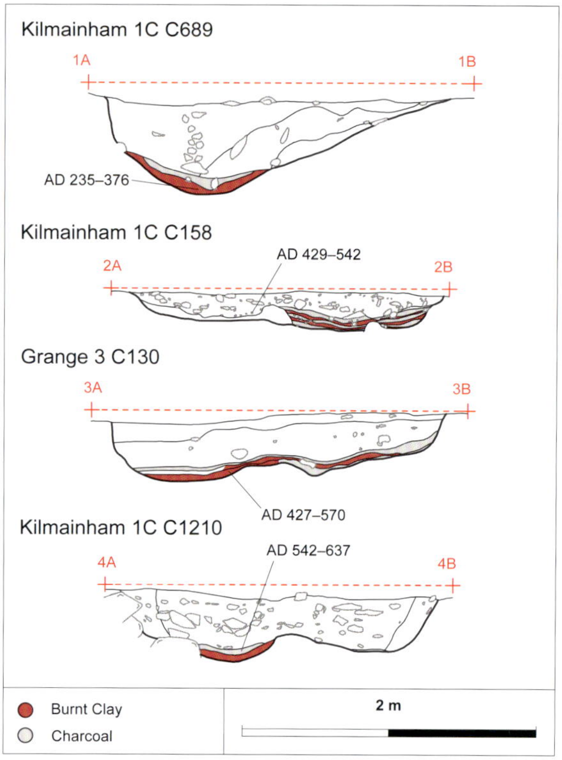

Illus. 8.4 Section drawings of selected cereal-drying kilns from Grange and Kilmainham. Burnt clay and charcoal are typical basal deposits (*IAC Ltd*).

dated to AD 235–376 (UBA-12929) and AD 269–432 (UBA-12926), but most of the kilns at Kilmainham 1C seemed to belong to a single phase of organised crop-processing at this location, as they were dated to a period from the early fifth to the mid-sixth century. There were eight kilns in this group. They were all figure-of-eight-shaped and most of them had fire bowls towards the northern end. The earliest (C3151) of the group was dated to AD 412–535 (UBA-12931) and the latest (C2986) to AD 425–562 (UBA-15486). Beyond this, there was a single late outlier (C1210), which may properly be regarded as an early medieval kiln. It was also figure-of-eight-shaped and was dated to AD 542–637 (UBA-15485).

Some of the kilns (C156, C157 and C158) had successive lenses of burnt clay and charcoal in the fire bowl, representing multiple working cycles. Deposits of stone in some kilns (e.g. C103 and C158) might be the collapsed remains of kiln superstructures.

Other kilns in the Kilmainham area

The other kilns in Kilmainham and neighbouring Gardenrath produced similar dates to the main phase at Kilmainham 1C, broadly from the early fifth to the mid-sixth century. There were four kilns at Kilmainham 1B, one at Kilmainham 1A and one at Gardenrath 2. The Gardenrath kiln was oval in plan. The Kilmainham kilns were all figure-of-eight-shaped, with one exception, at Kilmainham 1B. This kiln (C144) was very irregular in plan and had an unusually long flue (c. 1.5 m) extending from a fire bowl at the northern end. There was no surviving trace of a drying chamber at the opposite, southern end, so this part of the kiln may have been constructed entirely above ground.

Grange 3

Towards the south-eastern end of the road corridor another, smaller group of kilns was recorded at Grange 3. Only one of these was radiocarbon-dated. At AD 427–570 (UBA-12073) the result is broadly similar to dates for kilns in the main group at Kilmainham.

2 The early medieval enclosure is outside the scope of this present book but is fully described in the final archaeological excavation report on Grange 3 (https://repository.dri.ie/catalog/h7033n15g).

3 The place-name Grange derives from the Latin word for a granary (*granica*) and in later medieval times came to refer to a farm belonging to a monastery or a convent, proving the old archaeological adage that ‘the good land is good in all periods’.

The three kilns in Grange 3 were also figure-of-eight-shaped and were probably all of a single phase.

A subrectangular earthwork enclosure at Grange 3 produced dates from the upper ditch fills of AD 617–666 (UBA-12055) (barley) and AD 669–772 (UBA-15476) (cattle bone).[2] One of the kilns (C596) was inside the enclosure; the other two were c. 75 m east of it. The kilns probably pre-date the construction of the enclosure but, taken all together, these features indicate a long continuity of land use and settlement in Grange, from at least the Iron Age/early medieval transition period. This is corroborated by the Sites and Monuments Record for County Meath, which records an early medieval ringfort (ME024-007) and an early church and burial-ground (ME 024-088) elsewhere in Grange, c. 300 m south of the road project.[3]

Illus. 8.5 Barley was the dominant cereal type found in the excavated cereal-drying kilns. The absence of weed seeds and chaff in samples from the kilns indicates a clean crop that was processed before it was dried *(Jerry O'Sullivan)*.

Kiln products and fuel wood

Examination of the charred grain and charcoals from the kilns reveals a consistent pattern in the crops processed and the available fuel wood. Barley was the dominant grain (Illus. 8.5) and was found in all of the kilns. It was the only grain found in two of the kilns at Kilmainham 1C, but more often it was accompanied by smaller quantities of wheat and/or oats and, in two instances, by rye. Where the wheat could be identified to species it was most often bread/club wheat, but spelt and emmer also occurred.

Small numbers of weed seeds—such as bindweed (*Fallopia convolvulus*), knotgrasses (*Polygonum* sp.), goosefoot/fat hen (*Chenopodium* sp.), pale persicaria (*Polygonum lapathifolium*), pea/vetch (*Vicia/Lathyrus* spp) and wild grasses (Gramineae spp)—were incidental inclusions in the harvested cereals. Chaff was almost entirely absent from the sample assemblages, which shows that the grain had already been threshed and winnowed, and brought to the kilns in a clean, prepared state (Lyons 2011).

The charcoals indicate that oak and hazel were the preferred fuel woods. Where hazel charcoal was dominant (e.g. C81 and C1210), this may represent the conflagration and collapse of a drying rack or a wattled superstructure rather than a preference for hazel over oak as a fuel wood.

Agriculture and society

The dating evidence for the 22 kilns recorded on our road project spans several centuries but, as we saw, there is a marked concentration of dates in the fifth and sixth centuries AD. Why did cereal-drying kilns become so important in the agricultural practices of this period? Europe experienced a colder, wetter and windier climate in the period AD 400–900. The effects of a deteriorating climate may have been exacerbated by population pressure. There is palaeoenvironmental and historical evidence for a general increase in population in Ireland during our 'transition period', and especially in the Leinster region. Thus, in addition to climate change, there may also have been adverse human impacts on the environment at this time (Monk & Power 2012, 39). We can add to these long-term trends the shorter but more extreme climatic effects of two major Icelandic volcanic eruptions in AD 536 and AD 540 (Baillie & Brown 2011). Taking all these factors together—population pressure, less favourable conditions for tillage farming and the social stresses consequent to disastrous volcanic events—it is unsurprising that we find an increase in the use of drying kilns. In these conditions it would have been of critical importance to manage and preserve any food surpluses that could be produced.

Food-hoarding in a society under stress is not the whole explanation. There were other and more positive factors at work. As the veil of late prehistory is drawn aside, the early medieval society that we see emerging in Ireland was enterprising, sophisticated and hierarchical. The population continued to grow, but now managing food surpluses was driven by the need to maintain a new social order—in short, to feed people who were not themselves directly involved in subsistence farming (Monk & Power 2012, 41).

Settlement was dominated from the sixth century onwards by dispersed homesteads. They are still represented in the rural landscape today by innumerable ringforts and cashels—typically the homes of the freeman farmers described by early Irish law tracts. The people who occupied these homesteads and worked the fields around them were ultimately the dependants of larger ecclesiastical and secular estates, where some of their produce was collected, processed and rendered to their overlords, who could include senior clergy. These estates were centres of agricultural production that operated cereal-drying kilns and grain mills of their own. Like cereal-drying in hot kilns, milling grain in water-powered mills was another technology imported from the late Roman world. Early mills are well documented in the Irish archaeological record. On current evidence their floruit is later than that of cereal kilns, with at least 100 known mill sites from the period c. AD 600–900, including several excavated examples (Rynne 2013, 116–17).

We see a glimpse in the early Irish law tracts of the social order that both underpinned and depended on the management of food production. The lowest order of freeman farmer (*ocaire*) might have a share in the ownership of a kiln and a mill, while the freeman strong farmer (*bóaire*) and others of higher social rank could be expected to own their kilns and mills outright (Kelly 1998, 241 and 245). A *muilenn tuaithe* was a large mill, used by many farmers and likely to have been operated by a professional miller (*muilleoir*) (ibid., 484).

Early medieval estate management is a relatively new theme in Irish archaeology but has already been documented at several sites on national road schemes. Johnstown and Raystown, Co. Meath (Carlin et al. 2008, 55–85; Seaver 2016), and Balriggan, Co. Louth (Delaney et al. 2020, 106–13), are examples of very large earthwork enclosures containing, variously, burial-grounds, buildings, grain mills, butchered animal bones and craftwork or industrial areas. Such sites have been interpreted as large farmsteads with burial-grounds for an extended family or kin group but, we propose here, may equally be regarded as secular estate centres. These were similar in some respects to large monastic settlements of the same period. Kilbegly, Co. Roscommon, is an example of an early mill that was owned by an ecclesiastical estate (Devane 2013, 109–13). That the Irish word *muilenn*, a mill, is derived from the Latin *molina* is one reminder of the important role of the early monastic Church in Ireland as a vector for innovation in agriculture and food-processing.

On our own road project, the M3 Navan to Kells and N52 Kells Bypass, we have not discovered an estate centre but have seen instead the sort of large-scale crop-processing that was undertaken in the hinterlands of such places. Our cereal kilns in Kilmainham, Grange and Gardenrath may have been part of the supply chain for Kells/Hill of Lloyd, in whatever form it was settled and governed as a central place in the district, in the fifth and sixth centuries and beyond. No doubt the rich agricultural landscape of the Blackwater valley continued to supply Kells when it was rededicated as a Columban monastery in the ninth century.

Ironworking

In the fourth century BC metalworkers began smelting and smithing iron in Grange. There were 10 small pit or bowl furnaces at Grange 3, and this site was used intermittently for metalworking until the first century AD. Smelting iron was a noxious business and, like crop-processing (above), was often conducted away from settlement sites, in marginal places where raw materials (bog ore) and fuel wood (oak charcoal) were more readily available. Ore may have been extracted from Boheermeen Bog, which is the nearest large bog to Grange, about 4 km away to the south-west.

Early metalworking evidence is commonly found on or near burial-grounds. A shaft furnace was operated at Grange 2 sometime between the mid-third and mid-sixth centuries AD, when there was also a small burial-ground on this site. The transformative power of metalworking was seen as having spiritual and even magical power in early history and prehistory. Burial-grounds were spiritual places too—and became consecrated places in the Christian era.

Grange 3 Iron Age bowl furnaces

Ten small ironworking furnaces were scattered across the Grange 3 site. There were no discernible groupings, and there did not seem to be much planning involved in their locations. The furnaces were all small, bowl-shaped pits, with fired clay at the base, a middle layer of charcoal and an upper layer of mixed clay. The charcoals identified from the sampled pits were alder, ash and willow rather than the oak that one might expect from metalworking features.

Only four of the pits contained any metallurgical waste. The slag from three pits had the appearance of smithing slag lumps, which are formed during primary (refining the bloom) and secondary (manufacturing and repairing of artefacts) smithing. Charcoal (ash) from one of these pits was dated to 390–200 BC (SUERC-29330). The grey-black 'drippy slag' from a fourth pit suggests that it may have been the sunken base for an overground clay shaft furnace (Wallace & Anguilano 2010). Charcoal (alder) from this pit was dated to 191–5 BC (UBA-12057).

The other six pits had similar fill sequences to the slag-bearing pits—other than the absence of slag—and may have been used for roasting ore or for any other high-temperature activities associated with metalworking. Charcoal samples from two of them were dated to 346–60 BC (UBA-12056) (ash) and 190 BC–AD 30 (SUERC-29333) (alder).

Grange 2 shaft furnace

Small, simple bowl furnaces are common in the Irish archaeological record. Some of these may have the bases for simple shaft furnaces but often there is not enough surviving evidence to make this distinction. This was not the case at Grange 2, where the furnace was more elaborate and the lower, below-ground portion of the clay shaft survived.

The main element in a shaft furnace was a cylindrical chimney made of fired clay. Combustible material (wood) was placed in the base of the shaft. Oak charcoal and iron ore filled the remainder of the shaft at a ratio of 2:1. Once the fuel wood was set alight, a bellows was inserted into the shaft—via a clay nozzle called a *tuyère*—to blow air into the mix and thus maintain a supply of oxygen (Illus. 8.6). The aim was to bring the mass of charcoal and ore to a temperature of at least 1,000°C and to maintain it there while the ore resolved into molten metal (the bloom) and metallurgical waste (slag). A hole or arch at the base of the shaft allowed slag to be removed from the furnace at intervals during the smelt. The arch was otherwise kept sealed, perhaps with sods of earth. Eventually, the bloom could also be removed through the arch. This was a spongy mass of iron particles that was capable, with further

Illus. 8.6 (left) Grange 2: artist's impression of the shaft furnace being worked. One man blows air into the shaft with a leather bellows (right) while a smith beats a bloom of newly smelted iron into shape on his anvil *(Dan Tietzsch-Tyler)*.

Illus. 8.7 (right, inset) Grange 2: ceramic furnace shaft, conserved and reconstructed. Waste slag and the smelted iron ore 'bloom' were removed via the opening at the base, where a slag 'cake' is still in place in this example *(IAC Ltd)*.

Illus. 8.8 (right, main) Grange 2: a replica of the shaft furnace was successfully built and operated by Brendan O'Neill and Črtomir Lorenčič (pictured) at the Centre for Experimental Archaeology and Material Culture (CEMAC) at University College Dublin *(Aidan O'Sullivan)*.

25 mm

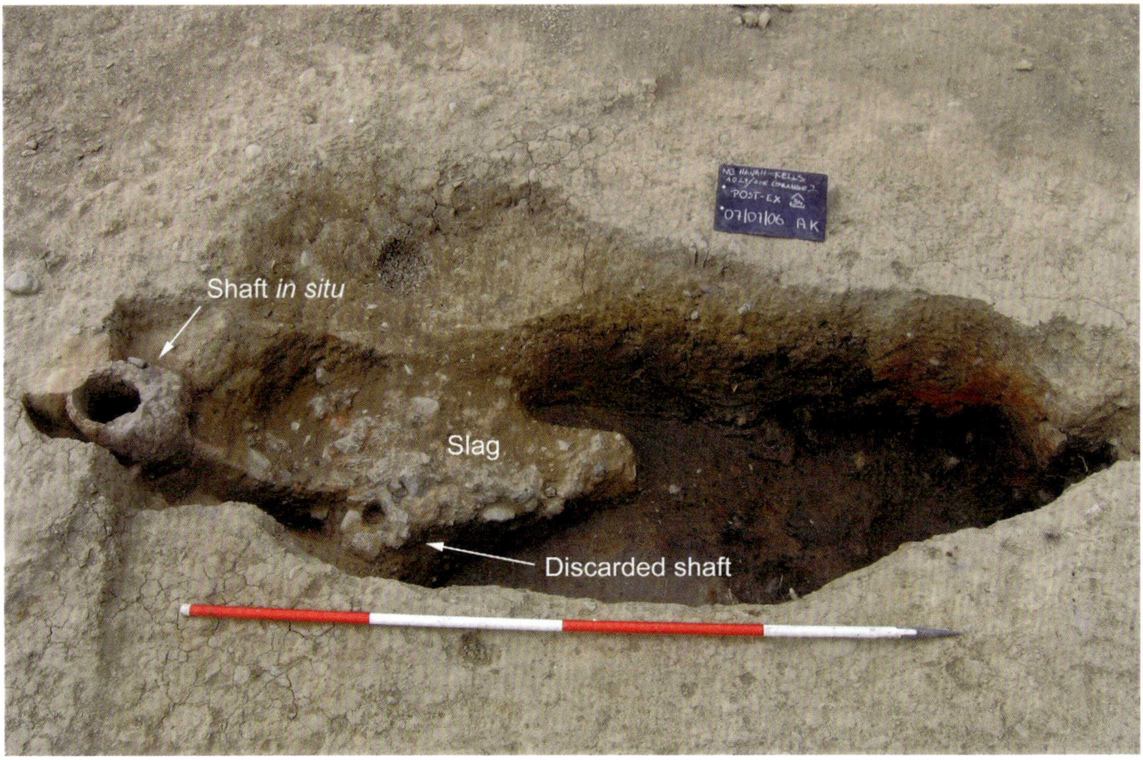

Illus. 8.9 Grange 2: the shaft furnace during excavation, looking north-west (scale rod 2 m). The ceramic shaft is set within the edge of the pit (left), with an issue of slag adjacent to it in the pit as well as a fragment of a discarded shaft. The base of the pit is stepped down to allow waste slag to be raked out and set aside more easily (*IAC Ltd*).

work, of being converted into smithing iron.

In our furnace at Grange 2 the surviving part of the shaft was a cylinder of clay, broader at the base and tapering gradually towards the top (Illus. 8.7 and 8.8). It was found *in situ* set into one end (south-west) of a large pit (c. 3.4 m long, 1 m wide and 0.8 m deep) (Illus. 8.9 and 8.10). There was no blow-hole for a *tuyère* in the surviving part of the shaft, presumably because the bellows would have been inserted into the upper or overground part of the shaft, which did not survive (probably truncated in some later episode of land use on the site). The base of the pit was stepped so that the shaft was in an elevated position relative to the pit bottom. This would have allowed waste products to be raked away from the shaft more easily. The base of the pit and the soils surrounding the edge of the shaft were hard and reddened by prolonged exposure to the intense heat of the shaft furnace and its waste products. A large deposit of solidified black slag was found *in situ* at the base of the shaft. Analysis of this material (Wallace & Anguilano 2011) identified a flow pattern emanating from the base of the shaft. Analysis also confirmed that the furnace was operated at a temperature of c. 1,100°C, which is typical of bloomery smelting.

A shaft furnace is a more elaborate structure than a pit furnace and is evidence of a permanent smithy on this site. There is

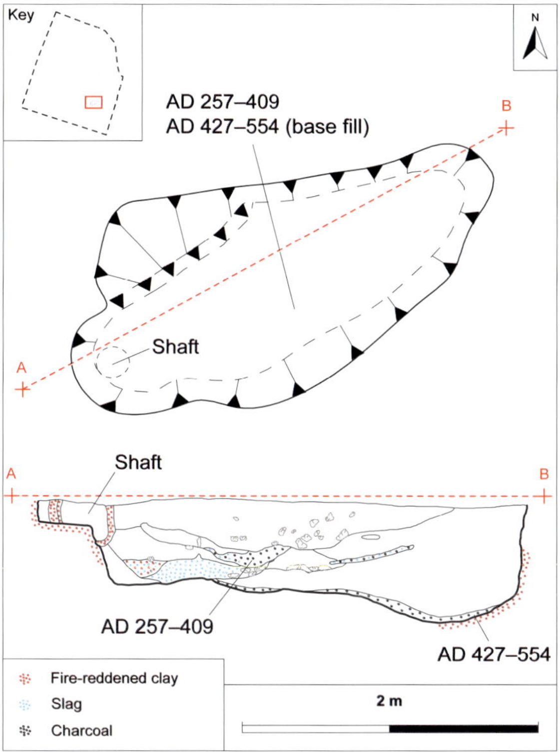

Illus. 8.10 Grange 2: plan and section drawing of the shaft furnace (*IAC Ltd*).

evidence that this particular furnace was used repeatedly. Part of a second shaft was found in the base of the pit. This was a discard from an earlier smelting cycle using the same pit.

A quantity of cereal grains was recovered from the basal fills of the pit, predominantly barley (> 60 grains) with a smaller amount of oats. Possibly the pit was originally used as a cereal-drying kiln and afterwards adapted for use as a smelting furnace. One of the barley grains was dated to AD 427–554 (UBA-12079). This is broadly contemporary with a nearby group of inhumation burials that were also found at Grange 2 (below) and with a cereal-drying kiln found at the neighbouring Grange 3 site (above), but a second and much earlier radiocarbon date of AD 257–409 (UBA-12077) was obtained from oak charcoal found at a stratigraphically higher level within the pit fills. This is puzzling. It is unlikely to be a result of the 'old wood effect' (i.e. sampled from the heartwood of an ancient oak tree) because the charcoal was identified as coming from coppiced oak (O'Donnell 2011). We therefore have to assume that the sampled charcoal was a residual inclusion, from some earlier episode on the same site, accidentally incorporated in the furnace pit fills.

We know of only one parallel for the Grange 2 shaft furnace in the Irish archaeological record. A similar furnace was excavated at Derrinsallagh, Co. Laois (Lennon 2006; Young 2008). This had a low, bottle-shaped shaft and a rake-out pit. The end-product was retrieved from the base rather than the top of the shaft, as at Grange 2 (Tim Young, pers. comm.). In Britain, broadly similar furnaces are known from Iron Age sites in north Wales (Crew 1991), while 'sunken shaft' furnaces are recorded on sites in England at Wakerley (Jackson et al. 1978) and perhaps Priors Hall, Corby, Northamptonshire (Hall 2006).

Grange 2 charcoal-rich pits

There are some other 'isolated' features of this period scattered throughout the road project site but, unlike the scattered pits of the earlier prehistoric periods, these Iron Age examples were much less numerous and did not attest to a high density of population or intensive land use.

Among a group of seven charcoal-rich pits at Grange 2, one was dated to 369–202 BC (UBA-12078) and another to 46 BC–AD 56 (UBA-12075). This latter pit contained a plain blue glass bead (Illus. 8.18, below). They may have been roasting-pits or hearths

Illus. 8.11 Cakestown Glebe 2: the barrow monument is at the south-western (top) end of the excavation site, on a ridge overlooking the River Blackwater (*Studio Lab*).

representing transient occupation, or were perhaps associated with the metalworkers at Grange 3.

Burial rites: from pagan to Christian

Burial monuments changed throughout Irish prehistory, from megalithic tombs in the Neolithic period to ring-ditches, barrows and cremation pits in the Bronze Age. In the Iron Age, ring-ditches, barrows and cremation burials are still strongly represented in the archaeological record and persist in smaller numbers into the early medieval period. But the Iron Age/early medieval transition also saw a major change, with the appearance of the first extended inhumation burials in grave-pits.

Burying an uncremated body in an oblong pit, in a burial-ground where multiple grave-pits are arranged in rows, is another behaviour acquired from the late Roman world. It was part of a cultural package that included literacy and Christianity. In all periods, burials are a focus for ritual behaviour and, by extension, an expression of religious beliefs. Ultimately, by the later medieval period, extended inhumation cemeteries became identical with churchyards, but the first inhumation burials in Ireland pre-dated the widespread adoption of Christianity and it is a moot point whether the people whose remains we find buried in them were among the last pagans or the first Christians.

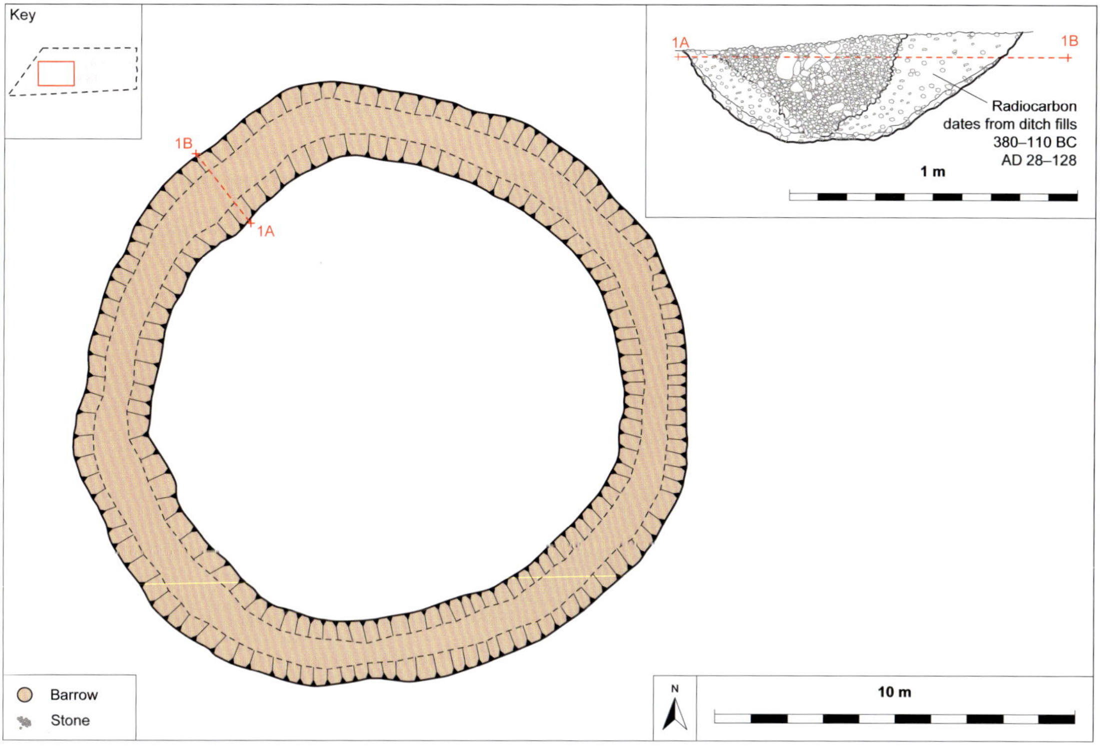

Illus. 8.12 Cakestown Glebe 2: plan and section drawing of the barrow monument. There was no break or causeway in the ditch to indicate an entrance. There was probably an internal mound or external bank originally (*IAC Ltd*).

Ring-ditch and barrow monument

Cakestown Glebe 2 barrow

The earliest funerary monument of the Iron Age discovered on our road project was a barrow at Cakestown Glebe 2. It stood on a gravel ridge overlooking the River Blackwater (Illus. 8.11)—a location probably chosen for its impressive landscape setting.

The monument itself was quite large, with an internal diameter of 12.5 m within a ditch with an average width of 2 m and depth of 1 m (Illus. 8.12 and 8.13). (The much earlier Bronze Age barrow at Grange 3 had similar dimensions.) There was no evidence, in the form of a break in the ditch or a causeway, for a formal entrance to the interior; a temporary bridge of wooden planks may have sufficed.

A small quantity of burnt bone was present. The fragments that could be identified were not human but rather the remains of sheep or pig. In spite of this we still interpret the barrow as a burial monument or, at least, a focus for funerary ceremonies. The animal bone—which was also present at Grange 3—is perhaps again evidence that the ceremonies included feasting or sacrifice, or both. Ring-ditches and barrows are very common in the Sites and Monuments Record for County Meath and 18 examples were discovered along the M3 Clonee to Kells motorway project. The closest contemporary parallel for the Cakestown Glebe 2 barrow was recorded on another sector of the M3, at Castlefarm 1, near Dunboyne (O'Connell & Clarke 2009).

Illus. 8.13 Cakestown Glebe 2: elevated view of the barrow monument, looking south-west (*Hawkeye*).

This Early–Middle Iron Age monument also produced burnt bone and, again, the only identifiable fragments were animal bones (dog and indeterminate animal).

Charcoal samples from the ditch fills at Cakestown Glebe 2 were dated to 380–110 BC (SUERC-29337) (hazel) and AD 28–128 (UBA-12069) (*Prunus* sp.). The dates are ambiguous: either one of them is a rogue date from intrusive or residual charcoal or they genuinely represent repeated uses of the same monument after many generations.

Commons of Lloyd 1 ring-ditch

A curvilinear ditch was found lying partly within the road project site at Commons of Lloyd 1 (Illus. 8.14) and is also interpreted as the remains of a ring-ditch funerary monument. This was located on a slight rise, on a site overlooked by the hillfort of Commons of Lloyd, 600 m away to the WSW. About one third of the ring-ditch was exposed and excavated. The ditch was up to 0.63 m deep and 0.85 m wide on average. The projected overall diameter of the monument is c. 20 m. Burnt bone and charcoal were recovered from the ditch fills but, again, none of the bone fragments could be positively identified as human.

Again, the dating evidence from this monument is ambiguous. A fragment of the burnt bone from the ditch fills was dated to 384–207 BC (UBA-12938), but a barley grain from the base of the ditch returned a date of AD 593–655 (UBA-12112). This later date cannot simply be dismissed as coming from intrusive sample material, as there was also an antler spindle-whorl—a typical early medieval artefact type—in the base of the ditch. So, just as at Cakestown Glebe 2 (above), there is tentative evidence at this site for repeated use of a late prehistoric monument, after many generations, in the early medieval period.

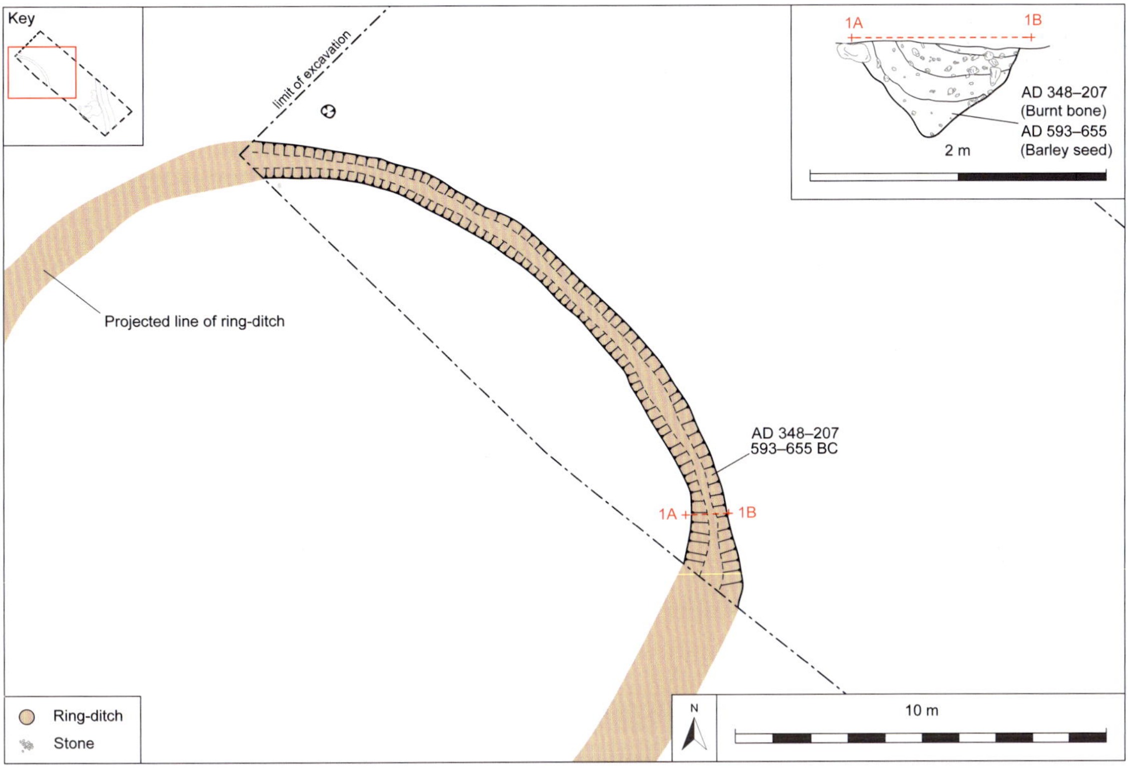

Illus. 8.14 Commons of Lloyd 1: plan and section of a ring-ditch that extended beyond the limit of the road project site. About a third of the monument was excavated (*IAC Ltd*).

Kilmainham 1C sanctuary and burials

The essential characteristic of a barrow, or a ring-ditch, is that it enclosed a defined space that was separated from the mundane world of the living. Ditched, circular ceremonial enclosures probably derived from such funerary monuments or, at any rate, were typologically related to them. A good example of this was discovered on another national road scheme in County Meath, at Cookstown, near Ashbourne, where a central area was enclosed by a pair of concentric ditches with an overall diameter of c. 14 m (Clutterbuck 2012). Such 'sacred spaces' could also take rectangular form and this is our interpretation of a rectangular ditched area recorded at Kilmainham 1C.

Kilmainham 1C sanctuary enclosure

The ceremonial enclosure at Kilmainham (Structure 8) was defined by a narrow trench or ditch forming three sides of a rectangular area measuring 16.2 m SE–NW by 14.1 m SW–NE (Illus 8.15 and Illus 8.16). The fourth or south-western side was open—i.e. there was no ditch on that side. Stony fills throughout the trench are interpreted as packing material for upright posts or planks and this is corroborated by several post-pipes (i.e. humic remnants of decayed posts) that were found within the southern part of the trench. These were not evidently structural members and, in any case, the area enclosed is simply too big to have been roofed, so the upright timbers erected in the trench were more likely to have formed a screen or palisade. There

Illus. 8.15: Kilmainham 1C: Late Iron Age/early medieval ceremonial enclosure or 'sanctuary'. There were two burials in shallow grave-pits less than 10 m beyond the enclosure on the open west side (*Hawkeye*).

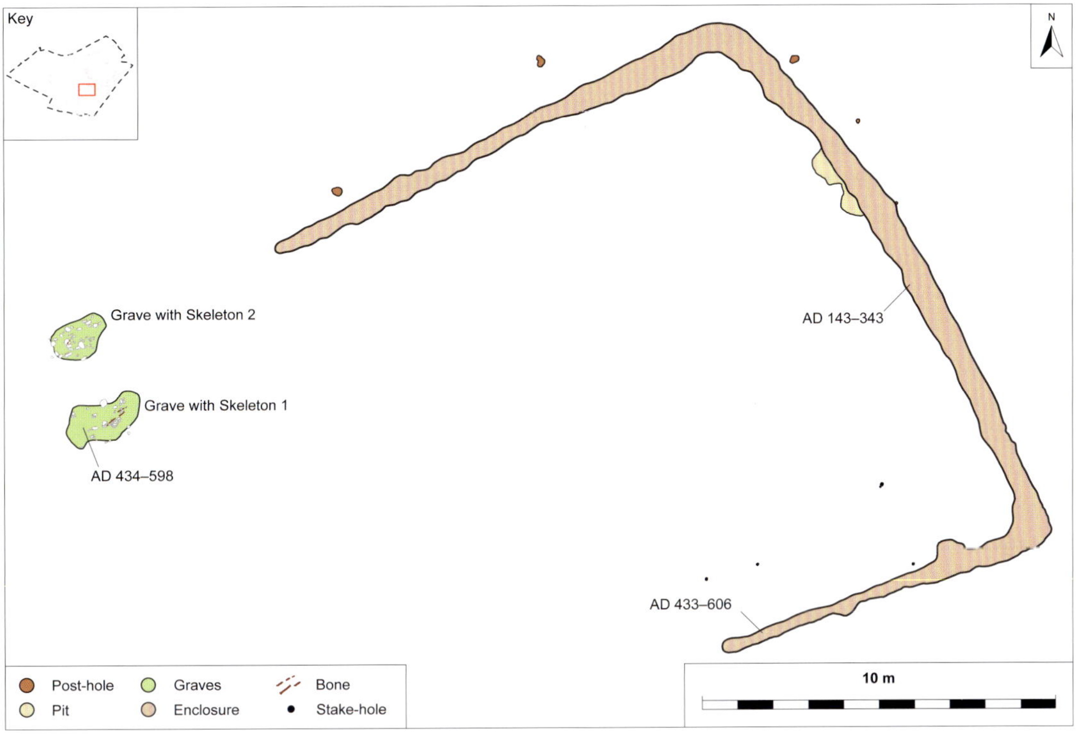

Illus. 8.16: Kilmainham 1C: plan of the sanctuary and associated burials, in two grave-pits west of the open side of the sanctuary enclosure (*IAC Ltd*).

were charcoal-rich fills in the upper part of the trench, with inclusions of burnt animal bone, a circular stone spindle-whorl (Illus. 8.17) and an ammonite (a spiral-shaped marine fossil) that was possibly used as a bead. The animal bone (148 fragments) was mostly unidentifiable but definitely included cattle and possibly sheep/goat or pig. None of the fills contained cereal grain and so the enclosure is very unlikely to have been used for crop-processing, though there was a group of Late Iron Age/early medieval cereal-drying kilns recorded on the same site (above).

Burnt animal bone (unidentified) from a primary fill of the trench was dated to AD 143–343 (UBA-15488). A charcoal sample (birch) from one of the upper fills was dated to AD 433–606 (UBA-12908). The later date is similar to a date from one of two inhumation burials (below) found near the open side of the trenched enclosure, less than 10 m west of it. One of the burials contained a bead made on an ammonite fossil, similar to the one from the trench fill.

Considering the orientation of the trenched enclosure, the proximity of contemporary graves to the west of it on the 'open' side and the presence of burnt animal bone in the upper fills, we must consider the possibility that the trench and its wooden palisade defined a sacred ceremonial space of the sort known elsewhere in northern Europe as a 'sanctuary'.

This type of monument is very rare in Ireland but is well known, though not very common, in southern Britain, northern

France and Germany. In a more evolved or, at least, more elaborate form of the monument type there is a little building inside the enclosure, interpreted as a 'shrine'. In lowland Britain there are over 30 recorded examples of small rectangular structures, with east-facing entrances, interpreted as Late Iron Age shrines, and many of them were enclosed by ditched or palisaded rectangular enclosures, forming sanctuaries (Woodward 1992; Historic England 2018). Worshippers would not have been admitted to the shrine but the sanctuary provided a space in which sacred objects taken from the shrine could be exposed for veneration (Cunliffe 1997, 202–5). Ritual deposition of weapons, coins and other objects is recorded at some such sites, and evidence for animal sacrifice and feasting has also been noted (Fitzpatrick 2009, 393).

There was no evidence of a shrine within the enclosure at Kilmainham, though a light portable structure would have left no archaeological footprint, if it existed. The evidence for animal sacrifice and feasting is inconclusive at best, as the quantity of burnt bone recovered (148 fragments) was small. A spindle-whorl and ammonite from the trench fills hardly amount to evidence of ritual deposition. And the open side faced west, not east. Nonetheless, the unusual rectangular form of this enclosure, its date and its association with adjacent burials signal that it is related to a diverse group of rectangular sanctuary enclosures of this period.

Among the few known Irish examples, the nearest candidate for a similar monument is a square building or enclosure (12 m by 12 m) formed by closely set posts that was recorded on the same site as a much larger timber circle at Lismullin, Co. Meath (O'Connell 2013, 57–60). Also in the region, at Collierstown 1, Co. Meath, two L-shaped foundation ditches appeared to represent a small, square building or enclosure (6 m by 6 m) beside an early medieval cemetery. Among the finds from this structure were sherds of imported pottery of the sort (Bii ware) used to import olive oil and wine from the eastern Mediterranean between the fourth and seventh centuries AD (O'Hara 2009).

'Caesar's Camp' at Heathrow in Middlesex is the classic English site (Historic England 2018, 3, fig. 2) where the foundation trench for a small rectangular structure (the shrine) was surrounded by a rectangular wooden palisade. Other examples include Capel Eithin on Anglesey in Wales (White & Smith 1999; Williams 2006, 15); Gallows Hill at Thetford (Fison Way) in Norfolk (Gregory 1992); Uley in Gloucestershire (Woodward & Leach 1993); and—on the European mainland—Écury-le-Repos in the Marne region (Roualet et al. 1982) and Gournay-

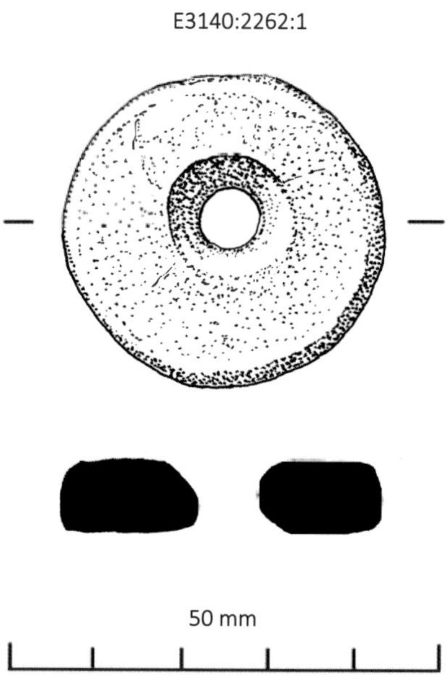

Illus. 8.17 Kilmainham 1C: stone spindle-whorl from the sanctuary enclosure trench (*Alva MacGowan for IAC Ltd*).

sur-Aronde in Oise (Brunaux 1987, 13–16), both in northern France. Some sites with simple beginnings evolved into much larger enclosures with multiple shrine buildings, like Gallows Hill, or were rededicated as Romanised temple sites, like Uley and Gournay-sur-Aronde, but the fundamental template of a sacred space defined by a rectangular enclosure remained a common thread throughout this evolution and it is this fundamental feature of the type that we find at Kilmainham 1C.

Kilmainham 1C inhumation burials

Two inhumation burials were found at Kilmainham 1C immediately west of the sanctuary enclosure (Illus. 8.16). They were in shallow grave-pits, close to each other, and less than 10 m from the rectangular ceremonial enclosure described above. The skeletal remains were very poorly preserved and extremely fragmented, with only tiny elements of each individual surviving. It was clear, however, that they represented extended, oriented (head to the west), supine inhumations in unlined graves—a burial form adopted from the late Roman world and which had become common in Ireland by the fourth century AD. The burials were located on the highest point of a broad, low gravel ridge and were partly truncated by tillage, so it may be that there were once other burials here which were entirely truncated, leaving no visible traces.

Skeleton 1 survived as poorly preserved remains of the right and left legs, left foot and a small number of pelvic fragments of an individual of unknown age or sex. A bone sample from Skeleton 1 was dated to AD 434–598 (UBA-12933). Skeleton 2 was also very poorly preserved and survived as a small number of skull and vertebral fragments. None of the bone from Skeleton 2 was suitable for dating but it is likely to have been contemporary with Skeleton 1. A single ammonite bead (Illus. 8.18), probably from a pendant or some such personal adornment, was found with Skeleton 2.

We do not know who was buried at Kilmainham 1C or their relationship to the adjacent ceremonial enclosure or sanctuary, other than the likelihood that they were contemporary with it. Perhaps the bodies of the deceased were exposed for a time in the enclosure, awaiting funeral rites and burial. Alternatively, the deceased may have been the priests or holy men who were guardians of the sanctuary and were privileged by being buried close to it.

Grange 2 cemetery

There was another group of Late Iron Age/ early medieval burials at Grange 2. Here, eight shallow graves were arranged roughly in two rows and, again, the burials were extended, oriented, supine inhumations (Illus. 8.19 and 8.20). One of the smallest graves (Skeleton 4) was neatly lined with limestone slabs. There was a partial rough lining in two other graves. Large stones placed near the heads in two graves (Skeletons 2 and 3) may have been grave-markers, though it is not clear that they would have been visible above ground in antiquity.

The skeletal remains were very poorly preserved. In two graves more than 50% of the bones survived. In five other graves there were only bone fragments or tooth enamel stains. There was no surviving bone in one grave. This limited the potential for osteological analysis (Coughlan 2011). Nonetheless, it is possible to say that the burials were all of adults or older juveniles, and probably included at least one female and

Illus. 8.18 Iron Age/early medieval beads. Clockwise from left: Phoenixtown 3 (E3130:1:62), polychrome bead from topsoil; Kilmainham 1C (E3140:3064:1), ammonite bead from a grave; Grange 2 (E3124:24:1), blue glass bead from a charcoal-rich pit group; Nugentstown 1 (E3136:1:10), yellow glass bead from topsoil (*IAC Ltd*).

one male. Fragments of a child's leg bones were found in the grave of the adult female (Skeleton 1) and may represent a double burial, or simply the disturbed residual remains of an earlier burial.

Samples of bone from two graves were dated to AD 431–571 (UBA-13957) and AD 424–568 (UBA-13958). Charred hazelnut shell from a third grave was dated to AD 432–591 (UBA-12076).

This little cemetery at Grange 2 was located within 30 m of an impressive Bronze Age barrow at neighbouring Grange 3. The choice of site is unlikely to have been a coincidence. In early medieval Irish literature the term sometimes used for an ancestral or kin-group burial-ground is *ferta*. In the archaeological record such burial-grounds are often found occupying the same sites as much older, prehistoric burial monuments, including ring-ditches and barrows. This has been interpreted as a declaration of patrimony—real or borrowed—to legitimise a claim to territory by those early medieval kin groups who buried their dead in such places (O'Brien & Bhreathnach 2011). The practice persisted until the Church finally established control over burials and burial-grounds in Ireland c. AD 800. Prehistory did not end abruptly with the first Christian missions to Ireland, by Palladius and Patrick, in the fifth century, but lingered for many generations among communities with 'histories' deeply rooted in the ancient funerary and ceremonial monuments among which they lived.

Illus. 8.19 (right, upper) Grange 2: plan of the Late Iron Age/early medieval cemetery. There were eight shallow grave-pits containing extended, oriented, supine burials of male and female adults, but with some disarticulated leg bones of a child accompanying one adult female skeleton (SK1) (*IAC Ltd*).

Illus. 8.20 (right, lower) Grange 2: the graves containing Skeletons 2 and 3 (right) (*IAC Ltd*).

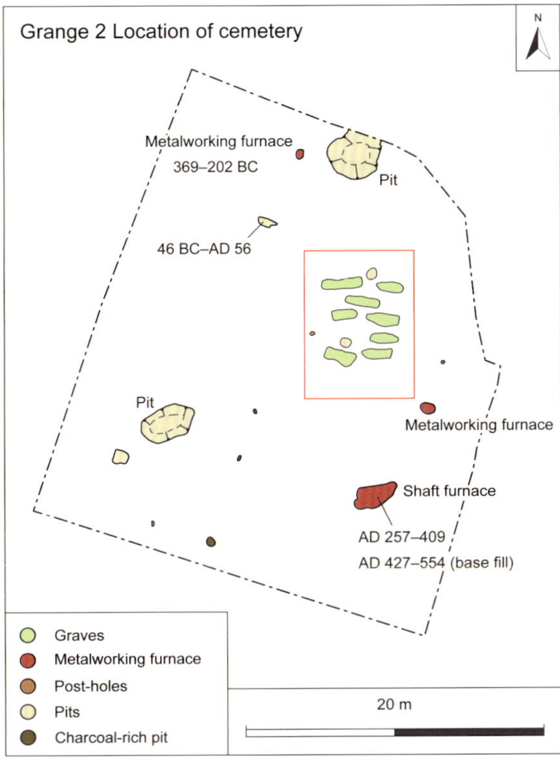
Grange 2 Location of cemetery
N
Metalworking furnace
369–202 BC
Pit
46 BC–AD 56
Pit
Metalworking furnace
Shaft furnace
AD 257–409
AD 427–554 (base fill)
Graves
Metalworking furnace
Post-holes
Pits
Charcoal-rich pit
20 m

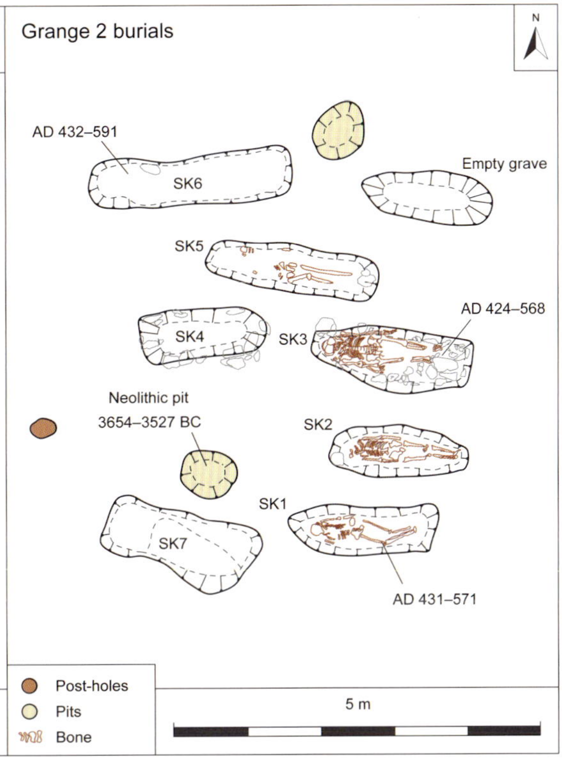
Grange 2 burials
N
AD 432–591
SK6
Empty grave
SK5
SK4
SK3
AD 424–568
Neolithic pit
3654–3527 BC
SK2
SK1
SK7
AD 431–571
Post-holes
Pits
Bone
5 m

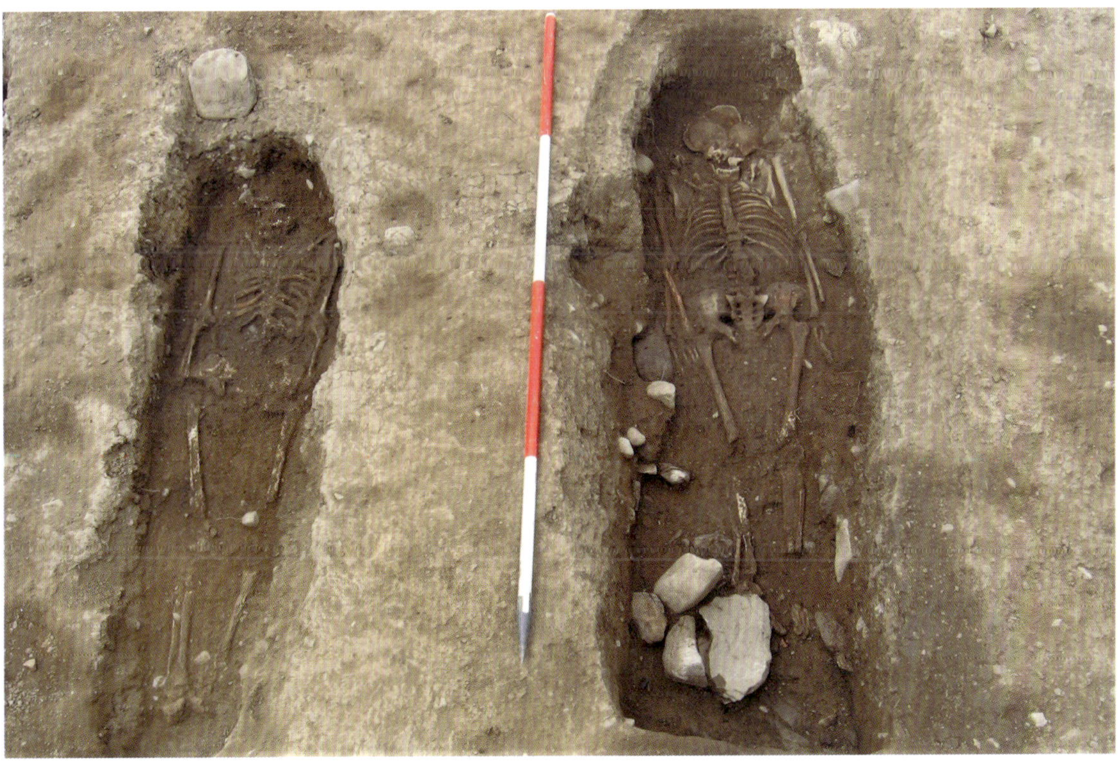

CHAPTER 9

A palimpsest of prehistory

Fintan Walsh and Jerry O'Sullivan

A palimpsest of prehistory

Kells is known worldwide for its eighth-century illuminated gospel-book, the Book of Kells. Early Irish manuscripts were written on vellum made from finest calfskin. This material was too valuable to be casually discarded. It was sometimes recycled by scraping off the text and overwriting it with a new one. A manuscript made in this way, with visible traces of an original text showing through, is called a 'palimpsest'. The word derives, through Latin, from the Greek words *palin* (again) and *psēstos* (rubbed smooth).

The monastic history of Kells is an important chapter in the story of the town and its hinterland, but it is only one chapter in a story that extends over several thousand years. All human landscapes are palimpsests where favourable locations are 'scraped clean' and reoccupied multiple times. The marks on the landscape of earlier occupations—pits, post-holes, hearths and ditches—are never entirely erased, however, and with patient care they can be exposed, understood and transcribed into the archaeological record. What we have tried to do in this book is to decipher a palimpsest of prehistory in the landscape around Kells and make each period 'legible' again to the extent that the evidence will allow.

The first people we met in this story were Mesolithic hunter-gatherers, in Cakestown Glebe, who gathered around a campfire on a gravel ridge by the River Blackwater over 6,000 years ago. This would have been a small, mobile group, moving from place to place on a seasonal basis, carrying only their tools and hunting weapons, bedding and baskets of food. The first farmers, of the Early Neolithic period, were immigrants who arrived here in the early fourth millennium BC, bringing new ideas, new technologies and a radically different way of life. We found extensive evidence of their settlements in the landscape around Kells, representing a community that lived in dispersed farmsteads centred around big, permanent, rectangular houses—with examples in Cookstown Great, Gardenrath, Kilmainham and Townparks. We do not know why the 'big houses' of the Early Neolithic disappeared after c. 3600 BC. There was a decline in population but not, evidently, a wholesale collapse, as elsewhere in County Meath, in the Middle Neolithic period, the passage tombs of Lough Crew and Brú na Bóinne attest to an organised and complex society. Perhaps the population was now locally concentrated, in smaller territories focused on highly visible monuments. In any case, by the Late Neolithic period, from c. 2900 BC, there is once again evidence for an established community in the lowlands of the Blackwater catchment. We found few traces of Late Neolithic domestic occupation on the road project, but the timber circle monument in Kilmainham gives us a vivid glimpse of a community with shared beliefs and the place where they assembled for public religious ceremonies.

The centuries that followed, in the Chalcolithic period, c. 2450–2200 BC, saw the advent of metallurgy and a distinctive material culture associated with Beaker pottery forms. Whether these changes in the archaeological record represent another influx of new migrants is currently a moot point. In any case, there was certainly a steady rise in population throughout the Early and Middle Bronze Age, extensive woodland clearance for farming and, by c. 1500 BC, a new horizon of prosperous farmsteads centred on big houses—this time round-houses with a distinctive post-ring construction style, as seen in Grange, Kilmainham and Phoenixtown. By the Late Bronze Age, however, the domestic buildings found on our road project were smaller and the structural evidence less coherent. Once again the population of the island began to decline. Society became more hierarchical and probably more warlike. Hillforts on the Commons of Lloyd and Faughan Hill were probably built towards the end of this period, c. 800 BC, as power was centralised in tribal chiefdoms and maintained by a warrior élite.

The Iron Age saw continuing population decline in Ireland, indicated by a paucity of settlement sites in the archaeological record and, especially in the Late Iron Age, by evidence for widespread woodland regeneration in the fossil pollen record. On our road project we found little evidence of a settled agricultural landscape around Kells at this time. The tide of life returned in full flow, however, in the Late Iron Age/early medieval transition period, c. AD 400–500. We recorded abundant evidence from this period—in the form of metalworking and crop-processing—for an organised and productive landscape. Cereal-drying kilns in Gardenrath, Grange and Kilmainham represent a crop surplus being processed on a large scale. This may have been to supply a focal settlement at Kells, perhaps a royal estate of the Uí Néill that would be gifted to the Church in the mid-sixth century and rededicated, in the ninth century, as a Columban monastery for monks from Iona.

The transition from paganism to Christianity, and from prehistory to early historic times, is heralded especially at one site in Kilmainham, where an enclosure interpreted as a Late Iron Age 'sanctuary' was associated with two grave-pits for extended inhumation burials. There were grave-pits at Grange too, arranged in rows. We do not know what sort of pre-Christian rites would have been performed in the sanctuary or whether those buried in the nearby grave-pits were Christians or pagans. But we can say that burying uncremated bodies in orderly rows of grave-pits is a practice adopted in Ireland from the late Roman world and that, ultimately, it would become synonymous with Christian burials in the consecrated ground surrounding churches. This is also a good reminder that incoming fashions, beliefs and technologies were not always delivered by mass migrations of peoples to Ireland. The Romans did not invade and govern Ireland. Their influence was transmitted instead by traders, raiders, missionaries and other travellers on the Irish Sea, including Irish colonists in western Britain in the fourth to sixth centuries.

Some things are constant throughout the millennia. The powerful human need for a place to call home is one of them. It is expressed in the archaeology of our road project by buildings and funerary monuments. We saw that people made offerings of buried artefacts in their houses in the Early Neolithic period and again in the

Middle Bronze Age. This is a practice still seen today in Ireland, where special or meaningful objects are placed within the foundations of new houses. In the Chalcolithic and Bronze Age periods the simple act of placing pottery in a pit may have signified an attachment or claim to a place, while later, in the Iron Age/early medieval transition period, human bodies were placed near already ancient monuments to legitimise occupation of the land by the people who buried them. These behaviours are ingrained in the human psyche—or, at least, we find them repeated throughout prehistory and early history, regardless of changes in technology and social organisation.

The M3 Navan to Kells and N52 Kells Bypass project provided the opportunity to sample a large tract of the landscape around Kells. The results demonstrate without any doubt that the area is rich in archaeological remains of all periods. The River Blackwater is integral to this landscape. In mundane terms it was a constant source of fresh food and water. In some periods it would also have had symbolic and spiritual importance, not

Illus. 9.1 River Blackwater near Teltown, Co. Meath (*Faith Bailey for IAC Ltd*).

least as a ceremonial routeway connecting people to major public monuments in the landscape, like the Neolithic timber circle complex in Kilmainham or, in a later period, the royal and ceremonial earthworks of Teltown, further downstream on the opposite bank. The Blackwater joins the Boyne at Navan and their combined waters reach the coast at Drogheda. In all periods of prehistory these rivers offered routeways from the interior to the Irish Sea coast and, conversely, from the coast into the heart of Meath; in this sense, they are themselves a kind of living monument.

Appendix 1 Radiocarbon dates

This table records the radiocarbon dates from the excavated archaeological sites on the Navan to Kells and N52 Kells Bypass section of the M3 Clonee to North of Kells national road scheme. The dates are listed in order of the lab codes (Beta = Beta Analytic, Florida; SUERC = Scottish Universities Environmental Research Centre at the University of Glagow; UBA = ^{14}CHRONO Centre at Queen's University Belfast). All dates are derived using the accelerator mass spectrometry (AMS) method. Radiocarbon ages are quoted in conventional years BP (before present = AD 1950). The δ^{13}C ‰ value is a measurement of the Carbon 13 isotope and can help to identify an anomalous result. Calibrated date ranges are in calendrical years expressed at one-sigma and two-sigma levels of confidence (1σ = 68% probability; 2σ = 95% probability). Calibrations were calculated for Beta dates using OxCal 4.2 (Bronk Ramsey 2020) in conjunction with Reimer et al. 2020. Calibrations were calculated for UBA dates using the CALIB programme (Revs 5.0.2 and 6.0.0) (Stuiver et al. 2005 and 2010) in conjunction with Stuiver & Reimer 1993. Calibrations for SUERC dates were calculated using the OxCal v.3.10 programme (Bronk Ramsey 2005) in conjunction with Reimer et al. 2004 and 2009. All dates quoted in the text are calibrated (calendrical) dates at two-sigma confidence level.

Lab code	Site	Sample and context	Yrs BP	δ^{13}C‰	Calibrated dates
Beta-235626	Kilmainham 1C	Peat deposit in pond (top)	3500 ± 40	-28.8	1890–1750 BC (1σ) 1930–1695 BC (2σ)
Beta-280826	Kilmainham 1C	Peat deposit in pond	3200 ± 40	-26.8	1500–1440 BC (1σ) 1540–1400 BC (2σ)
Beta-280827	Kilmainham 1C	Peat deposit in pond	3170 ± 40	-27.8	1500–1420 BC (1σ) 1510–1310 BC (2σ)
Beta-235627	Kilmainham 1C	Peat deposit in pond (base)	3460 ± 40	-28.0	1880–1695 BC (1σ) 1890–1640 BC (2σ)
Beta-235618	Newrath Little	Peat deposit in wetland area	5700 ± 40	-27.3	4600–4460 BC (1σ) 4680–4450 BC (2σ)
Beta-235619	Newrath Little	Peat deposit in wetland area	8790 ± 50	-29.0	7960–7740 BC (1σ) 8180–7610 BC (2σ)
Beta-235620	Newrath Little	Peat deposit in wetland area	12830 ± 70	-10.8	13500–13250 BC (1σ) 13620–13170 BC (2σ)

Lab code	Site	Sample and context	Yrs BP	$\delta^{13}C$‰	Calibrated dates
Poz-24082	Newrath Little, infilled fenland lake	Antler sample from remains of giant Irish deer found in basal lake marl	11430 ± 70	—	11400–11270 BC (1σ) 11480–11210 BC (2σ)
SUERC-29329	Grange 3 Bronze Age ditches	Pomaceous fruit-wood (Maloideae sp.) charcoal from the fill C399 of ditch C400	2810 ± 40	-24.5	1010–910 BC (1σ) 1090–840 BC (2σ)
SUERC-29330	Grange 3 Iron Age pit furnaces	Willow (*Salix* sp.) charcoal from a fill C92 of pit furnace C114	2235 ± 40	-24.7	380–200 BC (1σ) 390–200 BC (2σ)
SUERC-29331	Grange 3 Bronze Age Structure 1	Hazel (*Corylus avellana*) charcoal from the basal fill C227 of pit C228	3155 ± 40	-27.5	1495–1400 BC (1σ) 1520–1310 BC (2σ)
SUERC-29332	Grange 3 Bronze Age Structure 2	Hazel (*Corylus avellana*) charcoal from the fill C32 of pit C85	3190 ± 40	-23.6	1500–1430 BC (1σ) 1540–1390 BC (2σ)
SUERC-29333	Grange 3 Iron Age pit furnaces	Alder (*Alnus glutinosa*) charcoal from a fill C495 of pit furnace C497	2060 ± 40	-26	160 BC–AD 1 (1σ) 190 BC–AD 30 (2σ)
SUERC-29337	Cakestown Glebe 2 Iron Age barrow	Hazel (*Corylus avellana*) charcoal from a fill C4 of barrow ditch C5	2175 ± 40	-25	360–170 BC (1σ) 380–110 BC (2σ)
SUERC-29338	Cakestown Glebe 2 Bronze Age Structure 3	Oak (*Quercus* sp.) sapwood from a fill of (C58) post-hole C59	3730 ± 40	-26.7	2200–2040 BC (1σ) 2280–2020 BC (2σ)
SUERC-29339	Cakestown Glebe 2 Bronze Age Structure 2	Hazel (*Corylus avellana*) charcoal from the fill C215 of post-hole C263	6155 ± 40	-25.9	5210–5040 BC (1σ) 5220–4990 BC (2σ)
SUERC-29340	Kilmainham 3 Neolithic timber circle (Structure 2)	Hazel (*Corylus avellana*) charcoal from the fill C175 of post-hole C174	6600 ± 40	-25.6	5610–5490 BC (1σ) 5620–5480 BC (2σ)
SUERC-29341	Kilmainham 3 Neolithic timber circle (Structure 2)	Hazel (*Corylus avellana*) charcoal from the fill C100 of post-hole C144	4150 ± 40	-27	2870–2630 BC (1σ) 2880–2580 BC (2σ)

Lab code	Site	Sample and context	Yrs BP	δ^{13}C‰	Calibrated dates
SUERC-29342	Kilmainham 1C Bronze Age Structure VII	Hazel (*Corylus avellana*) charcoal from the fill C254 of post-hole C253	3400 ± 40	-25.6	1750–1630 BC (1σ) 1880–1530 BC (2σ)
SUERC-29343	Kilmainham 1C Neolithic Structure VI	Young oak (*Quercus* sp.) charcoal from the fill C2029 of post-hole C2028	4090 ± 40	-26.8	2850–2570 BC (1σ) 2870–2490 BC (2σ)
SUERC-29347	Kilmainham 1C Neolithic Structure 5	Oak (*Quercus* sp.) sapwood charcoal from the basal fill C1195 of post-hole C1193	5175 ± 40	-26.8	4040–3955 BC (1σ) 4060–3800 BC (2σ)
SUERC-29348	Kilmainham 1C Bronze Age post	20-year-old oak (*Quercus* sp.) sapwood from timber 18 from the track/ platform in pond C3193	4945 ± 40	-27	3770–3660 BC (1σ) 3800–3640 BC (2σ)
UBA-11080	Townparks 1 Bronze Age burnt mound	Hazel (*Corylus avellana*) charcoal from the fill C12 of trough C11	3716 ± 22	-25.4	2189–2042 BC (1σ) 2197–2034 BC (2σ)
UBA-11081	Townparks 1 Bronze Age burnt mound	Maloideae charcoal from the fill C26 of trough/ waterhole C28	2788 ± 21	-27	975–905 BC (1σ) 1005–855 BC (2σ)
UBA-11083	Cookstown Great 2 Bronze Age burnt mound-type pit	Hazel (*Corylus avellana*) charcoal from a fill C16 of cooking pit/trough C15	3807 ± 24	-26	2286–2204 BC (1σ) 2337–2144 BC (2σ)
UBA-11085	Cookstown Great 2 Bronze Age burnt mound	Young oak (*Quercus* sp.) charcoal from the fill C107 of pit C106	2910 ± 26	-31.8	1188–1046 BC (1σ) 1209–1012 BC (2σ)
UBA-11087	Cookstown Great 2 Bronze Age burnt mound	Ash (*Fraxinus* sp.) charcoal from the upper fill C144 of waterhole/trough C143	2870 ± 28	-26.6	1112–1003 BC (1σ) 1186–932 BC (2σ)
UBA-11088	Cookstown Great 2 Bronze Age burnt mound	Hazel (*Corylus avellana*) charcoal from the basal fill C170 of pit C167	3247 ± 26	-26.7	1602–1459 BC (1σ) 1607–1450 BC (2σ)

Lab code	Site	Sample and context	Yrs BP	δ13C‰	Calibrated dates
UBA-11089	Cookstown Great 3 Neolithic Structure A	Hazelnut shell (*Corylus avellana*) from a fill C30 of foundation trench C26	4851 ± 30	-30.9	3692–3544 BC (1σ) 3702–3536 BC (2σ)
UBA-11090	Cookstown Great 3 Neolithic Structure A	Hazelnut shell (*Corylus avellana*) from the fill C28 of pit/hearth C27	4811 ± 28	-26.6	3644–3536 BC (1σ) 3651–3526 BC (2σ)
UBA-11092	Cookstown Great 3 Bronze Age burnt mound	Burnt bone from the fill C36 of waterhole C35	2519 ± 27	-29.2	774–562 BC (1σ) 791–541 BC (2σ)
UBA-11093	Cookstown Great 3 Bronze Age Structure C	Alder (*Alnus glutinosa*) charcoal from the fill C83 of post-hole C82	3590 ± 26	-28.8	1973–1901 BC (1σ) 2023–1886 BC (2σ)
UBA-11094	Cookstown Great 3 Bronze Age Structure C	Alder (*Alnus glutinosa*) charcoal from hearth deposit C108	3614 ± 28	-29.6	2023–1938 BC (1σ) 2109–1892 BC (2σ)
UBA-11095	Cookstown Great 3 Bronze Age Structure D	Ash (*Fraxinus* sp.) from the secondary fill C135 of pit C133	3544 ± 21	-27.0	1928–1828 BC (1σ) 1948–1776 BC (2σ)
UBA-11096	Cookstown Great 3 Bronze Age Structure D	Alder (*Alnus glutinosa*) charcoal from a fill C155 of hearth/roasting-pit C141	3521 ± 27	-25.2	1894–1775 BC (1σ) 1923–1756 BC (2σ)
UBA-11097	Cookstown Great 3 Bronze Age burnt mound	Alder (*Alnus glutinosa*) charcoal from the basal fill C211 of trough C210	3500 ± 32	-34.3	1882–1772 BC (1σ) 1912–1742 BC (2σ)
UBA-11098	Newrath Little 3 Bronze Age burnt mound	Alder (*Alnus glutinosa*) charcoal from the secondary fill C34 of trough C15	2875 ± 28	-30.0	1113–1008 BC (1σ) 1188–937 BC (2σ)
UBA-11099	Grange 5 Iron Age/early medieval cereal-drying pits	Barley (*Hordeum* sp.) grain from a fill C26 of pit C24	1578 ± 23	-24.9	AD 433–534 (1σ) AD 424–541 (2σ)

Lab code	Site	Sample and context	Yrs BP	$\delta^{13}C$‰	Calibrated dates
UBA-11100	Grange 5 Bronze Age pit	Ash (*Fraxinus* sp.) charcoal from the fill C13 of pit C27	3810 ± 21	-26.1	2286–2205 BC (1σ) 2335–2148 BC (2σ)
UBA-11101	Townparks 6 burnt mound	Oak (*Quercus* sp.) twig charcoal from the fill C15 of post-hole C14	4901 ± 27	-28.8	3695–3653 BC (1σ) 3749–3640 BC (2σ)
UBA-11102	Phoenixtown 1 Bronze Age burnt mound	Hazel (*Corylus avellana*) charcoal from the fill C57 of post-hole C116	3066 ± 25	-25.3	1389–1313 BC (1σ) 1408–1269 BC (2σ)
UBA-11103	Phoenixtown 1 Bronze Age burnt mound	Alder (*Alnus glutinosa*) charcoal from a fill C115 of pit C172	3931 ± 31	-27.7	2475–2348 BC (1σ) 2559–2300 BC (2σ)
UBA-11104	Phoenixtown 1 Bronze Age burnt mound	Ash (*Fraxinus* sp.) charcoal from the fill C100 of post-hole C101	3846 ± 27	-27.6	2400–2209 BC (1σ) 2457–2205 BC (2σ)
UBA-11105	Phoenixtown 5 Neolithic structure	Hazel (*Corylus avellana*) charcoal from the fill C44 of pit C51	4124 ± 26	-27	2857–2628 BC (1σ) 2866–2580 BC (2σ)
UBA-11106	Phoenixtown 6 Bronze Age burnt mound	Ash (*Fraxinus* sp.) charcoal from a fill C18 of possible trough C19	3379 ± 26	-28.1	1730–1634 BC (1σ) 1742–1617 BC (2σ)
UBA-11107	Phoenixtown 6 Neolithic hearth	Hazelnut shell (*Corylus avellana*) from the fill C7 of possible hearth C23	4935 ± 27	-26.6	3757–3658 BC (1σ) 3770–3654 BC (2σ)
UBA-11108	Phoenixtown 6 Bronze Age burnt mound	Ash (*Fraxinus* sp.) charcoal from the fill C21 of trough C22	3622 ± 30	-25	2025–1946 BC (1σ) 2119–1895 BC (2σ)
UBA-11110	Phoenixtown 3 Bronze Age features	Hazelnut shell (*Corylus avellana*) from the fill C137 of pit C147	3393 ± 24	-31.4	1738–1643 BC (1σ) 1745–1628 BC (2σ)

Lab code	Site	Sample and context	Yrs BP	δ13C‰	Calibrated dates
UBA-11111	Phoenixtown 3 Bronze Age Structure A	Ash (*Fraxinus* sp.) charcoal from the fill C1049 of post-hole C1073	3152 ± 24	-26.2	1449–1409 BC (1σ) 1494–1392 BC (2σ)
UBA-11112	Phoenixtown 3 Bronze Age Structure A	Ash (*Fraxinus* sp.) charcoal from the fill C1044 of pit C1104	3188 ± 26	-28.9	1493–1434 BC (1σ) 1503–1415 BC (2σ)
UBA-11113	Phoenixtown 3 Bronze Age Structure A	Alder (*Alnus glutinosa*) charcoal from the fill C1041 of post-hole C1055	3113 ± 22	-26.4	1425–1326 BC (1σ) 1436–1316 BC (2σ)
UBA-11114	Phoenixtown 3 Bronze Age Structure A	Hazelnut shell (*Corylus avellana*) from the secondary fill C1147 of pit C1146	3102 ± 29	-23.1	1419–1319 BC (1σ) 1435–1303 BC (2σ)
UBA-11123	Townparks/ Commons of Lloyd Bronze Age Burnt Mound 1	Alder (*Alnus glutinosa*) charcoal from the fill C22 of pit C25	3614 ± 28	-27.4	2023–1938 BC (1σ) 2109–1892 BC (2σ)
UBA-11124	Townparks/ Commons of Lloyd Bronze Age Burnt Mound 2	Alder (*Alnus glutinosa*) charcoal from the basal fill C60 of trough	3864 ± 25	-29.9	2453–2290 BC (1σ) 2462–2212 BC (2σ)
UBA-11125	Commons of Lloyd 1 Bronze Age burnt mound	Hazel (*Corylus avellana*) from burnt mound spread C3	2850 ± 23	-24.2	1048–946 BC (1σ) 1113–928 BC (2σ)
UBA-11126	Grange 4 early medieval pit	Barley (*Hordeum* sp.) grains from the basal fill C69 of pit C7	1291 ± 27	-25.2	AD 673–767 (1σ) AD 666–772 (2σ)
UBA-11127	Grange 4 Neolithic/Bronze Age Structure A	Hazel (*Corylus avellana*) charcoal from the fill C73 of post-hole C25	3145 ± 23	-27.9	1442–1407 BC (1σ) 1493–1326 BC (2σ)
UBA-11128	Grange 4 Neolithic/Bronze Age Structure A	Hazelnut shell (*Corylus avellana*) from the fill C71 of post-hole C70	4008 ± 25	-28.0	2568–2487 BC (1σ) 2574–2474 BC (2σ)

Lab code	Site	Sample and context	Yrs BP	δ13C‰	Calibrated dates
UBA-11129	Grange 1 Iron Age/early medieval cereal-drying kiln	Barley (*Hordeum* sp.) grain from the secondary fill C32 of cereal-drying kiln C19	1562 ± 22	-23.8	AD 436–540 (1σ) AD 428–549 (2σ)
UBA-11130	Ballybeg 1 Bronze Age burnt mound	Hazel (*Corylus avellana*) charcoal from burnt mound material C12	2910 ± 25	-26.5	1188–1047 BC (1σ) 1208–1013 BC (2σ)
UBA-11131	Ballybeg 1 Bronze Age burnt mound	Alder (*Alnus glutinosa*) charcoal from the fill C20 of stake-hole C19	3057 ± 25	-29.1	1386–1305 BC (1σ) 1403–1265 BC (2σ)
UBA-11132	Nugentstown 3 Bronze Age occupation feature	Ash (*Fraxinus* sp.) charcoal from the fill C43 of post-hole C42	3314 ± 22	-25.7	1621–1534 BC (1σ) 1664–1522 BC (2σ)
UBA-11133	Nugentstown 2 burnt mound	Alder (*Alnus glutinosa*) charcoal from the burnt mound spread material (C3) in natural depression C9	4012 ± 24	-26.7	2569–2488 BC (1σ) 2575–2475 BC (2σ)
UBA-11134	Cookstown Great 1 Bronze Age/Iron Age pit	Bedstraw (*Galium* sp.) seeds from the fill C25 of pit C27	2491 ± 24	-25.8	757–546 BC (1σ) 768–521 BC (2σ)
UBA-12042	Gardenrath 2 Neolithic Structure 1	Maloideae sp. charcoal from the upper fill C49 of foundation trench C99/C193	5004 ± 28	-25.1	3894–3713 BC (1σ) 3938–3705 BC (2σ)
UBA-12043	Gardenrath 2 Neolithic building Structure 1	Hazel (*Corylus avellana*) charcoal from the fill C203 of post-hole C221	4953 ± 27	-27.2	3768–3698 BC (1σ) 3783–3660 BC (2σ)
UBA-12044	Gardenrath 2 Bronze Age pits	Barley (*Hordeum* sp.) grain from the fill C93 of linear feature C100	3282 ± 28	-25.2	1608–1520 BC (1σ) 1628–1496 BC (2σ)
UBA-12045	Gardenrath 2 early medieval cereal-drying kiln	Barley (*Hordeum* sp.) grain from the secondary fill C178 of kiln C181	1566 ± 26	-23.3	AD 435–539 (1σ) AD 425–552 (2σ)

Lab code	Site	Sample and context	Yrs BP	δ13C‰	Calibrated dates
UBA-12046	Townparks 5 Neolithic Structure B	Young oak (*Quercus* sp.) charcoal from the primary fill C26 of possible post-hole C25	4866 ± 24	-30.9	3691–3639 BC (1σ) 3698–3637 BC (2σ)
UBA-12047	Townparks 5 Neolithic Structure A	Indeterminate cereal grain from a fill C65 of pit C67	4922 ± 32	-26.5	3710–3653 BC (1σ) 3768–3647 BC (2σ)
UBA-12048	Townparks 5 Neolithic Structure B	Hazelnut shell (*Corylus avellana*) from a fill C116 of post-hole C117	4935 ± 27	-26.3	3757–3658 BC (1σ) 3770–3654 BC (2σ)
UBA-12049	Townparks 5 Neolithic Structure A	Charred hazelnut (*Corylus avellana*) shell from a fill C13 of foundation trench C14	4891 ± 29	-26.9	3695–3648 BC (1σ) 3709–3639 BC (2σ)
UBA-12050	Townparks 5 Neolithic Structure A	Charred hazelnut (*Corylus avellana*) shell from a fill C16 of foundation trench C14	4930 ± 27	-26.5	3747–3656 BC (1σ) 3768–3652 BC (2σ)
UBA-12051	Townparks 5 Neolithic Structure A	Charred hazelnut (*Corylus avellana*) shell from the upper fill C4 of hearth C59	4860 ± 31	-22.1	3693–3637 BC (1σ) 3705–3539 BC (2σ)
UBA-12052	Grange 3 Bronze Age Structure 2	Hulled barley (*Hordeum vulgare*) from deposit C54	1518 ± 30	-22.5	AD 470–599 (1σ) AD 433–611 (2σ)
UBA-12053	Grange 3 Bronze Age barrow	A fragment of a horse tibia from a fill C505 of barrow ditch	2753 ± 26	-20.5	919–843 BC (1σ) 974–828 BC (2σ)
UBA-12054	Grange 3 Bronze Age barrow	Alder (*Alnus glutinosa*)/hazel (*Corylus avellana*) charcoal from the fill C522 of barrow ditch C534	3001 ± 22	-27.5	1301–1212 BC (1σ) 1372–1131 BC (2σ)
UBA-12055	Grange 3 early medieval ditches	Hulled barley (*Hordeum vulgare*) grain from an upper fill C646 of ditch C584	1388 ± 20	-26.9	AD 643–659 (1σ) AD 617–666 (2σ)

Lab code	Site	Sample and context	Yrs BP	$\delta^{13}C$‰	Calibrated dates
UBA-12056	Grange 3 Iron Age pit furnaces	Ash (*Fraxinus* sp.) brushwood charcoal from the middle fill C633 of pit/furnace C632	2132 ± 21	-29.7	201–114 BC (1σ) 346–60 BC (2σ)
UBA-12057	Grange 3 Iron Age pit furnaces	Alder (*Alnus glutinosa*) charcoal from a fill C600 of pit C601	2082 ± 29	-30.6	158–52 BC (1σ) 191–5 BC (2σ)
UBA-12058	Grange 3 Bronze Age Structure 2	Ash (*Fraxinus* sp.) brushwood charcoal from the upper fill C10 of pit C90	3065 ± 24	-30.5	1388–1313 BC (1σ) 1408–1269 BC (2σ)
UBA-12059	Grange 3 pit	Oak (*Quercus* sp.) charcoal from the upper fill C245 of cereal-drying kiln C491	3858 ± 24	-27.9	2451–2236 BC (1σ) 2460–2210 BC (2σ)
UBA-12060	Nugentstown 1 Bronze Age Structure 3	Alder (*Alnus glutinosa*)/hazel (*Corylus avellana*) charcoal from the fill C45c of slot-trench C196	2880 ± 22	-29.6	1112–1013 BC (1σ) 1186–978 BC (2σ)
UBA-12061	Nugentstown 1 Bronze Age features	Alder (*Alnus glutinosa*) charcoal from the fill C313 of pit C373	3301 ± 25	-29.0	1611–1532 BC (1σ) 1657–1506 BC (2σ)
UBA-12062	Nugentstown 1 Bronze Age pit	Bedstraw (*Galium* sp.) seed from the fill C77 of possible post-hole C234 adjacent to Structure 2, a circular hut?	153 ± 23	-29	AD 1673–1952 (1σ) AD 1667–1953 (2σ)
UBA-12063	Newrath Little 2 Bronze Age burnt mound	Hazel (*Corylus avellana*) charcoal from the primary fill C12 of trough C10	3576 ± 28	-28.8	1955–1888 BC (1σ) 2023–1828 BC (2σ)
UBA-12064	Newrath Little 2 Bronze Age burnt mound	Hazel (*Corylus avellana*) charcoal from the tertiary fill C16 of trough C14	3535 ± 27	-31.1	1920–1780 BC (1σ) 1944–1771 BC (2σ)

Lab code	Site	Sample and context	Yrs BP	$\delta^{13}C$‰	Calibrated dates
UBA-12065	Kilmainham 2 Iron Age kiln	Barley (*Hordeum* sp.) from the fill C38 of kiln C33	2357 ± 25	-30.6	479–390 BC (1σ) 510–387 BC (2σ)
UBA-12066	Kilmainham 2 Bronze Age Structure 1	Hazel (*Corylus avellana*) charcoal from the fill C31 of post-hole C30	2844 ± 26	-26.4	1043–941 BC (1σ) 1112–921 BC (2σ)
UBA-12067	Kilmainham 1B Iron Age/ early medieval cereal-drying kiln	Hazel (*Corylus avellana*) charcoal from the secondary fill C143 of cereal-drying kiln C144	1606 ± 26	-28.2	AD 414–532 (1σ) AD 406–537 (2σ)
UBA-12068	Nugentstown 3 Bronze Age occupation feature	Alder (*Alnus glutinosa*) charcoal from the basal fill C6 of pit C5	3517 ± 23	-27.8	1889–1776 BC (1σ) 1915–1759 BC (2σ)
UBA-12069	Cakestown Glebe 2 Iron Age barrow	*Prunus* sp. charcoal from the fill C4 of barrow ditch C5	1921 ± 21	-30.3	AD 60–122 (1σ) AD 28–128 (2σ)
UBA-12070	Cakestown Glebe 2 Mesolithic cooking area	Oak (*Quercus* sp.) charcoal from a fill C240 of hearth C333	5595 ± 32	-28.8	4456–4370 BC (1σ) 4489–4356 BC (2σ)
UBA-12071	Cakestown Glebe 2 Bronze Age Structure 1	Maloideae sp. charcoal from the fill C185 of stake-hole C234	2864 ± 24	-28.3	1111–997 BC (1σ) 1122–939 BC (2σ)
UBA-12072	Cakestown Glebe 2 Bronze Age Structure 2	Hazel (*Corylus avellana*) charcoal from the fill C40 of post-hole C108	2915 ± 29	-27.4	1191–1048 BC (1σ) 1251–1013 BC (2σ)
UBA-12073	Grange 3 early medieval cereal-drying kiln	Hulled barley (*Hordeum vulgare*) from a fill C315 of cereal-drying kiln C130	1552 ± 28	-20.5	AD 435–549 (1σ) AD 427–570 (2σ)
UBA-12074	Grange 2 Neolithic pits	Hazelnut shell (*Corylus avellana*) from the upper fill C8 of pit C29	4819 ± 27	-21	3647–3537 BC (1σ) 3654–3527 BC (2σ)
UBA-12075	Grange 2 Iron Age metal-working	Ash (*Fraxinus* sp.) charcoal from a fill C24 of pit C31	2000 ± 23	-27.6	39 BC–AD 24 (1σ) 46 BC–AD 56 (2σ)

Lab code	Site	Sample and context	Yrs BP	$\delta^{13}C$‰	Calibrated dates
UBA-12076	Grange 2 early medieval graves	Hazelnut shell (*Corylus avellana*) from the fill C38 of grave-cut C39	1537 ± 28	-26.2	AD 438–569 (1σ) AD 432–591 (2σ)
UBA-12077	Grange 2 Iron Age metal-working	Coppiced oak (*Quercus* sp.) charcoal from a fill C37 of furnace C34	1700 ± 24	-26.1	AD 263–390 (1σ) AD 257–409 (2σ)
UBA-12078	Grange 2 Iron Age/early medieval metal-working	Hazelnut shell (*Corylus avellana*) from the fills (C61, C65 and C60) of possible pit furnace C62	2210 ± 25	-25.2	358–207 BC (1σ) 369–202 BC (2σ)
UBA-12079	Grange 2 Iron Age/early medieval metal-working	Barley (*Hordeum* sp.) grain from the fill C78 of furnace C34	1561 ± 24	-18.7	AD 435–541 (1σ) AD 427–554 (2σ)
UBA-12080	Kilmainham 3 Neolithic features	Hazelnut shell (*Corylus avellana*) from the fill C13 of post-hole C18	4873 ± 27	-26	3693–3640 BC (1σ) 3702–3638 BC (2σ)
UBA-12081	Kilmainham 3 Neolithic Structure 1	Hazelnut shell (*Corylus avellana*) from the fill C63 of post-hole C64	4138 ± 27	-22.3	2862–2634 BC (1σ) 2872–2622 BC (2σ)
UBA-12082	Kilmainham 3 Neolithic Structure 1	Hazelnut shell (*Corylus avellana*) from a fill C66 of pit C65	4085 ± 30	-25.8	2835–2575 BC (1σ) 2858–2496 BC (2σ)
UBA-12083	Kilmainham 3 Bronze Age ring-ditch	Hazelnut shell (*Corylus avellana*) from the fill C27 of ring-ditch C26	3671 ± 26	-20.8	2131–1982 BC (1σ) 2137–1965 BC (2σ)
UBA-12084	Kilmainham 3 Neolithic timber circle (Structure 2)	Barley (*Hordeum* sp.) grain from the fill C165 of post-hole C164	1396 ± 24	-22	AD 634–660 (1σ) AD 608–665 (2σ)
UBA-12085	Kilmainham 3 Neolithic timber circle (Structure 2)	Hazelnut shell (*Corylus avellana*) from the primary fill C131 of post-hole C129	4740 ± 38	-23	3632–3384 BC (1σ) 3637–3377 BC (2σ)

Lab code	Site	Sample and context	Yrs BP	$\delta^{13}C$‰	Calibrated dates
UBA-12086	Kilmainham 3 Neolithic timber circle: pit in central structure	Hazelnut shell (*Corylus avellana*) from the fill C125 of pit C211	4131 ± 24	-23.9	2859–2633 BC (1σ) 2871–2586 BC (2σ)
UBA-12087	Kilmainham 3 Iron Age features	Maloideae sp. charcoal from the fill C259 of possible post-hole C258	2011 ± 21	-28	42 BC–AD 16 (1σ) 51 BC–AD 52 (2σ)
UBA-12088	Kilmainham 3 Neolithic features (possible cremation pit)	Hazelnut shell (*Corylus avellana*) from the fill C268 of pit C270	4094 ± 39	-25.7	2849–2575 BC (1σ) 2866–2495 BC (2σ)
UBA-12089	Kilmainham 3 Neolithic features (possible cremation pit)	Hazel (*Corylus avellana*) charcoal from the fill C214 of pit C228	4184 ± 25	-24.5	2878–2703 BC (1σ) 2885–2677 BC (2σ)
UBA-12090	Kilmainham 3 Neolithic features (possible cremation pit)	Hazel (*Corylus avellana*) charcoal from the fill C213 of pit C224	4131 ± 24	-26.2	2859–2633 BC (1σ) 2871–2586 BC (2σ)
UBA-12091	Kilmainham 3 Neolithic Structure 3	Hazelnut shell (*Corylus avellana*) from the fill C256 of pit/post-hole C255	6085 ± 26	-26.7	5033–4958 BC (1σ) 5197–4913 BC (2σ)
UBA-12092	Kilmainham 3 Neolithic Structure 3	Hazelnut shell (*Corylus avellana*) from the fill C252 of pit/post-hole C265	4261 ± 27	-22.8	2902–2883 BC (1σ) 2918–2779 BC (2σ)
UBA-12093	Kilmainham 3 Neolithic Structure 3	Hazelnut shell (*Corylus avellana*) from the fill C72 of pit C223	4079 ± 28	-27.1	2834–2506 BC (1σ) 2855–2496 BC (2σ)
UBA-12094	Kilmainham 3 Neolithic Structure 3	Hazelnut shell (*Corylus avellana*) from a fill C215 of pit C222	4164 ± 25	-24.9	2873–2681 BC (1σ) 2878–2637 BC (2σ)
UBA-12095	Ballybeg 3 Bronze Age burnt mound	Ash (*Fraxinus* sp.) charcoal from the basal fill C6 of trough C7	3224 ± 25	-27.8	1514–1454 BC (1σ) 1600–1431 BC (2σ)

Lab code	Site	Sample and context	Yrs BP	δ^{13}C‰	Calibrated dates
UBA-12096	Ballybeg 3 Bronze Age burnt mound	Hazel (*Corylus avellana*) charcoal from the basal fill C25 of hearth C23	3459 ± 25	-26.8	1873–1699 BC (1σ) 1879–1693 BC (2σ)
UBA-12097	Kilmainham 1A Bronze Age features	*Prunus* spp charcoal from the fill C42 of gully C43	3179 ± 24	-27.8	1493–1428 BC (1σ) 1497–1415 BC (2σ)
UBA-12098	Kilmainham 1A Bronze Age Structure 3	Alder (*Alnus glutinosa*)/birch (*Betula* sp.) charcoal from the secondary fill C38 of pit C55	4958 ± 30	-24.2	3772–3702 BC (1σ) 3791–3659 BC (2σ)
UBA-12099	Kilmainham 1A Bronze Age Structure 3	Hazel (*Corylus avellana*) charcoal from the fill C292 of post-hole C295	3111 ± 25	-26.5	1425–1324 BC (1σ) 1436–1314 BC (2σ)
UBA-12100	Kilmainham 1A Neolithic Structure 2	Hazelnut shell (*Corylus avellana*) from the fill C258 of post-hole C303	4878 ± 26	-23.2	3693–3642 BC (1σ) 3701–3639 BC (2σ)
UBA-12101	Kilmainham 1A Neolithic Structure 2	Hazel (*Corylus avellana*) charcoal from a fill C33 of house floor cut C306	3989 ± 25	-26.6	2564–2473 BC (1σ) 2571–2468 BC (2σ)
UBA-12102	Kilmainham 1A Bronze Age Structure 3	Alder (*Alnus glutinosa*) charcoal from the fill C320 of post-hole C321	3085 ± 29	-25	1410–1316 BC (1σ) 1426–1271 BC (2σ)
UBA-12103	Kilmainham 1A Bronze Age Structure 3	Alder (*Alnus glutinosa*) charcoal from the fill C332 of post-hole C333	3080 ± 29	-26.1	1406–1316 BC (1σ) 1419–1269 BC (2σ)
UBA-12104	Kilmainham 1A early medieval cereal-drying kiln	Hazelnut shell (*Corylus avellana*) from a basal fill C608 of cereal-drying kiln C606	1568 ± 27	-24	AD 435–538 (1σ) AD 423–552 (2σ)
UBA-12105	Kilmainham 1A Bronze Age Structure 2	Hazelnut shell (*Corylus avellana*) from the fill C305 of house floor cut C306	3121 ± 29	-23.6	1433–1325 BC (1σ) 1452–1313 BC (2σ)

Lab code	Site	Sample and context	Yrs BP	δ^{13}C‰	Calibrated dates
UBA-12106	Kilmainham 1A Neolithic Structure 2	Hazelnut shell (*Corylus avellana*) from the fill C424 of post-hole C667	4902 ± 31	-24.1	3697–3653 BC (1σ) 3760–3639 BC (2σ)
UBA-12107	Kilmainham 1A Bronze Age cremations	Hazelnut shell (*Corylus avellana*) from the upper fill C610 of cremation pit C668	3267 ± 29	-23.8	1606–1500 BC (1σ) 1619–1458 BC (2σ)
UBA-12108	Phoenixtown 5 Neolithic structure	Hazel (*Corylus avellana*) charcoal from the fill C13 of post-hole C40	4122 ± 31	-23.5	2857–2624 BC (1σ) 2867–2579 BC (2σ)
UBA-12109	Phoenixtown 5 Neolithic structure	Hazel (*Corylus avellana*) charcoal from the fill C9 of pit C53	4047 ± 23	-29.7	2618–2495 BC (1σ) 2831–2487 BC (2σ)
UBA-12111	Phoenixtown 3 Bronze Age waste pits	Hazel (*Corylus avellana*) charcoal from the upper fill C1001 of pit C1166	3203 ± 24	-27.7	1496–1448 BC (1σ) 1515–1428 BC (2σ)
UBA-12112	Commons of Lloyd 1 ring-ditch	Hulled barley (*Hordeum vulgare*) from the basal fill C8 of ring-ditch C5	1427 ± 22	-26.4	AD 614–646 (1σ) AD 593–655 (2σ)
UBA-12113	Cookstown Great 1 occupation site	Holly (*Ilex aquifolium*) charcoal from the fill C3 of cut/depression C13	5250 ± 26	-28.6	4220–3989 BC (1σ) 4227–3978 BC (2σ)
UBA-12114	Townparks 2 Mesolithic/ Neolithic occupation site	Young oak (*Quercus* sp.) charcoal from a fill C32 of hearth/fire pit C33	5400 ± 26	-27.1	4324–4245 BC (1σ) 4334–4179 BC (2σ)
UBA-12115	Townparks 3 Bronze Age Structure 1	Holly (*Ilex aquifolium*) charcoal from the fill C24 of post-hole/pit C42	2815 ± 22	-28	999–931 BC (1σ) 1019–906 BC (2σ)

Lab code	Site	Sample and context	Yrs BP	δ13C‰	Calibrated dates
UBA-12895	Kilmainham 1C Neolithic Structure 1	Emmer wheat (*Triticum dicoccum*) grain from the packing fill C1424 of post-hole C1418	4938 ± 25	-21.7	3758–3660 BC (1σ) 3770–3656 BC (2σ)
UBA-12896	Kilmainham 1C Neolithic Structure 1	Emmer wheat (*Triticum dicoccum*) grain from the post-pipe C1294 of post-hole C1293	4943 ± 25	-23.6	3761–3664 BC (1σ) 3773–3657 BC (2σ)
UBA-12897	Kilmainham 1C Neolithic features	Blackthorn (*Prunus* sp.) charcoal from the basal fill C1337 of hearth C1285	5164 ± 38	-25.2	4037–3952 BC (1σ) 4045–3811 BC (2σ)
UBA-12898	Kilmainham 1C Bronze Age Structure 2	Ash (*Fraxinus* sp.) charcoal from the fill C2859 of post-hole C2858	3546 ± 24	-23.8	1936–1828 BC (1σ) 1953–1774 BC (2σ)
UBA-12899	Kilmainham 1C Neolithic Structure 3	Hazel (*Corylus avellana*) charcoal from a fill C3202 of post-hole C3201	5028 ± 29	-25	3937–3773 BC (1σ) 3944–3713 BC (2σ)
UBA-12900	Kilmainham 1C Bronze Age fence Structure D	Blackthorn (*Prunus* sp.) charcoal from the fill C2132 of stake-hole C2131	3483 ± 23	-26.4	1877–1754 BC (1σ) 1882–1745 BC (2σ)
UBA-12901	Kilmainham 1C Bronze Age/ Iron Age fence Structure D	Blackthorn (*Prunus* sp.) charcoal from the fill C2136 of stake-hole C2135	2552 ± 22	-25.1	793–672 BC (1σ) 799–566 BC (2σ)
UBA-12902	Kilmainham 1C Neolithic features	Maloideae sp. charcoal from the fill C1332 of stake-hole C1331	4096 ± 23	-25.8	2835–2580 BC (1σ) 2857–2573 BC (2σ)
UBA-12903	Kilmainham 1C Neolithic Structure 1	Hazel (*Corylus avellana*) charcoal from the fill C1669 of stake-hole C1668	4927 ± 24	-25.2	3708–3660 BC (1σ) 3765–3651 BC (2σ)

Lab code	Site	Sample and context	Yrs BP	δ13C‰	Calibrated dates
UBA-12904	Kilmainham 1C Bronze Age/ Iron Age hearth	Blackthorn (*Prunus* sp.) charcoal from the upper fill C368 of hearth C367	2603 ± 22	-24	804–789 BC (1σ) 810–773 BC (2σ)
UBA-12905	Kilmainham 1C Bronze Age Structure I	Hazel (*Corylus avellana*) charcoal from the fill C1723 of post-hole C1722	3103 ± 33	-27.1	1424–1318 BC (1σ) 1443–1293 BC (2σ)
UBA-12906	Kilmainham 1C Neolithic Structure IV	Hazel (*Corylus avellana*) charcoal from the fill C2063 of post-hole C2062	4948 ± 24	-26.9	3764–3671 BC (1σ) 3776–3659 BC (2σ)
UBA-12908	Kilmainham 1C Iron Age/ early medieval Structure 8 ('sanctuary')	Birch (*Betula* sp.) charcoal from a fill C2244 of foundation trench C2218	1523 ± 30	-25.3	AD 465–596 (1σ) AD 433–606 (2σ)
UBA-12909	Kilmainham 1C Bronze Age cremations	A human femur fragment from the basal fill C1516 of cremation pit C1535	3493 ± 23	-25.6	1879–1771 BC (1σ) 1885–1749 BC (2σ)
UBA-12910	Kilmainham 1C Iron Age/early medieval pits	Barley (*Hordeum* sp.) grain from the basal fill C1800 of possible cereal-drying kiln C1598	1585 ± 20	-23.6	AD 429–533 (1σ) AD 425–537 (2σ)
UBA-12911	Kilmainham 1C Bronze Age features	Barley (*Hordeum* sp.) grain from the secondary fill C1885 of cooking pit C1878	3368 ± 27	-26.4	1690–1624 BC (1σ) 1742–1540 BC (2σ)
UBA-12912	Kilmainham 1C Bronze Age fence Structure J	Hazel (*Corylus avellana*) charcoal from the fill C1530 of stake-hole C1575	3392 ± 29	-26.6	1738–1641 BC (1σ) 1751–1616 BC (2σ)
UBA-12913	Kilmainham 1C Iron Age/early medieval pits	Ash (*Fraxinus* sp.) charcoal from the secondary fill C3003 of pit C3001	1566 ± 24	-26.4	AD 435–538 (1σ) AD 426–549 (2σ)

Lab code	Site	Sample and context	Yrs BP	δ13C‰	Calibrated dates
UBA-12914	Kilmainham 1C Bronze Age Structure 7	Hazel (*Corylus avellana*)/alder (*Alnus glutinosa*) charcoal from the post-pipe (C2990) in post-hole C2989	2857 ± 26	-29	1055–942 BC (1σ) 1119–932 BC (2σ)
UBA-12915	Kilmainham 1C Iron Age ditches	Holly (*Ilex aquifolium*) charcoal from the basal fill C41 of ditch C5	2117 ± 26	-26.9	191–107 BC (1σ) 203–51 BC (2σ)
UBA-12916	Kilmainham 1C Bronze Age ditch	Hazel (*Corylus avellana*) charcoal from the secondary fill C2861 of ditch C2697	2878 ± 22	-24.7	1112–1011 BC (1σ) 1128–977 BC (2σ)
UBA-12917	Kilmainham 1C Bronze Age boundary ditch	Blackthorn (*Prunus* sp.) charcoal from a fill C2698 of ditch C2657	3116 ± 23	-24.3	1428–1326 BC (1σ) 1440–1316 BC (2σ)
UBA-12918	Kilmainham 1C Bronze Age features	Barley (*Hordeum* sp.) grain from charcoal-rich spread C2785	3601 ± 37	-24.8	2019–1911 BC (1σ) 2122–1831 BC (2σ)
UBA-12919	Kilmainham 1C Chalcolithic Structure V	Human skull fragment from the fill C2717 of post-hole C2718	4375 ± 24	-26.9	3013–2928 BC (1σ) 3086–2913 BC (2σ)
UBA-12920	Kilmainham 1C Structure 6	Alder (*Alnus glutinosa*) charcoal from the fill C2591 of post-hole C2592	3824 ± 26	-24.2	2296–2205 BC (1σ) 2433–2148 BC (2σ)
UBA-12921	Kilmainham 1C Neolithic/ Bronze Age features	Hazel (*Corylus avellana*) charcoal from the secondary post-pipe fill C650 of post-hole C610	3960 ± 23	-25.2	2559–2463 BC (1σ) 2569–2350 BC (2σ)
UBA-12922	Kilmainham 1C Bronze Age platform	Ash (*Fraxinus* sp.) charcoal from spread C338	3509 ± 23	-23.8	1885–1775 BC (1σ) 1896–1752 BC (2σ)

Lab code	Site	Sample and context	Yrs BP	$\delta^{13}C$‰	Calibrated dates
UBA-12923	Kilmainham 1C Bronze Age platform	Ash (*Fraxinus* sp.) charcoal from deposit C11	3467 ± 44	-24.1	1878–1700 BC (1σ) 1906–1683 BC (2σ)
UBA-12924	Kilmainham 1C Bronze Age Burnt Mound 1	Alder (*Alnus glutinosa*) charcoal from the fill C2924 of stake-hole C2919	2903 ± 26	-27.7	1128–1028 BC (1σ) 1208–1007 BC (2σ)
UBA-12925	Kilmainham 1C Burnt Mound 2	Alder (*Alnus glutinosa*) charcoal from the fill C1545 of pit/trough C1804	4003 ± 23	-25.3	2566–2482 BC (1σ) 2573–2472 BC (2σ)
UBA-12926	Kilmainham 1C Iron Age cereal-drying kiln	Barley (*Hordeum* sp.) grain from the basal fill C24 of cereal-drying kiln C13	1654 ± 21	-22.3	AD 383–423 (1σ) AD 269–432 (2σ)
UBA-12927	Kilmainham 1C Iron Age cereal-drying kiln	Barley (*Hordeum* sp.) grain from the basal fill C82 of cereal-drying kiln C81	1924 ± 20	-20.7	AD 57–121 (1σ) AD 27–127 (2σ)
UBA-12928	Kilmainham 1C Iron Age/ early medieval cereal-drying kiln	Barley (*Hordeum* sp.) grain from the basal fill C169 of cereal-drying kiln C158	1568 ± 20	-22.9	AD 436–537 (1σ) AD 429–542 (2σ)
UBA-12929	Kilmainham 1C Iron Age cereal-drying kiln	Barley (*Hordeum* sp.) grain from the basal fill C888 of cereal-drying kiln C689	1750 ± 20	-25.3	AD 247–327 (1σ) AD 235–376 (2σ)
UBA-12930	Kilmainham 1C Iron Age/ early medieval cereal-drying kiln	Barley (*Hordeum* sp.) grain from the basal fill C2979 of cereal-drying kiln C2963	1579 ± 20	-23.4	AD 433–534 (1σ) AD 427–538 (2σ)
UBA-12931	Kilmainham 1C Iron Age/ early medieval cereal-drying kiln	Barley (*Hordeum* sp.) grain from the basal fill C3156 of cereal-drying kiln C3151	1603 ± 22	-23	AD 417–532 (1σ) AD 412–535 (2σ)
UBA-12933	Kilmainham 1C Iron Age/early medieval grave	A sample of the right tibia from Skeleton 1 from grave-cut C3053	1529 ± 22	-20.8	AD 444–578 (1σ) AD 434–598 (2σ)

Lab code	Site	Sample and context	Yrs BP	δ13C‰	Calibrated dates
UBA-12934	Kilmainham 1B Bronze Age pits	Burnt bone from a fill C90 of timber-lined pit C89	2708 ± 23	-21.3	895–821 BC (1σ) 902–812 BC (2σ)
UBA-12935	Gardenrath 1 Bronze Age occupation site	Oak (*Quercus* sp.) charcoal from the fill C14 of hearth C35	3915 ± 27	-24.8	2469–2348 BC (1σ) 2473–2301 BC (2σ)
UBA-12936	Gardenrath 2 Neolithic/ Bronze Age pits	Burnt bone from the fill C35 of pit C75	3838 ± 25	-28.9	2341–2209 BC (1σ) 2457–2202 BC (2σ)
UBA-12937	Grange 3 Bronze Age Structure 1	Unidentified burnt bone from the middle fill C28 of pit C30	3182 ± 25	-25	1493–1430 BC (1σ) 1499–1415 BC (2σ)
UBA-12938	Commons of Lloyd 1 ring-ditch	Burnt bone from the basal fill C8 of ring-ditch C5	2233 ± 22	-27.2	373–213 BC (1σ) 384–207 BC (2σ)
UBA-12939	Grange 1 Bronze Age pit	Human bone from the fill C31 of cremation pit C30	3262 ± 25	-24.1	1605–1498 BC (1σ) 1613–1459 BC (2σ)
UBA-12940	Phoenixtown 2 medieval roadway	Unidentified burnt bone from the deposit (C199) that filled ditches C197 and C198 and covered cobbled road surface C199	2068 ± 23	-26.9	147–45 BC (1σ) 169–3 BC (2σ)
UBA-12941	Phoenixtown 3 Bronze Age waste pits	Alder (*Alnus glutinosa*) charcoal from the basal fill C1168 of pit C1166	3247 ± 22	-29.2	1599–1461 BC (1σ) 1607–1451 BC (2σ)
UBA-12942	Grange 3 pit (poss. cremation)	Bone from the fill C67 of pit C203	3083 ± 24	-26	1408–1316 BC (1σ) 1420–1294 BC (2σ)
UBA-12943	Cakestown Glebe 2 Bronze Age Structure 1	Human bone from the fill C125 of hearth C268 and stake-holes C269 and C270	2768 ± 24	-28.9	971–849 BC (1σ) 993–838 BC (2σ)

Lab code	Site	Sample and context	Yrs BP	δ13C‰	Calibrated dates
UBA-12944	Cakestown Glebe 2 Bronze Age cremation	Human bone from the fill C129 of cremation pit C353	3687 ± 22	-23.3	2132–2033 BC (1σ) 2141–1981 BC (2σ)
UBA-12945	Kilmainham 1A Bronze Age cremations	Human bone from the basal fill C686 of cremation pit C687	2756 ± 26	-24.3	923–844 BC (1σ) 975–830 BC (2σ)
UBA-13019	Kilmainham 1C Neolithic Structure 3	Hazelnut shell (*Corylus avellana*) from a fill C3275 of post-hole C3274	4824 ± 30	-28.5	3651–3537 BC (1σ) 3659–3525 BC (2σ)
UBA-13020	Kilmainham 1C Bronze Age Structure 4	Hazelnut shell (*Corylus avellana*) from the fill C372 of post-hole C371	3639 ± 25	-28.6	2032–1959 BC (1σ) 2128–1926 BC (2σ)
UBA-13021	Kilmainham 1C Structure 6	Hazelnut shell (*Corylus avellana*) from the secondary fill C2350 of hearth C2588	3770 ± 26	-27.1	2272–2141 BC (1σ) 2287–2061 BC (2σ)
UBA-13957	Grange 2 early medieval graves	Human left femur from SK1 in the fill C42 of grave-cut C43	1544 ± 23	-22	AD 438–559 (1σ) AD 431–571 (2σ)
UBA-13958	Grange 2 early medieval graves	Human left femur from SK3 in the fill C54 of grave-cut C49	1558 ± 31	-18.8	AD 434–544 (1σ) AD 424–568 (2σ)
UBA-13960	Newrath Little 1 Neolithic features	Hazelnut shell (*Corylus avellana*) from the basal fill C35 of pit C36	4957 ± 27	-19.1	3769–3702 BC (1σ) 3788–3661 BC (2σ)
UBA-13961	Kilmainham 1C Bronze Age track/platform	30-year-old oak (*Quercus* sp.) wood from T21, a timber from pond C3193	7834 ± 27	-29.2	6685–6640 BC (1σ) 6745–6599 BC (2σ)
UBA-13962	Ardbraccan 6 Bronze Age burnt mound	Alder (*Alnus glutinosa*) wood from stake C20, in the base of trough C6	3665 ± 21	-28.4	2126–1981 BC (1σ) 2134–1963 BC (2σ)

Lab code	Site	Sample and context	Yrs BP	δ¹³C‰	Calibrated dates
UBA-14139	Kilmainham 1C Large Beaker pit	Accreted organic matter from internal surface of pot from the tertiary fill C2284 of pit C2208	3766 ± 28	-27.9	2272–2139 BC (1σ) 2287–2051 BC (2σ)
UBA-15475	Grange 3 Bronze Age pit (poss. cremation)	Unidentifiable burnt bone from the fill C229 of pit C275	2726 ± 37	-30.9	902–832 BC (1σ) 971–807 BC (2σ)
UBA-15476	Grange 3 early medieval ditches	A fragment of a cow ulna from an upper fill C653 of ditch C656	1287 ± 25	-23.8	AD 676–768 (1σ) AD 669–772 (2σ)
UBA-15477	Kilmainham 1B Iron Age/ early medieval cereal-drying kiln	Barley (*Hordeum* sp.) grain from the secondary fill C152 of cereal-drying kiln C154	1559 ± 26	-28.4	AD 435–542 (1σ) AD 427–560 (2σ)
UBA-15478	Kilmainham 1B Iron Age/ early medieval cereal-drying kiln	Barley (*Hordeum* sp.) grain from the secondary fill C140 of cereal-drying kiln C137	1631 ± 20	-21.7	AD 391–501 (1σ) AD 355–532 (2σ)
UBA-15479	Kilmainham 1B Iron Age/ early medieval cereal-drying kiln	Barley (*Hordeum* sp.) grain from the secondary fill C72 of cereal-drying kiln C57	1564 ± 20	-23.2	AD 436–539 (1σ) AD 429–545 (2σ)
UBA-15480	Kilmainham 1C Chalcolithic Structure V	Young oak (*Quercus* sp.) charcoal from the fill C2552 of post-hole C2578	3918 ± 23	-26.8	2469–2349 BC (1σ) 2474–2309 BC (2σ)
UBA-15481	Kilmainham 1C Bronze Age pits	Alder (*Alnus glutinosa*) charcoal from the fill C513 of pit C512	2965 ± 26	-28.2	1258–1130 BC (1σ) 1299–1059 BC (2σ)
UBA-15482	Kilmainham 1C Iron Age/ early medieval cereal-drying kiln	Barley (*Hordeum* sp.) grain from basal fills C301/ C302 of cereal-drying kiln C156	1576 ± 21	-24	AD 434–534 (1σ) AD 427–540 (2σ)

Lab code	Site	Sample and context	Yrs BP	δ^{13}C‰	Calibrated dates
UBA-15483	Kilmainham 1C Iron Age/ early medieval cereal-drying kiln	Barley (*Hordeum* sp.) grain from the secondary fill C311 of cereal-drying kiln C157	1589 ± 21	-24.5	AD 427–533 (1σ) AD 422–537 (2σ)
UBA-15484	Kilmainham 1C Iron Age/ early medieval cereal-drying kiln	Barley (*Hordeum* sp.) grain from the basal fill C151 of cereal-drying kiln C103	1590 ± 22	-24.3	AD 426–533 (1σ) AD 421–537 (2σ)
UBA-15485	Kilmainham 1C early medieval cereal-drying kiln	Barley (*Hordeum* sp.) grain from the secondary fill C1212 of cereal-drying kiln C1210	1484 ± 26	-22.5	AD 558–607 (1σ) AD 542–637 (2σ)
UBA-15486	Kilmainham 1C Iron Age/ early medieval cereal-drying kiln	Barley (*Hordeum* sp.) grain from the secondary fill C3016 of cereal-drying kiln C2986	1561 ± 29	-25.5	AD 435–542 (1σ) AD 425–562 (2σ)
UBA-15488	Kilmainham 1C Iron Age/ early medieval Structure 8 ('sanctuary')	Unidentifiable burnt animal bone from a fill C2264 of foundation trench C2218	1769 ± 23	-28.4	AD 235–323 (1σ) AD 143–343 (2σ)

Appendix 2 Summary data from excavated burnt mounds

Radiocarbon dates in the summary data table below are calibrated calendrical dates at a two-sigma degree of confidence (2σ = 95% probability).

Site name	Ardbraccan 6 (E3120)
Description	Pits and subcircular trough with four *in situ* wooden stakes (alder and ash) with evidence of possible hazel wattle lining. Sealed by flattened burnt mound deposit.
Landscape setting	Adjacent to a stream on level, boggy land
Artefacts	—
Charcoal/wood	Charcoals and preserved wood of ash, alder and hazel
Plant remains	Unburnt seeds of elder, bramble, buttercup and pale persicaria (*Fal-lopia persicaria*)
Animal bone	—
Period	Early Bronze Age
Radiocarbon date (cal. 2σ)	2134–1963 BC (UBA-13962)
Site name	**Ballybeg 1 (E3132)**
Description	Small pit, group of five stake-holes sealed by shallow spreads of burnt mound material.
Landscape setting	Immediately adjacent to a stream
Artefacts	A few sherds of medieval and modern pottery; roof slate
Charcoal	Alder and hazel with some fruitwood (Maloideae), wild/bird cherry and oak
Plant remains	—
Animal bone	—
Periods	Middle–Late Bronze Age

Site name	Ballybeg 1 (E3132)
Radiocarbon dates (cal. 2σ)	1403–1265 BC (UBA-11131) 1208–1013 BC (UBA-11130)
Site name	**Ballybeg 3 (E3160)**
Description	Rectangular trough, two hearths, two post-holes. Pockets of truncated, flattened burnt mound material.
Landscape setting	Flat arable land
Artefacts	Flint blade, flake and debitage
Charcoal	Hazel and oak with some ash, wild/bird cherry and fruitwood (Maloideae)
Plant remains	Single charred cereal grain (bread/club wheat); wild goosefoot seeds
Animal bone	Cattle molar from a hearth
Periods	Early–Middle Bronze Age
Radiocarbon dates (cal. 2σ)	1879–1693 BC (UBA-12095) 1600–1431 BC (UBA-12096)
Site name	**Commons of Lloyd 1 (E3175)**
Description	Flattened burnt mound spread, one small pit.
Landscape setting	Gentle north-facing slope in pasture (ponds shown locally on early Ordnance Survey maps)
Artefacts	—
Charcoal	Hazel, alder, elm, ash and fruitwood (Maloideae)
Plant remains	Charred barley and oats; wild sun spurge and persicaria
Animal bone	—
Period	Late Bronze Age
Radiocarbon date (cal. 2σ)	1113–928 BC (UBA-11125)
Site name	**Cookstown Great 2 (E3138)**
Description	*Phase 1*—Two pits with burnt fills, heat-affected stone. *Phase 2*—Burnt mound spread, pits and troughs/cooking pits, deep well-pit or cistern.
Landscape setting	Gentle NE-facing slope by stream
Artefacts	—

Site name	Cookstown Great 2 (E3138)
Charcoals	*Phase 1*—Hazel and oak with some elm *Phase* 2—Alder, hazel, ash, wild/bird cherry, fruitwood (Maloideae), oak and elm
Plant remains	*Phase 2*—Charred hazelnut, cereal grain (bread/club wheat)
Animal bone	—
Periods	Early Bronze Age, Late Bronze Age
Radiocarbon dates (cal. 2σ)	*Phase 1*—2337–2144 BC (UBA-11083) *Phase 2*—1186–932 BC (UBA-11087)

Site name	Cookstown Great 3 (E3139)
Description	*Burnt Mound Area A*—Deep well pit or cistern, pits, post-hole and stake-holes; residual burnt mound spreads. *Burnt Mound Area B*—Two deep well pits or cisterns, several small troughs or cooking pits, residual burnt mound spreads. Stake-built structure nearby (Structure D sauna hut?).
Landscape setting	Sloping land adjacent to a stream
Artefacts	*Burnt Mound Area B*—Chert flakes
Charcoal	*Burnt Mound Area A*—Ash *Burnt Mound Area B*—Alder, hazel, ash, wild/bird cherry, oak
Plant remains	—
Animal bone	—
Periods	Early Bronze Age, Late Bronze Age/Iron Age
Radiocarbon dates (cal. 2σ)	*Burnt Mound Area A*—791–541 BC (UBA-11092) *Burnt Mound Area B*—1912–1742 BC (UBA-11097)

Site name	Kilmainham 1C (E3140)
Description	*Burnt Mound 1*—Well-defined rectangular trough with stake-holes in four corners (hazel) and decayed plank lining (probably alder and ash). Second (possible) circular trough with irregularly arranged stake-holes. Well-defined burnt mound deposit downslope towards seasonal pond. *Burnt Mound 2*—Several pits, possible trough, residual burnt mound spread.
Landscape setting	*Burnt Mound 1*—Low east-facing slope near seasonal pond *Burnt mound 2*—Low north-facing slope
Artefacts	*Burnt mound 2*—Burnt flint knife

Site name	Kilmainham 1C (E3140)
Charcoal	*Burnt Mound 1*—Alder, hazel, ash, fruitwood (Maloideae) *Burnt mound 2*—Alder, hazel, oak
Plant remains	—
Animal bone	—
Periods	Chalcolithic and Late Bronze Age
Radiocarbon dates (cal. 2σ)	*Burnt Mound 1*—1208–1007 BC (UBA-12924) *Burnt Mound 2*—2573–2472 BC (UBA-12925)
Site name	**Newrath Little 2 (E3154)**
Description	Three circular troughs. One with decayed timber lining. Possible wooden structure c. 2.5 m in diameter defined by a cluster of stake-holes and gullies adjacent to the troughs. Elongated pit represents possible water management. Flattened burnt mound deposit.
Landscape setting	Flat grassland pasture
Artefacts	—
Charcoal	Hazel, ash, oak, holly
Plant remains	Weed seeds, goosefoot, knotgrass, spurge
Animal bone	—
Period	Early Bronze Age
Radiocarbon dates (cal. 2σ)	2023–1828 BC (UBA-12063) 1944–1771 BC (UBA-12064)
Site name	**Newrath Little 3 (E3134)**
Description	Rectangular trough with stake-holes at four corners and plank impressions in base of the trough (no surviving wood). Four pits and a gully or water channel immediately adjacent to the trough. Two pits contained burnt mound material.
Landscape setting	On the brow of a low hill overlooking bogland
Artefacts	—
Charcoal	Oak, ash, hazel, alder, wild/bird cherry
Plant remains	Charred hazelnut shell, four wheat grains (emmer?)
Period	Late Bronze Age
Radiocarbon date (cal. 2σ)	1188–937 BC (UBA-11098)

Site name	Phoenixtown 1 (E3128)
Description	Large burnt mound complex. Two troughs, circular and rectangular. Post-holes at the corners of the rectangular trough indicate a wooden lining (none survived). Circular wooden structure defined by stake-holes interpreted as possible hut or sweat-house. Numerous pits sealed by and adjacent to the burnt mound may have been cooking pits. Circular trough and numerous pits sealed by flattened burnt mound deposit.
Artefacts	—
Environmental material	—
Landscape setting	Adjacent to former wetland area
Periods	Early and Middle Bronze Age
Radiocarbon dates (cal. 2σ)	2559–2300 BC (UBA-11103) 1408–1269 BC (UBA-11102)
Site name	**Phoenixtown 6 (E3127)**
Description	Two troughs, one rectangular (earlier) and one circular (later). Sealed by flattened burnt mound deposit. Small burnt deposit and pit adjacent to this.
Landscape setting	Flat pasture field with drainage ditch, adjacent to former wetland area
Artefacts	Flint barbed-and-tanged arrowhead, flint burin spall
Charcoal	Alder, hazel, ash, fruitwood (Maloideae), oak, elm
Plant remains	Hazelnut shell
Animal bone	—
Period	Early Bronze Age
Radiocarbon dates (cal. 2σ)	2119–1895 BC (UBA-11108) 1742-1617 BC (UBA-11106)
Site name	**Townparks 1 (E3157)**
Description	*Burnt Mound Area A*—Rectangular trough, pit, deep well pit or cistern, flattened burnt mound deposit. *Burnt Mound Area B*—Oval trough, pits, flattened burnt mound deposit.
Landscape setting	Flat, arable but poorly drained field
Artefacts	—
Charcoal	*Burnt Mound Area A*—Hazel, oak, birch *Burnt Mound Area B*—Hazel, oak, alder, fruitwood (Maloideae), birch, holly

Site name	Townparks 1 (E3157)
Plant remains	—
Animal bone	—
Periods	Early Bronze Age, Late Bronze Age
Radiocarbon dates (cal. 2σ)	*Burnt Mound Area A*—2197–2034 BC (UBA-11080) *Burnt Mound Area B*—1005–855 BC (UBA-11081)
Site name	**Townparks 6 (E3152)**
Description	Subrectangular trough with stake-holes/post-holes at three corners. Linear gully running from trough towards flattened burnt mound deposit. Second, circular, trough c. 10 m to NW.
Landscape setting	Adjacent to stream
Artefacts	—
Charcoal	Alder, hazel, oak, fruitwood (Maloideae)
Plant remains	—
Animal bone	—
Period	Early Neolithic.
Radiocarbon date (cal. 2σ)	3749–3640 BC (UBA-11101)
Site name	**Townparks/Commons of Lloyd (E3156)**
Description	*Burnt Mound 1*—Rectangular trough with lenses of decayed wood and a piece of timber on its base, and remains of clay lining on its sides. Circular trough with evidence of decayed wood lining. Three large circular pits. Flattened 'horseshoe' burnt mound deposit. *Burnt Mound 2*—Three large circular pits, one of which had layer of large flat stones at base. All sealed by flattened burnt mound deposit. *Burnt Mound 3*—Two small pits with large, shallow, flattened burnt mound deposit.
Landscape setting	Low-lying and wet.
Artefacts	—
Charcoal	*Burnt Mound 1*—Alder, hazel, ash, oak *Burnt Mound 2*—Alder, hazel, ash, oak
Plant remains	—
Animal bone	—
Periods	Chalcolithic, Early Bronze Age
Radiocarbon dates (cal. 2σ)	*Burnt Mound 1*—2109–1892 BC (UBA-11123) *Burnt Mound 2*—2462–2212 BC (UBA-11124)

Appendix 3 Summary data from excavated cereal-drying kilns

Radiocarbon dates in the summary data table below are calibrated calendrical dates at a two-sigma degree of confidence (2σ = 95% probability).

Gardenrath 2	Kiln C181
Dimensions	L 2.55 m x W 2.4 m x D 0.73 m
Shape	Subcircular
Fire bowl orientation	West
Cereals	Barley (*Hordeum* sp.) and indeterminate cereal grains
Charcoals	Hazel (*Corylus avellana*), oak (*Quercus* sp.), holly (*Ilex aquifolium*) and alder (*Alnus*)
Radiocarbon date (cal.2σ)	AD 425–552 (UBA-12045)
Grange 3	**Kiln C130**
Dimensions	L 2.35 m x W 1.1 m x D 0.49 m
Shape	Figure-of-eight
Fire bowl orientation	North
Cereals	Barley (*Hordeum* sp.) with a small quantity of wheat (*Triticum* sp.), oats (*Avena* sp.) and indeterminate grains
Charcoals	Oak (*Quercus* sp.), smaller quantities of alder (*Alnus* sp.), ash (*Fraxinus excelsior* sp.), hazel (*Corylus avellana* sp.) and elm (*Ulmus* sp.)
Radiocarbon date (cal.2σ)	AD 427–570 (UBA-12073)
Grange 3	**Kiln C273**
Dimensions	L 2.63 m x W 1.32 x D 0.76
Shape	Figure-of-eight
Fire bowl orientation	WNW
Cereals	Barley (*Hordeum vulgare*) with lesser volumes of wheat (*Triticum* sp.) and oats (*Avena* sp.)

Grange 3	Kiln C273
Charcoals	Oak (*Quercus* sp.) and hazel (*Corylus avellana*), smaller amounts of Maloideae (a sub-family of fruiting trees including apples), *Prunus* sp. (a diverse genus of fruiting trees including wild cherry and blackthorn), ash (*Fraxinus excelsior*), willow (*Salix* sp.) and alder (*Alnus*)
Radiocarbon date (cal.2σ)	–
Grange 3	**Kiln C596**
Dimensions	L 2.6 m x W 1.1 m x D 0.3 m
Shape	Figure-of-eight
Fire bowl orientation	South
Cereals	Barley (*Hordeum* sp.), with smaller quantities of wheat (*Triticum* sp.) and indeterminate grains
Charcoals	Oak (*Quercus* sp.)
Radiocarbon date (cal.2σ)	–
Kilmainham 1A	**Kiln C606**
Dimensions	L 2.27 m x W 1.3 m x D 0.55 m
Shape	Figure-of-eight
Fire bowl orientation	–
Cereals	Bread/club wheat (*Triticum aestivo/compactum*), with barley (*Hordeum* sp.), oats (*Avena*) and rye (*Secale cereale*)
Charcoals	Hazel (*Corylus avellana*) with elm (*Ulmus*), holly (*Ilex aquifolium*), alder (*Alnus*), oak (*Quercus* sp.), *Prunus* sp., Maloideae and ash (*Fraxinus excelsior*)
Radiocarbon date (cal.2σ)	AD 423–552 (UBA-12104)
Kilmainham 1B	**Kiln C57**
Dimensions	L 1.98 m x W 0.88 m x D 0.35 m
Shape	Figure-of-eight
Fire bowl orientation	NNW
Cereals	Barley (*Hordeum* sp.)
Charcoals	Oak (*Quercus* sp.), *Prunus* sp., hazel (*Corylus avellana*) and ash (*Fraxinus excelsior*)
Radiocarbon date (cal.2σ)	AD 429–545 (UBA-15479)

Kilmainham 1B	Kiln C137
Dimensions	L 2.16 m x W 1.12 m x D 0.44 m
Shape	Figure-of-eight
Fire bowl orientation	North
Cereals	Barley (*Hordeum* sp.) and oats (*Avena*)
Charcoals	Hazel (*Corylus avellana*) with alder (*Alnus*), ash (*Fraxinus excelsior*), Maloideae, *Prunus* sp., oak (*Quercus* sp.) and willow (*Salix* sp.)
Radiocarbon date (cal.2σ)	AD 355–532 (UBA-15478)

Kilmainham 1B	Kiln C144
Dimensions	L 2.6 m x W 1.5 m x D 0.37 m
Shape	Irregular (truncated)
Fire bowl orientation	North
Cereals	Barley (*Hordeum* sp.) with lesser amounts of bread/club wheat (*Triticum aestivum/compactum*) and oats (*Avena*)
Charcoals	Hazel (*Corylus avellana*), ash (*Fraxinus excelsior*), oak (*Quercus* sp.) and willow (*Salix* sp.)
Radiocarbon date (cal.2σ)	AD 406–537 (UBA-12067)

Kilmainham 1B	Kiln C154
Dimensions	L 2.14 m x W 0.75 m x D 0.35 m
Shape	Figure-of-eight
Fire bowl orientation	North
Cereals	Large quantities of barley (*Hordeum* sp.) and oats (*Avena*)
Charcoals	Birch (*Betula* sp.), alder (*Alnus*) and oak (*Quercus* sp.)
Radiocarbon date (cal.2σ)	AD 427–560 (UBA-15477)

Kilmainham 1C	Kiln C13
Dimensions	L 1.75 m x W 0.8 m x D 0.28 m
Shape	Figure-of-eight
Fire bowl orientation	NNW
Cereals	Barley (*Hordeum* sp.) with oats (*Avena*), a small amount of wheat (*Triticum* sp.) and further indeterminate cereal grain
Charcoals	Hazel (*Corylus avellana*) with oak (*Quercus* sp.), ash (*Fraxinus excelsior*), Maloideae and birch (*Betula* sp.)
Radiocarbon date (cal.2σ)	AD 269–432 (UBA-12926)
Kilmainham 1C	**Kiln C81**
Dimensions	L 1.3 m x W 0.88 m x D 0.41 m
Shape	Oval
Fire bowl orientation	–
Cereals	Barley (*Hordeum* sp.) and indeterminate grain
Charcoals	Hazel (*Corylus avellana*), oak (*Quercus* sp.), alder (*Alnus*) and holly (*Ilex aquifolium*)
Radiocarbon date (cal.2σ)	AD 27–127 (UBA-12927)
Kilmainham 1C	**Kiln C103**
Dimensions	L 2.2 m x W 1.5 m x D 0.37 m
Shape	Figure-of-eight
Fire bowl orientation	NW
Cereals	Barley (*Hordeum* sp.) with oats (*Avena*) and indeterminate grain
Charcoals	Oak (*Quercus* sp.) with hazel (*Corylus avellana*), alder (*Alnus*), *Prunus* sp., willow (*Salix* sp.) and ash (*Fraxinus excelsior*)
Radiocarbon date (cal.2σ)	AD 421–537 (UBA-15484)

Kilmainham 1C	Kiln C156
Dimensions	L 2.23 m x W 1.1 m x D 0.36 m
Shape	Figure-of-eight
Fire bowl orientation	NNW
Cereals	Barley (*Hordeum* sp.) with oats (*Avena*) and wheat (*Triticum* sp.) and further indeterminate grains
Charcoals	Oak (*Quercus* sp.), ash (*Fraxinus excelsior*), alder (*Alnus*), hazel (*Corylus avellana*), birch (*Betula* sp.), blackthorn (*Prunus spinosa*) and elm (*Ulmus*)
Radiocarbon date (cal.2σ)	AD 427–540 (UBA-15482)
Kilmainham 1C	**Kiln C157**
Dimensions	L 2.4 m x W 1.2 m x D 0.29 m
Shape	Figure-of-eight
Fire bowl orientation	NNW
Cereals	Predominantly barley (*Hordeum* sp.) with oats (*Avena*), wheat (*Triticum* sp.) including bread/club wheat (*Triticum aestivo/compactum*), and a small quantity of indeterminate grain
Charcoals	Hazel (*Corylus avellana*), alder (*Alnus*), oak (*Quercus* sp.), ash (*Fraxinus excelsior*) and Maloideae
Radiocarbon date (cal.2σ)	AD 422–537 (UBA-15483)
Kilmainham 1C	**Kiln C158**
Dimensions	L 2.15 m x W 0.95 m x D 0.25 m
Shape	Figure-of-eight
Fire bowl orientation	NNW
Cereals	Barley (*Hordeum* sp.) and oats (*Avena*)
Charcoals	Oak (*Quercus* sp.), with smaller amounts of hazel (*Corylus avellana*), alder (*Alnus*) and Maloideae
Radiocarbon date (cal.2σ)	AD 429–542 (UBA-12928)

Kilmainham 1C	Kiln C689
Dimensions	L 2.35 m x W 1.25 m x D 0.6 m
Shape	Figure-of-eight
Fire bowl orientation	SSE
Cereals	Barley (*Hordeum* sp.) with wheat (*Triticum* sp.), including some spelt wheat (*Triticum* cf. *spelta*), oats (*Avena* sp.), a single rye (*Secale cereale*) grain and frequent indeterminate grains
Charcoals	Single fragments of hazel (*Corylus avellana*) and elm (*Ulmus*)
Radiocarbon date (cal.2σ)	AD 235–376 (UBA-12929)
Kilmainham 1C	**Kiln C1210**
Dimensions	L 2.17 m x W 1.3 m x D 0.4 m
Shape	Figure-of-eight
Fire bowl orientation	NW
Cereals	Mainly barley (*Hordeum* sp.) grains with oats (*Avena*) and a large quantity of indeterminate grain
Charcoals	Hazel (*Corylus avellana*) with oak (*Quercus* sp.), ash (*Fraxinus excelsior*) and wild/bird cherry (*Prunus avium/padus*)
Radiocarbon date (cal.2σ)	AD 542–637 (UBA-15485)
Kilmainham 1C	**Kiln C1598/1599**
Dimensions	L 2.1 m x W 0.82 m x D 0.1 m
Shape	Figure-of-eight
Fire bowl orientation	—
Cereals	Barley (*Hordeum* sp.) with very small amounts of wheat (*Triticum* sp.) and oats (*Avena* sp.)
Charcoals	—
Radiocarbon date (cal.2σ)	AD 425–537 (UBA-12910)

Kilmainham 1C	Kiln C2963
Dimensions	L 2.35 m x W 1.05 m x D 0.3 m
Shape	Figure-of-eight
Fire bowl orientation	NNW
Cereals	Barley (*Hordeum* sp.) with wheat (*Triticum* sp.) and oats (*Avena* sp.) as well as some indeterminate grain
Charcoals	Oak (*Quercus* sp.), hazel (*Corylus avellana*), ash (*Fraxinus excelsior*) and alder (*Alnus*)
Radiocarbon date (cal.2σ)	AD 427–538 (UBA-12930)
Kilmainham 1C	**Kiln C2986**
Dimensions	L 2.22 m x W 1.16 m x D 0.56 m
Shape	Figure-of-eight
Fire bowl orientation	NNW
Cereals	Barley (*Hordeum* sp.) with very small quantities of wheat (*Triticum* sp.) and oats (*Avena*)
Charcoals	Mainly hazel (*Corylus avellana*) with oak (*Quercus* sp.), ash (*Fraxinus excelsior*), Maloideae, *Prunus* sp., willow (*Salix* sp.) and birch (*Betula* sp.)
Radiocarbon date (cal.2σ)	AD 425–562 (UBA-15486)
Kilmainham 1C	**Kiln C3151**
Dimensions	L 2.49 m x W 1.14 m x D 0.83 m
Shape	Figure-of-eight
Fire bowl orientation	South
Cereals	Barley (*Hordeum* sp.), including hulled barley (*Hordeum vulgaris*); wheat (*Triticum* sp.), including bread/club wheat (*Triticum aestivo/compactum*) and emmer wheat (*Triticum dicoccum*); and oats (*Avena*)
Charcoals	—
Radiocarbon date (cal.2σ)	AD 412–535 (UBA-12931)

Kilmainham 2	Kiln C33
Dimensions	L 1.12 m x W 0.64 m x D 0.24 m
Shape	Oval
Fire bowl orientation	–
Cereals	Barley (*Hordeum vulgare*)
Charcoals	Alder (*Alnus*), ash (*Fraxinus excelsior*), hazel (*Corylus avellana*), Maloideae, *Prunus* sp., willow (*Salix* sp.) and oak (*Quercus* sp.)
Radiocarbon date (cal.2σ)	510–387 BC (UBA-12065)

Appendix 4 Archaeological reports in the TII Digital Heritage Collections

The following final excavation reports on archaeological sites on the Navan to Kells and N52 Kells Bypass section of the M3 Clonee to North of Kells national road scheme are all available on the Internet, free to view and download, in the TII Digital Heritage Collections at the Digital Repository of Ireland (repository.dri.ie/catalog/v6936m966). The reports are listed in alphabetical order by site name.

<table>
<tr><th>Filename</th><th>Excav. Director</th><th>DRI Identifier</th></tr>
<tr><td>E3119_Ardbraccan_5.pdf</td><td>Carmel Duffy</td><td>repository.dri.ie/catalog/gf06vh43d</td></tr>
<tr><td colspan="3">Three small rectangular buildings (wall trenches), undated. Modern plough furrows and drains.</td></tr>
<tr><td>E3120_Ardbraccan_6.pdf</td><td>Ciara MacManus</td><td>repository.dri.ie/catalog/gm80x911k</td></tr>
<tr><td colspan="3">Early Bronze Age burnt spread with pits, trough and stakes (possible wicker lining). Truncated by post-medieval drains.</td></tr>
<tr><td>E3132_Ballybeg_1.pdf</td><td>Patricia Lynch</td><td>repository.dri.ie/catalog/k069np278</td></tr>
<tr><td colspan="3">Middle to Late Bronze Age burnt spreads with pit and stake-holes.</td></tr>
<tr><td>E3133_Ballybeg_ 2.pdf</td><td>Patricia Lynch</td><td>repository.dri.ie/catalog/k643qf95p</td></tr>
<tr><td colspan="3">Modern path and field ditches on Ballybeg Demesne.</td></tr>
<tr><td>E3160_Ballybeg_3.pdf</td><td>Tim Coughlan</td><td>repository.dri.ie/catalog/st74s5231</td></tr>
<tr><td colspan="3">Early to Middle Bronze Age burnt mound with trough, pits, post-holes and hearths; truncated by post-medieval furrows and field ditches.</td></tr>
<tr><td>E3162_Ballybeg_4.pdf</td><td>Patricia Lynch</td><td>repository.dri.ie/catalog/t148tx91k</td></tr>
<tr><td colspan="3">Subterranean heating system possibly associated with greenhouses on Ballybeg Demesne. Modern drains and field boundaries. Modern china, brick, glass and metal.</td></tr>
<tr><td>E3159_Cakestown_Glebe_ 1.pdf</td><td>Patricia Lynch</td><td>repository.dri.ie/catalog/sn00qc55k</td></tr>
<tr><td colspan="3">Prehistoric pits and post-holes with flint flakes. Remnants of three modern buildings. Modern pottery and clay pipes.</td></tr>
</table>

Filename	Excav. Director	DRI Identifier
E3158_Cakestown_Glebe_2.pdf	Patricia Lynch	repository.dri.ie/catalog/sf26nk87c
Late Mesolithic hearth and post-holes. Early Bronze Age small, square building (post-holes) and cremation pit. Late Bronze Age stake-holes, pits, post-holes and hearths representing two possible buildings; associated chipped stone assemblage. Iron Age barrow with burnt mammal bones (sheep or pig?). Modern furrows, field ditches and drains, and pits.		
E3157_Commons_of_Lloyd_ 1.pdf	Yvonne Whitty	repository.dri.ie/catalog/s752kt19p
Late Bronze Age burnt spread and pit. Remnants of an Iron Age or early medieval ring-ditch with burnt bone (possibly human), seeds and charcoals, and an antler spindle-whorl.		
E3137_Cookstown_Great_1.pdf	Patricia Lynch	repository.dri.ie/catalog/m039zk67w
Pits and hearth. Burnt spread with Early Neolithic pottery. One pit dated to the Late Bronze Age/Early Iron Age.		
E3138_Cookstown_Great_2.pdf	Gill McLoughlin	repository.dri.ie/catalog/m6141c357
Early Bronze Age troughs/cooking pits with burnt fills. Early/Middle Bronze Age pit with cordoned urn pottery. Late Bronze Age burnt mound with pits and troughs. Undated pits and linear ditch post-dating the burnt mound. Undated hearth. Modern drains and furrows.		
E3139_Cookstown_Great_3.pdf	Gill McLoughlin	repository.dri.ie/catalog/mc883503p
Two oblong/rectangular buildings (wall trenches and post-holes) with Early Neolithic pottery. Small Early Bronze Age circular or D-shaped buildings (post-holes) with hearths/cooking pits and Early Bronze Age bowl food vessel and encrusted urn pottery. Early Bronze Age burnt mound with pits and troughs. Late Bronze Age burnt mound. Early medieval/medieval pits and linear trench or ditch; associated charcoals, burnt bone, charred seeds, ash, pottery and iron objects. Post-medieval/modern ditches. Disused railway line.		
E3146_Gardenrath_1.pdf	David Bayley	repository.dri.ie/catalog/q237x6710
Chalcolithic/Early Bronze Age hearth, pits and stake-holes.		
E3145_Gardenrath_2.pdf	David Bayley	repository.dri.ie/catalog/pv63vf038
Early Neolithic square building (wall trench, post-holes) with associated carinated bowl sherds and chipped flint; adjacent pits and soil spreads. Chalcolithic/Early Bronze Age hearth, pits and soil spread with Early Neolithic (residual?) pottery sherd, Beaker pottery and worked flint. Middle Bronze Age pit. Transitional Iron Age/early medieval cereal-drying kiln with barley grains and baked clay. Undated trackway with wheel ruts. Post-medieval/modern furrows and field ditch.		
E3125_Grange_ 1.pdf	Patricia Lynch	repository.dri.ie/catalog/hm517651b
Middle Bronze Age pit. Transitional Iron Age/early medieval cereal-drying kiln. Undated ditches and metalled surfaces.		

<table>
<tr><th>Filename</th><th>Excav. Director</th><th>DRI Identifier</th></tr>
<tr><td>E3124_Grange_2.pdf</td><td>Amanda Kelly</td><td>repository.dri.ie/catalog/hd775d834</td></tr>
<tr><td colspan="3">Early Neolithic pits with carinated bowl pottery sherds and worked flint. Iron Age metalworking evidence, pit and associated blue glass bead. Group of transitional Iron Age/early medieval oriented graves with poorly preserved human skeletal remains. Iron Age or transitional Iron Age/early medieval shaft furnace with iron slag and charred cereal grains.</td></tr>
<tr><td>E3123_Grange_3.pdf</td><td>Amanda Kelly</td><td>repository.dri.ie/catalog/h7033n15g</td></tr>
<tr><td colspan="3">Chalcolithic/Early Bronze Age cereal-drying kiln, burnt spread and pit. Middle/Late Bronze Age round-houses (post-holes, stake-holes), metalled surfaces and pits; associated chipped stone assemblage (chert) and coarse stone tools (hammerstones, saddle quern, axehead, spindle-whorl). Middle/Late Bronze Age barrow with adjacent pits and post-holes. Middle and Late Bronze Age pits with burnt bone (unidentifiable). Late Bronze Age ditches. Iron Age ironworking pits. Transitional Iron Age/early medieval cereal-drying kilns with charred grain, and early medieval ditches forming a small, subrectangular enclosure with associated ring-pin, pin fragments and bone needle. Modern field ditches, drains and furrows.</td></tr>
<tr><td>E3122_Grange_4.pdf</td><td>Carmel Duffy</td><td>repository.dri.ie/catalog/h1291v478</td></tr>
<tr><td colspan="3">Possible Early Neolithic building remains (post-holes, stake-holes), curvilinear gully and pits, with associated Early Neolithic pottery. Some features dated to the Late Neolithic and Middle Bronze Age periods. Early medieval curvilinear gully and pits.</td></tr>
<tr><td>E3121_Grange_5.pdf</td><td>Amanda Kelly</td><td>repository.dri.ie/catalog/gt550279x</td></tr>
<tr><td colspan="3">Chalcolithic/Early Bronze Age pit(s). Transitional Iron Age/early medieval pit(s) with burnt fills including charred grain. Undated post-holes and curvilinear ditches or gullies.</td></tr>
<tr><td>E3141_Kilmainham_1A.pdf</td><td>Ed Lyne</td><td>repository.dri.ie/catalog/p267m931c</td></tr>
<tr><td colspan="3">Two Early Neolithic oblong/rectangular buildings (post-holes) with associated pits and stake-holes. Middle Bronze Age round-house (post-holes) and (possible) linear palisade trench. Middle and Late Bronze Age cremation pits. Transitional Iron Age/early medieval cereal-drying kiln. Undated metalled surfaces and ditches.</td></tr>
<tr><td>E3142_Kilmainham_1B.pdf</td><td>David Bayley</td><td>repository.dri.ie/catalog/p841p2999</td></tr>
<tr><td colspan="3">Pit with Early Neolithic pottery. Scattered pits, post-holes and hearths with associated Beaker sherds and Early Bronze Age vase urn pottery. Late Bronze Age wood- and stone-lined pit with burnt bone (including red deer antler), burnt clay and possible clay mould fragments. Transitional Iron Age/early medieval cereal-drying kilns with charred grain and charcoal. Post-medieval/modern field ditches and drains. Undated pits, post-holes, stake-holes, hearths and metalled surfaces.</td></tr>
</table>

Filename	Excav. Director	DRI Identifier
E3140_Kilmainham_1CVol_1_Text.pdf	Fintan Walsh	repository.dri.ie/catalog/nv93jh63v
A large site with extensive evidence of settlement, ritual and industrial activity from the Early Neolithic to the medieval period. Numerous Neolithic and Bronze Age buildings, including three or more Early Neolithic houses, a Chalcolithic/Early Bronze Age stone platform and a wide range of other probable prehistoric features, including fence lines (stake-holes), pits, hearths, burnt mounds, a pond and boundary ditches. Late Iron Age/early medieval cereal-drying kilns; two burials associated with a large rectangular structure (wall or palisade trenches with post-holes), possibly a sanctuary or shrine; and a long ditch enclosing or bounding part of the site. Medieval pits. Post-medieval furrows.		
E3140_Kilmainham_1C_Images.pdf	Fintan Walsh	repository.dri.ie/catalog/np19gq95p
Photographs. See E3140_Kilmainham_1CVol_1_Text.pdf for summary.		
E3140_Kilmainham_1C_Volume_2.pdf	Fintan Walsh	repository.dri.ie/catalog/mp495t552
Appendices. See E3140_Kilmainham_1CVol_1_Text.pdf for summary.		
E3140_Kilmainham_1C_Figure_1_20.pdf	Fintan Walsh	repository.dri.ie/catalog/mw237m238
Figures 1–20. See E3140_Kilmainham_1CVol_1_Text.pdf for summary.		
E3140_Kilmainham_1C_Figure_21_40.pdf	Fintan Walsh	repository.dri.ie/catalog/n2979c91z
Figures 21–40. See E3140_Kilmainham_1CVol_1_Text.pdf for summary.		
E3140_Kilmainham_1C_Figure_1_60.pdf	Fintan Walsh	repository.dri.ie/catalog/n871c559p
Figures 41–60. See E3140_Kilmainham_1CVol_1_Text.pdf for summary.		
E3140_Kilmainham_1C_Figure_61_83.pdf	Fintan Walsh	repository.dri.ie/catalog/ng45dz270
Figures 61–83. See E3140_Kilmainham_1CVol_1_Text.pdf for summary.		
E3143_Kilmainham_2_Text.pdf	David Bayley	repository.dri.ie/catalog/pg15qv67m
Late Bronze Age four-post structure, surrounding pits with Bronze Age pottery and charred seeds. Iron Age (possible) cereal-drying kiln.		
E3144_Kilmainham_3.pdf	Yvonne Whitty	repository.dri.ie/catalog/pn89sn352
Early Neolithic pits and post-holes. Late Neolithic timber circle (post-holes) and two smaller buildings (post-holes; trapezoidal and subrectangular), associated pits with burnt bone (unidentified) and Grooved Ware pottery. Early Bronze Age ring-ditch. Middle Iron Age pit with metalworking evidence (slag, burnt clay). Post-medieval field ditches. Worked flint and chert.		
E3155_Newrath_Little_1.pdf	James Kyle	repository.dri.ie/catalog/rv04g783n
Cluster of Early Neolithic pits and hearth with pottery (one pit) and cremated human bone (one pit).		
E3154_Newrath_Little_2.pdf	Yvonne Whitty	repository.dri.ie/catalog/rn30dg15z
Early Bronze Age burnt mound with troughs, gullies (water conduits?) and stake-holes.		

Filename	Excav. Director	DRI Identifier
E3153_Newrath_Little_3.pdf	James Kyle	repository.dri.ie/catalog/rf56bp47r
Late Bronze Age burnt mound, with adjacent pits, and a trough with corner post-holes and impressions of planking in the base.		
E3136_Nugentstown_1.pdf	Patricia Lynch	repository.dri.ie/catalog/ks65ws99c
Early Bronze Age vase pottery. Middle Bronze Age hearth and associated pits, post-holes and stake-holes. Late Bronze Age subrectangular building (wall trenches) with associated pits and post-holes. Numerous undated features, including pits, stake-holes and two small circular buildings. Post-medieval/modern field ditches and drains. Chipped stone assemblage, including Middle Neolithic hollow scrapers and post-medieval gunflints. Yellow bead, Iron Age or early medieval.		
E3135_Nugentstown_2.pdf	Patricia Lynch	repository.dri.ie/catalog/kk91v131b
Late Neolithic/Early Bronze Age burnt spreads. Post-medieval/modern field drain.		
E3134_Nugentstown_3.pdf	Patricia Lynch	repository.dri.ie/catalog/kd17s7635
Early and Middle Bronze Age pits and post-holes with Beaker pottery and chipped stone in one pit.		
E3128_Phoenixtown_1.pdf	Ed Lyne	repository.dri.ie/catalog/j673dj552
Pits and post-holes with Early Neolithic pottery. Late Neolithic/Early Bronze Age burnt mound with troughs, pits and a small circular building (sweat-house?). One post-hole dated to the Middle Bronze Age. Worked flint, including two thumbnail scrapers.		
E3129_Phoenixtown_2.pdf	Ed Lyne	repository.dri.ie/catalog/jd47gb23j
Later medieval metalled road, animal-powered mill, cereal-drying kilns, building remnants, a possible well and water-pit/cistern; numerous pits with burnt or charcoal-rich fills, animal bone and medieval pottery.		
E3130_Phoenixtown_3.pdf	Ed Lyne	repository.dri.ie/catalog/jm21j391z
Middle Neolithic broad-rimmed bowl. Pits with Early Bronze Age food vessel pottery. Middle Bronze Age circular building or round-house (post-holes, gullies) with adjacent ditch and associated pottery. Saddle quern and flint debitage. Medieval ditch and pits with pottery. Undated post-holes and pits.		
E3131_Phoenixtown_4.pdf	Ed Lyne	repository.dri.ie/catalog/js95kw59r
Two red-brick furnaces or kilns with stone flag bases. Modern field ditch. Fragments of glass and barrel hoops, modern pottery, Irish George III (1805) copper penny.		
E3126_Phoenixtown_ 5.pdf	Tim Coughlin	repository.dri.ie/catalog/ht259019b
Possible rectangular building (L-plan post-holes) with Late Neolithic Grooved Ware pottery, chipped stone scraper and debitage, hammerstone, burnt bone fragments (unidentified).		
E3127_Phoenixtown_6.pdf	Ed Lyne	repository.dri.ie/catalog/j099br87v
Early Neolithic hearth. Early Bronze Age burnt mound with troughs. Barbed-and-tanged arrowhead. Modern ditch.		

Filename	Excav. Director	DRI Identifier
E3147_Townparks_1.pdf	Gill McLoughlin	repository.dri.ie/catalog/q8120039v
Early and Late Bronze Age burnt spreads (two) with associated troughs and pits.		
E3148_Townparks_2.pdf	Catriona Gleeson	repository.dri.ie/catalog/qf861s074
Late Mesolithic/Early Neolithic hearth(s) and associated post-holes. Modern furrows and refuse pit. Modern pottery, iron nails, worked flint (two flakes, scraper and blade).		
E3149_Townparks_3.pdf	Catriona Gleeson	repository.dri.ie/catalog/qn603j75j
Late Bronze Age possible building (post-holes) with Middle to Late Bronze Age pottery. Early medieval pit with charred cereal grain and a worked antler comb. Remnants of a post-medieval/modern house with outbuildings and a well; drains, ditches and furrows.		
E3150_Townparks_4.pdf	Yvonne Whitty	repository.dri.ie/catalog/qv345b431
Undated burnt spread. No finds.		
E3151_Townparks_5.pdf	Yvonne Whitty	repository.dri.ie/catalog/r2087411j
Two Early Neolithic subrectangular buildings (post-holes, wall trenches), with adjacent pits and post-holes, carinated bowl sherds and a chert 'laurel leaf' projectile head. Charred cereal grains and hazelnut shells. Middle Neolithic broad-rimmed bowl sherds from a soil spread.		
E3152_Townparks_6.pdf	Yvonne Whitty	repository.dri.ie/catalog/r7828w798
Early Neolithic burnt spread with two troughs (one with corner posts) and a gully or conduit trench.		
E3156_Townparks_Commons_of-Lloyd_1.pdf	David Bayley	repository.dri.ie/catalog/s178j1514
Three Chalcolithic period/Early Bronze Age burnt mounds with associated pits and troughs; plank lining in one trough and stone lining in another. Post-medieval/modern drains, including a deep ditch along the townland boundary.		

Bibliography

Allison, E, Carrott, J & Foster, A 2011 'Appendix 2.14. Insect and other macrofossil invertebrate remains from early Bronze Age and medieval deposits associated with a pond at Kilmainham 1C, Co. Meath', *in* F Walsh, *Archaeological Excavation Report E3141 Kilmainham 1C, Co. Meath. Vol. 2: Appendices*. Unpublished report by Irish Archaeological Consultancy Ltd for Meath County Council. TII Digital Heritage Collections: https://doi.org/10.7486/DRI.mp495t552.

Allman, E 2009 *A Review of the Construction of Irish Bronze Age Domestic Buildings circa 2300–600 BC*. Unpublished MA thesis, University College Dublin, Dublin.

Annals of the Four Masters = O'Donovan, J (ed. and trans.) 1848–51 *Annals of the Kingdom of Ireland by the Four Masters from the Earliest Period to the Year 1616* (7 vols). Hodges & Smith, Dublin. Corpus of Electronic Texts, University College Cork: https://celt.ucc.ie//published/T100005A/.

Annals of Ulster = Mac Airt, S & Mac Niocaill, G (eds & trans.) 1983 *The Annals of Ulster (to AD 1131)*. Dublin Institute for Advanced Studies, Dublin. Corpus of Electronic Texts, University College Cork: https://celt.ucc.ie/published/T100001A/index.html.

ApSimon, A 1976 'Ballynagilly at the beginning and end of the Irish Neolithic', *in* S J de Laet (ed.), *Acculturation and Continuity in Atlantic Europe*, 15–38. Dissertationes Archaeologicae Gandenses, Bruges.

Armit, I, Swindles, T, Becker, K, Plunkett, G & Blau, M 2014 'Rapid climate change did not cause population collapse at the end of the European Bronze Age', *Proceedings of the National Academy of Sciences of the United States of America*, Vol. 111, No. 48, 17045–49. National Academy of Science: https://www.pnas.org/content/111/48/17045.

Baillie, M G L & Brown, D M 2011 'Dendrochronology and Deer Park Farms', *in* C J Lynn & J A McDowell, *Deer Park Farms. The excavation of a raised rath in the Glenarm Valley, Co. Antrim*, 558–67. Stationery Office, Belfast.

Becker, K 2009 'Iron Age Ireland. Finding an invisible people', *in* G Cooney, K Becker, J Coles, M Ryan & S Sievers (eds), *Relics of Old Decency: archaeological studies in later prehistory. A festschrift for Barry Raftery*, 353–62. Wordwell, Dublin.

Becker, K 2012 'Re-defining the Irish Iron Age', *in* C Corlett & M Potterton (eds), *Life and Death in Iron Age Ireland in the Light of Recent Archaeological Excavations*, 1–14. Wordwell, Dublin.

Bhreathnach, E 2005 'The medieval kingdom of Brega', *in* E Bhreathnach (ed.), *The Kingship and Landscape of Tara*, 410–22. Discovery Programme/Four Courts Press, Dublin.

Bhreathnach, E 2011 'Transforming

kingship and cult: the provincial ceremonial capitals in early medieval Ireland', *in* R Schot, C Newman & E Bhreathnach (eds), *Landscapes of Cult and Kingship*, 126–48. Four Courts Press, Dublin.

Binchy, D A 1958 'The fair of Tailtiú and the feast of Tara', *Ériu*, Vol. 18, 113–38.

Bolger, T 2011 *Archaeological Excavation Report 01E0294 Rathmullan 6, Co. Meath*. Unpublished report by Irish Archaeological Consultancy Ltd for Meath County Council. TII Digital Heritage Collections: https://doi.org/10.7486/DRI.dn409g29j.

Bolger, T 2012 *Archaeological Excavation Report 00E0813 Rathmullan 10, Co. Meath*. Unpublished report by Irish Archaeological Consultancy Ltd for Meath County Council. TII Digital Heritage Collections: https://doi.org/10.7486/DRI.0c48h013x.

Bradley, J 1991 'Excavations at Moynagh Lough, County Meath', *Journal of the Royal Society of Antiquaries of Ireland*, Vol. 121, 5–26.

Bradley, J 2001 'A Late Mesolithic settlement site in Eastern Ireland', *in* B Raftery & J Hickey (eds), *Recent Developments in Wetland Research*, 299–306. Monograph Series Vol. 2. Department of Archaeology, University College Dublin, Dublin.

Breen, C & Forsythe W 2004 *Boats and Shipwrecks of Ireland*. The History Press Ltd, Stroud.

Brindley, A L 1999 'Irish Grooved Ware', *in* R Cleal & A MacSween (eds), *Grooved Ware in Britain and Ireland*, 23–35. Neolithic Studies Group Seminar Papers 3. Oxbow Books, Oxford.

Bronk Ramsey, C 2005 OxCal Program v.3.10: https://c14.arch.ox.ac.uk/oxcal/OxCal.html.

Bronk Ramsey, C 2020 OxCal Program v. 4.2: https://c14.arch.ox.ac.uk/oxcal/OxCal.html.

Brück, J 1999 'Houses, lifecycles and deposition on Middle Bronze Age settlements in southern England', *Proceedings of the Prehistoric Society*, Vol. 65, 145–66.

Brunaux, J-L 1987 *The Celtic Gauls. Gods, rites and sanctuaries*. Routledge, London.

Byrne, F J 1973 *Irish Kings and High-Kings*. Four Courts Press, Dublin.

Byrnes, E 1999 'Recent excavations at Richardstown, Co. Louth', *Archaeology Ireland*, Vol. 13, No. 4, 33.

Campbell, K 2004 'Staleen, Co. Meath: ring-ditch with urn burials', Excavation Licence No. 04E0625. Database of Irish Excavation Reports No. 1342: https://excavations.ie/report/2004/Meath/0012464/.

Carlin, N 2018 *The Beaker Phenomenon. Understanding the character and context of social practices in Ireland 2500–2000 BC*. Sidestone Press, Leiden.

Carlin, N, Clarke, L & Walsh, F 2008 *The Archaeology of Life and Death in the Boyne Floodplain. The linear landscape of the M4*. NRA Scheme Monographs 2. National Roads Authority, Dublin.

Clarke, L 2008 *Archaeological Excavation Report E3112, Boyerstown 7, Co. Meath*. Unpublished report by Archaeological Consultancy Services Ltd for Meath County Council. TII Digital Heritage Collections: https://doi.org/10.7486/DRI.f188f1678.

Clarke, L & Carlin, N 2008 *Archaeological Excavation Report E3087, Ardsallagh 2, Co. Meath*. Unpublished report by Archaeological Consultancy Services Ltd for Meath County Council. TII

Digital Heritage Collections: https://doi.org/10.7486/DRI.8336wg67c.

Cleary, K 2005 'Skeletons in the closet: the dead among the living on Irish Bronze Age settlements', *Journal of Irish Archaeology*, Vol. 14, 23–42.

Cleary, K 2006 'Irish Bronze Age settlements: more than meets the eye?', *Archaeology Ireland*, Vol. 20, No. 2, 18–21.

Cleary, R M 1983 'Ceramic assemblage', *in* M J O'Kelly, R M Cleary & D Lehane, *Newgrange, Co. Meath, Ireland. The Late Neolithic/Beaker period settlement*, 58–117. British Archaeological Reports, International Series 190. Oxford.

Clutterbuck, R 2012 'Iron Age ritual and settlement at Cookstown, Co. Meath', *in* C Corlett & M Potterton (eds), *Life and Death in Iron Age Ireland in the Light of Recent Archaeological Excavations*, 35–51. Wordwell, Bray.

Cooney, G 2000 *Landscapes of Neolithic Ireland*. Taylor and Francis Group, Routledge, London.

Cooney, G, Bayliss, A, Healy, F, Whittle, A, Danaher, E, Cagney, L, Mallory, J, Smyth, J, Kador, T, O'Sullivan, M, 'Ireland', 2011 *in* A Whittle, F Healy & A Bayliss (eds), *Gathering Time. Dating the Early Neolithic enclosures of southern Britain and Ireland* (2 vols), Vol. 1, 562–681. Oxbow Books, Oxford.

Cooney, G & Grogan, E 1994 *Irish Prehistory: a social perspective*. Wordwell, Dublin.

Coughlan, J 2011 'Appendix 2.8: Human remains', *in* A Kelly, *Archaeological Excavation Report E3124, Grange 2, Co. Meath*. Unpublished report by Irish Archaeological Consultancy Ltd for Meath County Council. TII Digital Heritage Collections: https://doi.org/10.7486/DRI.hd775d834.

Crew, P 1991 'The experimental production of prehistoric bar iron', *Historical Metallurgy*, Vol. 25, 1–36.

Crothers, N 1996 'Ballyharry's game', *Archaeology Ireland*, Vol. 38, No. 4, 12–14.

Cunliffe, B 1997 *The Ancient Celts*. Oxford University Press, Oxford.

Daly, A & Grogan, E 1993 'Excavation of four barrows in Mitchelstown West, Knocklong, County Limerick', *Discovery Programme Reports*, Vol. 1, 44–60.

Darvill, T 1996 'Neolithic buildings in England, Wales and the Isle of Man', *in* T Darvill & J Thomas (eds), *Neolithic Houses in Northwest Europe and Beyond*, 77–112. Oxbow Monograph 57. Oxbow Books, Oxford.

Davies, O 1949 'Excavations at the horned cairn at Ballymarlagh, Co. Antrim', *Ulster Journal of Archaeology*, Vol. 12, 26–42.

Davies, S 2009 'Location, location: a landscape-based study of early Neolithic longhouses in Britain', *Rosetta*, Vol. 7, 57–101: http://www.rosetta.bham.ac.uk/issue7/location-longhouses.

Deevy, M & Murphy, D 2009 *Places Along the Way. First findings on the M3*. NRA Scheme Monographs 5. National Roads Authority, Dublin.

Delaney, S, Bayley, D, Lyne, E, Nunan, J & McNamara, S 2012 'Burnt mounds: kitchen sinks of the Bronze Age', *in* S Delaney, D Bayley, E Lyne, S McNamara, J Nunan & K Molloy, *Borderlands. Archaeological excavations along the M18 Gort to Crusheen road scheme*, 57–108. NRA Scheme Monographs 9. National Roads Authority, Dublin.

Delaney, S, Bayley, D & McKeon, J 2020 *Around the Bay of Dundalk. Archaeological investigations along the route of the M1 Dundalk Western Bypass*. TII Heritage 10. Transport Infrastructure Ireland, Dublin.

Devane, C 2013 'The history of Kilbegly and

its environs', *in* N Jackman, *The Mill at Kilbegly. An archaeological investigation on the route of the N6 Ballinasloe to Athlone national road scheme*, 97–114. NRA Scheme Monographs 12. National Roads Authority, Dublin.

Doody, M 2000 'Bronze Age houses in Ireland', *in* A Desmond, G Johnston & M McCarthy (eds), *New Agendas in Irish Prehistory. Papers in commemoration of Liz Anderson*, 135–60. Wordwell, Bray.

Doody, M 2008 *The Ballyhoura Hills Project*. Discovery Programme Monograph No. 7. Wordwell, Bray.

Dowd, M & Carden R F 2016 'First evidence of a Late Upper Palaeolithic presence in Ireland', *Quaternary Science Reviews* 139 (2016), 158–63. http://dx.doi.org/10.10.16/j.quascirev.2016.02.029

Dowling, G 2015 'Exploring the hidden depths of Tara's hinterland: geophysical survey and landscape investigations in the Meath–north Dublin region, Ireland', *Proceedings of the Prehistoric Society* (FirstView Article), November 2015, 1–25. Published online 28 August 2015. DOI: https://10.1017/ppr.2015.11.

Dowling, G & Cahill Wilson, J 2014 'Tracing the footprints of our ancestors', *Archaeology Ireland*, Vol. 28, No. 1, 20–2.

Driscoll, K 2009 'Constructing Later Mesolithic landscapes', *in* N Finlay, S McCartan, N Milner & C Wickham-Jones (eds), *From Bann Flakes to Bushmills. Papers in honour of Professor Peter Woodman*, 101–12. Prehistoric Society Research Papers 1. Oxbow Books, Oxford.

Duffy, C 2000 'Hill of Rath, prehistoric complex, Co. Louth', Excavation Licence No. 00E0535. Database of Irish Excavation Reports No. 0688: https://excavations.ie/report/2000/Louth/0005514/.

Dunlop, C & Barkley, J 2012 'Late Neolithic timber circle—focus on Armalughey (Site 20)', *in* C Dunlop & J Barkley, *Road to the West. A Road to the Past, Vol. 2. Archaeology of the A4/A5 Road Improvements Scheme from Dungannon to Ballygradey*, 36–44. Northern Archaeological Consultancy Ltd, Belfast.

Elder, E & Ginn, V 2009 *Archaeological Excavation Report E3041, Johnstown 1, County Meath*. Unpublished report by Archaeological Consultancy Services Ltd for Meath County Council. TII Digital Heritage Collections: https://doi.org/10.7486/DRI.xs560s823.

Elder, S, O'Connor, E & Owen, J 2009 *Archaeological Excavation Report E3038, Raynestown 1, Co. Meath*. Unpublished report by Archaeological Consultancy Services Ltd for Meath County Council. TII Digital Heritage Collections: https://doi.org/10.7486/DRI.x633tf78s.

Elliot, R 2007 'Whitehall/Paulstown 2, Co. Kilkenny. Beaker activity', Excavation Registration No. E3632. Database of Irish Excavation Reports No. 1023: https://excavations.ie/report/2007/Kilkenny/0018009.

Elliott, R 2009 *Archaeological Excavation Report E3632, Paulstown 2, Co. Kilkenny*. Unpublished preliminary excavation report by Irish Archaeological Consultancy Ltd for the National Monuments Service, Dublin.

Eogan, G 1984 *Excavations at Knowth 1. Smaller passage tombs, Neolithic occupation and Beaker activity*. Royal Irish Academy, Dublin.

Eogan, G 2012 *Excavations at Knowth 5. The archaeology of Knowth in the first and second millennia AD*. Royal Irish Academy, Dublin.

Eogan, G & Roche, H 1997 *Excavations at Knowth 2*. Royal Irish Academy, Dublin.

Eogan, J 1998 'Bettystown, Co. Meath: prehistoric, multi-period site', Excavation Licence No. 98E0072. Database of Irish Excavation Reports No. 503: https://excavations.ie/report/1998/Meath/0003681/.

Eogan, J 1999 'Recent excavations at Bettystown, Co. Meath', *Irish Association of Professional Archaeologists Newsletter*, No. 30, 9.

Evans, E E 1953 *Lyles Hill. A Late Neolithic site in County Antrim*. Archaeological Research Publications 2. HMSO, Belfast.

Feachem, R W 1965 *The North Britons. The prehistory of a border people*. Hutchinson, London.

Fitzpatrick, A 2009 'The champion's portion: feasting in the Celtic pre-Roman Iron Age', *in* G Cooney, K Becker, J Coles, M Ryan & S Sievers (eds), *Relics of Old Decency: archaeological studies in later prehistory. A festschrift for Barry Raftery*, 389–404. Wordwell, Dublin.

Foley, C 1988 'Only an old pile of stones. Creggandevesky court tomb, Co. Tyrone', *in* A Hamlin & C Lynn (eds), *Pieces of the Past*, 3–5. HMSO, Belfast.

Gallagher, D & Ginn, V 2008 *Archaeological Excavation Report E3184, Derver 4, Co. Meath*. Unpublished report by Archaeological Consultancy Services Ltd for Meath County Council. TII Digital Heritage Collections: https://doi.org/10.7486/DRI.zc7864878.

Gearey, B R, Hopla, E J & Hill, T 2011 'Appendix 2.16: Palynological analyses of deposits from Clowanstown 1, Kilmainham 1C and Lismullin Sample Site 1', *in* F Walsh, *Archaeological Excavation Report E3141 Kilmainham 1C, Co. Meath. Volume 2: Appendices*. TII Digital Heritage Collections: https://doi.org/10.7486/DRI.mp495t552.

Geissel, H 2006 *A Road on the Long Ridge. In search of the ancient highway on the Esker Riada*. CRS Publications, Newbridge.

Ginn, V & Plunkett, G 2020 'Filling the gaps: a chronology of Bronze Age settlement in Ireland', *Journal of Irish Archaeology*, Vol. 29, 41–61.

Ginn, V & Rathbone, S (eds) 2012 *Corrstown: a coastal community. Excavation of a Bronze Age village in Northern Ireland*. Oxbow Books, Oxford.

Gowen, M 1988 *Three Irish Gas Pipelines. New archaeological evidence in Munster.* Wordwell, Bray.

Gregory, T 1992 *Excavations in Thetford, 1980–82, Fison Way* (2 vols). East Anglian Archaeology Report No. 53. East Anglian Archaeology, Norwich.

Grogan, E 2002 'Neolithic houses in Ireland: a broader perspective', *Antiquity*, Vol. 76, 517–25.

Grogan, E 2004 'The implications of Irish Neolithic houses', *in* I Shepard & G Barclay (eds), *Scotland in Ancient Europe. The Neolithic and Early Bronze Age of Scotland in their European context*, 103–14. Society of Antiquaries of Scotland, Edinburgh.

Grogan, E 2005a *The North Munster Project. Volume 1. The prehistoric landscape of south-east Clare*. Discovery Programme Monographs 6. Wordwell, Bray.

Grogan, E 2005b *The North Munster Project. Volume 2. The prehistoric landscape of north Munster*. Discovery Programme Monographs 6. Wordwell, Bray.

Grogan, E 2013 'The development of the Neolithic and Bronze Age landscape in the Tara region', *in* M O'Sullivan, C Scarre & M Doyle (eds), *Tara—from the Past to the Future. Towards a new research agenda*, 335–62. UCD School of Archaeology/Wordwell, Bray.

Grogan, E & Roche, H 2009 *Prehistoric*

Pottery Assemblage from Paulstown 2, Co. Kilkenny (AR146, E3632). N9/N10 Rathclogh to Powerstown. Unpublished report for Irish Archaeological Consultancy Ltd.

Grogan, E & Roche, H 2011 'Appendix 2.1: Prehistoric pottery', *in* P Lynch, *Archaeological Excavation Report E3158, Cakestown Glebe 2, County Meath*. Unpublished report by Irish Archaeological Consultancy Ltd for Meath County Council. TII Digital Heritage Collections: https://doi.org/10.7486/DRI.sf26nk87cM3.

Hall, R 2006 *Excavations at Priors Hall, Corby, Northamptonshire. An Iron Age and Romano-British ironworking complex*. Archaeological Project Services Report No. 4/08: doi.org/10.5284/1023760.

Hannah, E & McLaughlin, T 2019 'Long-term archaeological perspectives in new genomic and environmental evidence from early medieval Ireland', *Journal of Archaeological Science*, Vol. 106, 23–28: https://doi.org/10.1016/j.jas.2019.04.001.

Hartwell, B 1998 'The Ballynahatty Complex', *in* A Gibson & D Simpson (eds), *Prehistoric Ritual and Religion*, 32–44. Sutton Publishing, Stroud.

Hartwell, B 2002 'A Neolithic ceremonial timber complex at Ballynahatty, Co. Down', *Antiquity*, Vol. 76, 526–32.

Hawkes, A 2018 *The Archaeology of Prehistoric Burnt Mounds in Ireland*. Archaeopress, Oxford.

Hencken, H O'Neill 1950 'Lagore Crannog: an Irish royal residence from the seventh to tenth centuries', *Proceedings of the Royal Irish Academy*, Vol. 53C, 1–247.

Hickie, D 2002 *Native trees and forests of Ireland*. Gill & Macmillan, Dublin.

Historic England 2018 [first issued 2011] *Later Prehistoric Shrines and Ritual Structures:* historicengland.org.uk/images-books/publications/iha-later-prehist-shrines-ritual-structures/.

Inland Fisheries Ireland 2020 'Fishing in Ireland: the Kells Blackwater', https://fishinginireland.info/trout/east/meath/kellsblackwater/.

Jackson, D A, Ambrose, T M, Pacitto, A L, Woods, P J, Jenkins, F, Goodburn, R, Butcher, S A, Bayley, J, Jones, R, Evans, J G & Arthur, J R B 1978 'Excavations at Wakerley, Northants, 1972–75', Britannia, Vol. 9, 115-242; Cambridge Journals Online: https://www.jstor.org/stable/525939?origin=crossref&seq=1.

Jobey, G & Tait, J 1966 'Excavations on palisaded settlement and cairnfields at Alnham, Northumberland', *Archaeologia Aeliana* (4th ser.), Vol. 44, 5–48.

Jones, C 1998 'The discovery and dating of the prehistoric landscape of Roughan Hill, Co. Clare', *Journal of Irish Archaeology*, Vol. 9, 27–43.

Kelly, E 2002 'Antiquities from Irish holy wells and their wider context', *Archaeology Ireland*, Vol. 16, No. 2, 24–8.

Kelly, F 1998 *Early Irish Farming. A study based on the law tracts of the 7th and 8th centuries AD*. Dublin Institute for Advanced Studies, Dublin.

Kiely, J 2003 'A Neolithic house at Cloghers, Co. Kerry', *in* I Armit, E Murphy, E Nelis & D Simpson (eds), Neolithic Settlement *in Ireland and Western Britain*, 182–87. Oxbow Books, Oxford.

Lennon, A M 2006 'Derrinsallagh 4 Co. Laois: industrial pits', Excavation Licence No. E2180. Database of Irish Excavation Reports No. 1163: https://excavations.ie/report/2006/Laois/0015907/.

Lipscombe, M & Stokes, J 2008 *Trees and How to Grow Them*. Think Books, London.

Lock, G & Ralston, I 2017 *Atlas of Hillforts of Britain and Ireland*. University of Edinburgh and Oxford University: https://hillforts.arch.ox.ac.uk/.

Logue, P 2003 'Excavations at Thornhill, Co. Derry', *in* I Armit, E Murphy, E Nelis & D Simpson (eds), *Neolithic Settlement in Ireland and Western Britain*, 149–55. Oxbow Books, Oxford.

Lowe, J J, Walker, M J C, Scott, E M, Harkness, D D, Bryant, C L & Davies, S M 2004 'A coherent high-precision radiocarbon chronology for the Late-glacial radiocarbon sequence at Sluggan Bog, Co. Antrim, Northern Ireland', *Journal of Quaternary Science*, Vol. 19, No. 2, 147–58.

Lunde, P & Stone, C (trans.) 2011 *Ibn Fadlan and the Land of Darkness. Arab travellers in the far north*. Penguin Classics, London.

Lynch, F & Musson, C 2001 'A prehistoric and early medieval complex at Llandegai, near Bangor, North Wales', *Archaeologia Cambrensis*, Vol. 150, 17–142.

Lyne, E 2010 *Archaeological Excavation Report E3128 Phoenixtown 1, County Meath*. Unpublished report by Irish Archaeological Consultancy Ltd for Meath County Council. TII Digital Heritage Collections: https://doi.org/10.7486/DRI.j673dj552.

Lyne, E 2012 'Multiphase prehistoric settlement at Rathwilladoon', *in* S Delaney, D Bayley, E Lyne, S McNamara, J Nunan & K Molloy, *Borderlands. Archaeological excavations along the M18 Gort to Crusheen road scheme*, 39–56. NRA Scheme Monographs 9. National Roads Authority, Dublin.

Lyons, S 2011 'Appendix 2.6: Plant remains', *in* F Walsh, *Archaeological Excavation Report E3141 Kilmainham 1C, Co. Meath. Volume 2: Appendices*. Unpublished report by Irish Archaeological Consultancy Ltd for Meath County Council. TII Digital Heritage Collections: https://doi.org/10.7486/DRI.mp495t552.

McQuade, M 2005 'Archaeological excavation of a multi-period prehistoric settlement at Waterunder, Mell, Co. Louth', *County Louth Archaeological and Historical Journal*, Vol. 26, 31–66.

McQuade, M, Molloy, B & Moriarty, C 2009 *In the Shadow of the Galtees. Archaeological excavations along the N8 Cashel to Mitchelstown road scheme*. NRA Scheme Monographs 4. National Roads Authority, Dublin.

McSparron, C 2008 'Have you no homes to go to?', *Archaeology Ireland*, Vol. 22, No. 3, 18–21.

Mallory, J P, Nelis, E & Hartwell, B 2011 *Excavations on Donegore Hill, Co. Antrim*. Wordwell, Bray.

Mandal, S 2011 'Appendix 2.11: Petrological analysis of stone samples', *in* F Walsh, *Archaeological Excavation Report E3141 Kilmainham 1C, Co. Meath. Volume 2: Appendices*. Unpublished report by Irish Archaeological Consultancy Ltd for Meath County Council. TII Digital Heritage Collections: https://doi.org/10.7486/DRI.mp495t552.

Meath County Council 2013 'Landscape Character Assessment', *Meath County Development Plan 2013–2019*, Appendix 7. Meath County Council, Navan.

Meehan, R 2007 *The Making of Meath: the county's natural landscape history*. Meath County Council, Navan.

Mitchell, F 1972 'Some Ultimate Larnian sites at Lake Derravaragh, Co. Westmeath', *Journal of the Royal Society of Antiquaries of Ireland*, Vol. 102, 160–73.

Mitchell, F 1990 *Shell Guide to Reading the Irish Landscape*. Country House, Dublin.

Molloy, K & O'Connell, M 2004 'Holocene vegetation and land-use dynamics in the karstic environment of Inis Oírr, Aran Islands, western Ireland: pollen analytical evidence evaluated in the light of the archaeological record', *Quaternary International*, Vol. 113, 41–64.

Monk, M & Kelleher, E 2005 'An assessment of the archaeological evidence for Irish corn-drying kilns in the light of the results of archaeological experiments and archaeobotanical studies', *Journal of Irish Archaeology*, Vol. 14, 77–114.

Monk, M & Power, O 2012 'More than a grain of truth emerges from a rash of corn-drying kilns?', *Archaeology Ireland*, Vol. 26, No. 2, 38–41.

Moore, D 2012 *Archaeological Excavation Report 00E0810 Sheephouse 2, Co. Meath*. Unpublished report by Irish Archaeological Consultancy Ltd for Meath County Council. TII Digital Heritage Collections: https://doi.org/10.7486/DRI.0000cd770.

Moore, D & Walsh, F 2011 *Archaeological Excavation Final Report 01E0129 Lagavooren 5, Co. Meath*. Unpublished report by Irish Archaeological Consultancy Ltd for Meath County Council. TII Digital Heritage Collections: https://doi.org/10.7486/DRI.6q18g089p.

Moore, D G 2003 'Neolithic houses in Ballyharry townland, Islandmagee, Co. Antrim', *in* I Armit, E Murphy, E Nelis & D Simpson (eds), *Neolithic Settlement in Ireland and Western Britain*, 156–3. Oxbow Books, Oxford.

Moore, M (ed.) 1987 *Archaeological Inventory of County Meath*. Office of Public Works, Dublin.

Mossop, M, Ginn, V & Ruddle, E 2009 *Archaeological Excavation Report E3116, Ardbraccan 2, Co. Meath*. Unpublished report by Archaeological Consultancy Services Ltd for Meath County Council. TII Digital Heritage Collections: https://doi.org/10.7486/DRI.ft84p5395.

Mossop, M & Mossop, E 2009 *Archaeological Excavation Report on E3064 Clowanstown 2, Co. Meath*. Unpublished report by Archaeological Consultancy Services Ltd for Meath County Council. TII Digital Heritage Collections: https://doi.org/10.7486/DRI.3b59dq352.

Mount, C 1995 'A look at the burials of the Bronze Age', *Archaeology Ireland*, Vol. 9, No. 1, 18–21.

Mount, C 2012 'A note on some Beaker period pit burials in Ireland', *Journal of Irish Archaeology*, Vol. 21, 1–6.

Nelis, D 2011 *Archaeological Excavation Report 01E0390 Rathmullan 9, Co. Meath*. Unpublished report by Irish Archaeological Consultancy Ltd for Meath County Council. TII Digital Heritage Collections: https://doi.org/10.7486/DRI.h7033n13x.

Nelis, D 2012 *Archaeological Excavation Report 00E0811 Sheephouse 3, Co. Meath*. Unpublished report by Irish Archaeological Consultancy Ltd for Meath County Council. TII Digital Heritage Collections: https://doi.org/10.7486/DRI.0574f645f.

Nelis, E 2010 'Appendix 2.3: Lithics analysis', *in* Y Whitty, *Archaeological Excavation Report E3151 Townparks 5, Co. Meath*. Unpublished report by Irish Archaeological Consultancy Ltd for Meath County Council. TII Digital Heritage Collections: https://doi.org/10.7486/DRI.r2087411j.

Nelis, E 2011a 'Appendix 2.3: Lithic report', *in* F Walsh, *Archaeological Excavation Report E3141, Kilmainham 1C, Co. Meath. Volume 2: Appendices*. Unpublished report by Irish Archaeological Consultancy Ltd for Meath County Council. TII Digital Heritage Collections: https://doi.org/10.7486/DRI.mp495t552.

Nelis, E 2011b 'Appendix 2.3: Lithics analysis', in E Lyne, *Archaeological Excavation Report E3141 Kilmainham 1A, Co. Meath*. Unpublished report by Irish Archaeological Consultancy Ltd for Meath County Council. TII Digital Heritage Collections: https://doi.org/10.7486/DRI.p267m931c.

Ní Bhrolcháin, M 2011 'Death tales of the early kings of Tara', *in* R Schot, C Newman & E Bhreathnach (eds), *Landscapes of Cult and Kingship*, 44–65. Four Courts Press, Dublin.

NPWS 2020 National Parks and Wildlife Service, 'River Boyne and River Blackwater SAC': https://www.npws.ie/protected-sites/sac.

O'Brien, E & Bhreathnach, E 2011 'Irish boundary *ferta*, their physical manifestation and historical context', *in* F Edmonds & P Russell (eds), *TOME: Studies in Medieval Celtic History and Law in honour of Thomas Charles Edwards*, 53–64. Boydell Press, Woodbridge.

O'Brien, R 2010a 'Appendix 2.4.3: Worked stone', *in* A Kelly, *Archaeological Excavation Report E3123, Grange 3, Co. Meath, on the M3 Clonee to North of Kells National Road Project*. Unpublished report by Archaeological Consultancy Services Ltd for Meath County Council. TII Digital Heritage Collections: https://doi.org/10.7486/DRI.h7033n15g.

O'Brien, R 2010b 'Appendix 2.4: Stone bead', *in* D Bayley, *Archaeological Excavation Report E3143, Kilmainham 2, Co. Meath*. Unpublished report by Irish Archaeological Consultancy Ltd for Meath County Council. TII Digital Heritage Collections: https://doi.org/10.7486/DRI.pg15qv67m.

O'Brien, W 2004 *Ross Island. Mining, metal and society in early Ireland*. Bronze Age Studies 6. Department of Archaeology, National University of Ireland, Galway.

O Carroll, E 2011 'Appendix 2.14: Wood analysis', *in* F Walsh, *Archaeological Excavation Report E3141 Kilmainham 1C, Co. Meath. Volume 2: Appendices*. Unpublished report by Irish Archaeological Consultancy Ltd for Meath County Council. TII Digital Heritage Collections: https://doi.org/10.7486/DRI.mp495t552.

O'Connell, A 2009 *Archaeological Excavation Report E3074, Lismullin 1, Co. Meath* (3 vols). Unpublished report by Archaeological Consultancy Services Ltd for Meath County Council. TII Digital Heritage Collections: https://doi.org/10.7486/DRI.5425zr47m.

O'Connell, A 2013 *Harvesting the Stars. A pagan temple at Lismullin, Co. Meath*. NRA Scheme Monographs 11. National Roads Authority, Dublin.

O'Connell, A & Clarke, A 2009 *Archaeological Excavation Report E3023, Castlefarm 1, Co. Meath*. Unpublished report by Archaeological Consultancy Services Ltd for Meath County Council. TII Digital Heritage Collections: https://doi.org/10.7486/DRI.0k22jw69q.

O'Connor, E 2007 *Fulacht Fiadh, Burnt Mounds and Hot Stone Technology on the M3*. Unpublished report for Archaeological Consultancy Services Ltd and Meath County Council.

O'Donnell, L 2007 'Wood and charcoal', *in* E Grogan, L O'Donnell and P Johnston (eds), *The Bronze Age Landscapes of the Pipeline to the West: an integrated archaeological and environmental assessment*, 27–69. Wordwell, Bray.

O'Donnell, L 2011 'Appendix 2.5: Charcoal', *in* A Kelly, *Archaeological Excavation Report E3124, Grange 2, Co. Meath*. Unpublished report by Irish Archaeological Consultancy Ltd for Meath County Council. TII Digital Heritage Collections: https://doi.org/10.7486/DRI.hd775d834.

O'Donnell, L 2017 'Woodland dynamics and use during the Bronze Age: new evidence from Irish archaeological charcoal', *The Holocene*, Vol. 27, No. 8, 1078–91.

Ó Drisceoil, C 2003 'Archaeological excavations of a Neolithic settlement at Coolfore, Co. Louth', *in* I Armit, E Nelis & D Simpson (eds), *Neolithic Settlement in Ireland and Western Britain*, 176–81. Oxbow Books, Exeter.

Ó Drisceoil, C 2009 'Excavation of a Late Neolithic Grooved Ware settlement at Balgatheran, County Louth', *County Louth Archaeological and Historical Journal*, Vol. 27, No. 1, 77–102.

O'Hara, R 2009 *Archaeological Excavation Report E3068, Collierstown 1, Co. Meath*. Unpublished report by Archaeological Consultancy Services Ltd for Meath County Council. TII Digital Heritage Collections: https://doi.org/10.7486/DRI.3x81m239n.

O'Kelly, M, Cleary, R & Lehane, D (eds) 1983 *Newgrange, County Meath, Ireland*. British Archaeological Reports, International Series 190. Oxford.

Olalde, I, Brace, S, Allentoft, M E et al. 2018 'The Beaker phenomenon and the genomic transformation of northwest Europe', *Nature*, Vol. 555, No. 7695, 190–6.

O'Neill, T & O'Hara, R 2009 *Archaeological Excavation Report E3072 Skreen 2, Co. Meath*. Unpublished report by Archaeological Consultancy Services Ltd for Meath County Council. TII Digital Heritage Collections: https://doi.org/10.7486/DRI.4q77v611b.

Ó Ríordáin, B & Waddell, J 1993 *The Funerary Bowls and Vases of the Irish Bronze Age*. Galway University Press, Galway.

Ó Ríordáin, S P 1954 'Lough Gur excavations: Neolithic and Bronze Age houses on Knockadoon', *Proceedings of the Royal Irish Academy*, Vol. 56C, 297–459.

Ó Ríordáin, S P 1955 'A burial with faience beads at Tara', *Proceedings of the Prehistoric Society*, Vol. 21, 163–73.

O'Sullivan, A 2001 *Foragers, Farmers and Fishermen in a Coastal Landscape. An intertidal archaeological survey of the Shannon estuary*. Discovery Programme Monograph 5. Royal Irish Academy, Dublin.

O'Sullivan, M 2005 *Duma na nGiall. The Mound of the Hostages, Tara*. School of Archaeology, University College Dublin/Wordwell, Bray.

Parker Pearson, M 2013 'Researching Stonehenge: theories past and present', *Archaeology International*, Vol. 16, 72–83 (http://dx.doi.org/10.5334/ai.1601).

Parker Pearson, M, Pollard, J, Richards, C, Thomas, J, Tilley, C, Welham, K & Albarella, U 2006 'Materiality and Stonehenge: the Stonehenge Riverside Project and new discoveries', *Journal of Material Culture*, Vol. 11, 227–61.

Pope, R E 2015 'Bronze Age architectural traditions: dates and landscapes', *in* F Hunter & I B M Ralston (eds), *Scotland in Later Prehistoric Europe*, 159–84. Oxbow Books, Oxford.

Quinn, B & Moore, D 2009 '*Fulachta fiadh* and the beer experiment', *in* M Stanley, E Danaher and J Eogan (eds), *Dining and Dwelling*, 43–53. Archaeology and the National Roads Authority Monograph Series No. 6. National Roads Authority, Dublin.

Raftery, B 1994 *Pagan Celtic Ireland: the enigma of the Irish Iron Age*. Thames and Hudson, London.

Rajic, M 2012 'From Wexford to Clare in 5,600 years', *Seanda*, No. 7, 22–3.

Rathbone, S 2009 *Archaeological Excavation Report E3061, Garretstown 2, Co. Meath.* Unpublished report by Archaeological Consultancy Services Ltd for Meath County Council. TII Digital Heritage Collections: https://doi.org/10.7486/DRI.2j635k63v.

Rawlinson, G (trans.) 1910 *The History of Herodotus*. J M Dent, London.

Reimer, P J, Austin, W E N, Bard, E, Bayliss, A, Blackwell, P G, Bronk Ramsey, C, Butzin, M, Cheng, H, Lawrence Edwards, R, Friedrich, M, Grootes, P M, Guilderson, T P, Hajdas, I, Heaton, T J, Hogg, A G, Hughen, K A, Kromer, B, Manning, S W, Muscheler, R, Palmer, J G, Pearson, C, van der Plicht, J, Reimer, R, Richards, D A, Marian Scott, E, Southon, J R, Turney, C S M, Wacker, L Adolphi, F, Büntgen, U, Capano, M, Fahrni, S, Fogtmann-Schulz, A, Friedrich, R, Miyake, F, Olsen, J, Reinig, F, Sakamoto, M, Sookdeo, A & Talamo, S 2020 'The IntCal20 Northern Hemisphere radiocarbon age calibration curve (0–55 cal kBP)', Radiocarbon 62, 725–57.

Reimer, P J, Baillie, M G L, Bard, E, Bayliss, A, Beck, Bertrand, C Blackwell, P G, Buck, C E, Burr, G, Cutler, K B, Damon, P E, Edwards, R L, Fairbanks, R G, Friedrich, M, Guilderson, T P, Hughen, K A, Kromer, B, McCormac, F G, Manning, S, Bronk Ramsey, C, Reimer, R W, Remmele, S, Southon, J R, Stuiver, M, Talamo, S, Taylor, F W, van der Plicht, J and Weyhenmeyer, C E 2004 'IntCal04 terrestrial radiocarbon age calibration, 0-26 cal kyr BP', Radiocarbon 46, 1029–58.

Reimer, P J, Baillie, M G L, Bard, E, Bayliss, A, Beck, J W, Blackwell, P G, Bronk Ramsey, C, Buck, C E, Burr, G S, Edwards, R L, Friedrich, M, Grootes, P M, Guilderson, T P, Hajdas, I, Heaton, T J, Hogg, A G, Hughen, K A, Kaiser, K F, Kromer, B, McCormac, F G, Manning, S W, Reimer, R W, Richards, D A, Southon, J R, Talamo, S, Turney, C S M, van der Plicht, J and Weyhenmeyer, C E 2009 'IntCal09 and Marine09 radiocarbon age calibration curves, 0–50,000 years cal BP', Radiocarbon 51, 1111–50.

Reynolds, D M 1982 'Aspects of later timber construction in south-east Scotland', *in* D W Harding (ed.), *Later Prehistoric Settlement in South-East Scotland*, 44–56. Occasional Paper 8. Department of Archaeology, University of Edinburgh, Edinburgh.

Roche, H 2002 'Excavations at Ráith na Ríg, Tara, Co. Meath', *Discovery Programme Reports*, Vol. 5, 19–82.

Rohan, N 2006 'Kells Business Park Extension, Townparks, Kells, Meath: Multi-phase with Neolithic activity', Excavation Licence No. 05E0466 (ext.). Database of Irish Excavation Reports No. 1329: https://excavations.ie/report/2006/Meath/0016337/.

Rohan, N 2007 'Townparks, Kells, Meath: Palisaded and ditched enclosure', Excavation Licence No. 05E0446 (ext.). Database of Irish Excavation Reports No. 1329: https://excavations.ie/report/2007/Meath/0018306/.

Roualet, P, Rapin, A, Fluzin, P & Uran, L 1982 'Sépultures du Crayon à Écury-le-Repos, Marne', *Mémoires de la Société d'Agriculture, de Commerce, des Art et des Science du Départment de la Marne*, Vol. 97, 25–44.

Russell, I 2003a *Archaeological Excavation Report 01E0039, Claristown 2, Co. Meath, on the M1 Northern Motorway Project*. Unpublished report by Archaeological Consultancy Services Ltd for Meath County Council. TII Digital Heritage Collections: https://doi.org/10.7486/DRI.5425zr452.

Russell, I 2003b *Archaeological Excavation Report 01E0191, Kilsharvan 16, Co. Meath, on the M1 Northern Motorway Project*. Unpublished report by Archaeological Consultancy Services Ltd for Meath County Council. TII Digital Heritage Collections: https://doi.org/10.7486/DRI.bg25mv81p.

Ryan, M 1980 'An Early Mesolithic site in the Irish midlands', *Antquity*, Vol. 54, 46–47.

Ryan, M 1984 'Archaeological excavations at Lough Boora, Broughal townland, Co. Offaly, 1977', *in* M O'Rourke (ed.), *Proceedings of the 7th International Peat Congress, Dublin, June 18–23, 1984*, Vol. 1, 407–13. Bord na Móna, Dublin.

Rynne, C 2013 'Mills and milling in early medieval Ireland', *in* N Jackman, *The Mill at Kilbegly. An archaeological investigation on the route of the N6 Ballinasloe to Athlone national road scheme*, 115–47. NRA Scheme Monographs 12. National Roads Authority, Dublin.

Seaver, M 2016 *Meitheal. The archaeology of life, labour and beliefs at Raystown, County Meath*. TII Heritage 4. Transport Infrastructure Ireland, Dublin.

Shee Twohig, E, Roughley, C, Shell, C, O Reilly, P, Clarke, C & Swanton, G 2010 'Open air rock art at Loughcrew, Co. Meath', *Journal of Irish Archaeology*, Vol. 19, 1–28.

Shell, C 2005 'The Loughcrew Landscape Project', *Past: Newsletter of the Prehistoric Society*, No. 51, 1–3. University College London, London.

Shell, C & Roughley, C F 2004 'Exploring the Loughcrew landscape: a new approach with airborne lidar', *Archaeology Ireland*, Vol. 18, No. 2, 20–3.

Sheridan, A 2010 'The Neolithisation of Britain and Ireland: the big picture', in B Finlayson & G Warren (eds), *Landscapes in Transition*, 89–105. Oxbow Books, Oxford.

Sheridan, A 2013 Early Neolithic habitation structures in Britain and Ireland: a matter of circumstance and context', *in* D Hofmann & J Smyth (eds), *Tracking the Neolithic House in Europe*, 283–300. Springer, New York, Dordrecht, Heidelberg and London.

Simms, A 1990 *Irish Historic Towns Atlas: Kells*. Royal Irish Academy, Dublin.

Smyth, J 2006 'The role of the house in Early Neolithic Ireland', *European Journal of Archaeology*, Vol. 9, 229–57.

Smyth, J 2014 *Settlement in the Irish Neolithic. New discoveries at the edge of Europe*. Prehistoric Society Research Papers Vol. 6. Oxbow Books, Oxford and Philadelphia.

Smyth, J & Evershed, R P 2014 'Milk and molecules: secrets from prehistoric pottery', *in* B Kelly, N Roycroft and M Stanley (eds), *Fragments of Lives Past: archaeological objects from Irish road schemes*, 1–13. Archaeology and the National Roads Authority Monograph Series 11. National Roads Authority, Dublin.

Stafford, E 2012 *Archaeological Excavation Report 00E0914, Lagavooren 7, Co. Meath*. Unpublished report by Irish Archaeological Consultancy Ltd for Meath County Council. TII Digital Heritage

Collections: https://doi.org/10.7486/DRI.1j92vp21j.

Stout, G 1991 'Embanked enclosures of the Boyne region', *Proceedings of the Royal Irish Academy*, Vol. 91C, 245–84.

Stuijts, I 2005 'Wood and charcoal identification', *in* M Gowen, J Ó Néill & M Phillips (eds), *The Lisheen Mine Archaeological Project 1996–8*, 137–86. Wordwell, Bray.

Stuiver, M & Reimer, P J 1993 'Extended 14C database and revised CALIB 3.0 14C age calibration program', *Radiocarbon*, Vol. 35, 215–30.

Stuiver, M, Reimer, P J & Reimer, R W 1985–2020 CALIB radiocarbon calibration programme Revs 5.0.2 (2005) and 6.0.0 (2010): wwww.calib.org.

Suddaby, I 2003 'The excavation of two Late Bronze Age roundhouses at Ballyprior Beg, Islandmagee, County Antrim', *Ulster Journal of Archaeology*, Vol. 62, 45–91.

Sweetman, D 1976 'An earthen enclosure at Monknewtown, Slane, Co. Meath', *Proceedings of the Royal Irish Academy*, Vol. 76C, 25–73.

Tierney, J, Ryan, M & Richardson, A 2008 'Beaker settlement: Area 2, Graigueshoneen townland', *in* P Johnston, J Kiely & J Tierney, *Near the Bend in the River. Archaeology of the N25 Kilmacthomas National Road Scheme*, 33–8. NRA Scheme Monographs 3. National Roads Authority, Dublin.

Tipping, R, Davies, A, McCulloch, R & Tisdall, E 2008 'Response to late Bronze Age climate change of farming communities in north-east Scotland', *Journal of Archaeological Science*, Vol. 35, 2379–86.

Waddell, J 2010 *The Prehistoric Archaeology of Ireland*. Wordwell, Bray.

Wainwright, G J & Longworth, I H 1971 *Durrington Walls: excavations 1966–1968.* Report of the Research Committee of the Society of Antiquaries of London 29. Society of Antiquaries of London, London.

Wallace, A & Anguilano, L 2010 'Appendix 2.10: Metallurgy', *in* A Kelly, *Archaeological Excavation Report E3123, Grange 3, Co. Meath*. Unpublished report by Irish Archaeological Consultancy Ltd for Meath County Council. TII Digital Heritage Collections: https://doi.org/10.7486/DRI.h7033n15g.

Wallace, A & Anguilano, L 2011 'Appendix 2.11: Metallurgy', *in* A Kelly, *Archaeological Excavation Report E3124, Grange 2, Co. Meath*. Unpublished report by Irish Archaeological Consultancy Ltd for Meath County Council. TII Digital Heritage Collections: https://doi.org/10.7486/DRI.hd775d834.

Walsh, F 2006 'Neolithic Monanny, County Monaghan', *in* J O'Sullivan & M Stanley (eds), *Settlement, Industry and Ritual*, 1–17. Archaeology and the National Roads Authority Monograph Series 3. National Roads Authority, Dublin.

Walsh, F 2011a *Archaeological Excavation Report E3141 Kilmainham 1C, Co. Meath* (2 vols). Unpublished report by Irish Archaeological Consultancy Ltd for Meath County Council. TII Digital Heritage Collections: https://doi.org/10.7486/DRI.nv93jh63v (Vol. 1, text), https://doi.org/10.7486/DRI.np19gq95p (Vol. 1, images), https://doi.org/10.7486/DRI.mp495t552 (Vol. 2, Appendices).

Walsh, F 2011b 'Excavation and conjecture of a Late Bronze Age farmstead at Tober, Co. Offaly', *Journal of the Royal Society of Antiquaries of Ireland*, Vol. 141, 9–31.

Walsh, F 2011c 'Archaeology of two townlands (part 1): from Stone Age settlers to 19th-century farmers at Monanny and Cloghvally Upper, Co.

Monaghan', *Clogher Record*, Vol. 20, No. 3, 500–20.

Walsh, F, Lyons, S & McClatchie, M 2011 'A post-built early Neolithic house at Kilmainham, Co. Meath', *Archaeology Ireland*, Vol. 25, No. 3, 35–7.

White, S I & Smith, G 1999 'A funerary and ceremonial centre at Capel Eithin, Gaerwen, Anglesey: excavations of Neolithic, Bronze Age, Roman and early medieval features in 1980 and 1981', *Anglesey Antiquarian Society and Field Club Transactions* (1999), 11–166.

Whitty, Y 2011 *Archaeological Excavation Report E3144 Kilmainham 3, Co. Meath*. Unpublished report by Irish Archaeological Consultancy Ltd for Meath County Council. TII Digital Heritage Collections: https://doi.org/10.7486/DRI.pn89sn352.

Williams, H 2006 *Death and Memory in Early Medieval Britain*. Cambridge University Press, Cambridge.

Woodman, P 1981 'A Mesolithic camp in Northern Ireland', *Scientific American*, Vol. 245 (August 1981), 120–32.

Woodman, P 1985 *Excavations at Mount Sandel 1973–1977*. HMSO, Belfast.

Woodman, P C, Anderson, E & Finlay, N 1999 *Excavations at Ferriter's Cove 1983–95. Last foragers/first farmers in the Dingle Peninsula*. Wordwell, Dublin.

Woodward, A 1992 *Shrines and Sacrifice*. English Heritage/Batsford, London.

Woodward, A & Leach, P E 1993 *The Uley Shrines. Excavation of a ritual complex on West Hill, Uley, Gloucestershire, 1977–9*. Historic Buildings and Monuments Commission for England Archaeological Report 17. English Heritage/British Museum Press, London.

Young, T 2008 *Detailed Recording of Furnace C397, Derrinsallagh 4 (E2180), M7/M8 Contract 2: GeoArch Report 2008/34*. Unpublished specialist report for Archaeological Consultancy Services Ltd.

Index

Note: Tables are indicated by (table) following the page number and illustrations are indicated by page numbers in *italics*.